CHALLENGING THE STATE

The 1980s and 1990s posed great challenges to governments in Latin America and Africa. Deep economic crisis and significantly heightened pressure for political reform severely taxed their capacity to manage economic and political tasks. These crises pointed to the intense need to reform the state and redefine its relationship to the market and civic society. This book is about the paradox of states that have been weakened by crisis just as their capacity to encourage economic development and provide for effective governance most needs to be strengthened.

Case studies of Mexico and Kenya document the challenge of dealing with this paradox. In these two countries, crisis underscored the need for the state to strengthen, reform, or reinvent itself. In assessing responses to pressure to improve the institutional, technical, administrative, and political capacities of government, this book analyzes the opportunities available for political leadership in moments of crisis. It also provides insight into the constraints set by leadership goals and existing economic and political structures on the potential for innovation.

Political leaders and institutions are frequently held to blame for the failure to introduce more effective relationships among state, economy, and society. But this book indicates that political leadership and structures of political power, while frequently part of the problem, are also part of the solution to building more efficient, effective, and responsive states. Engendering a shared vision of the future, building coalitions of interests, mobilizing electoral support, attracting talented people to public service, encouraging responsiveness to public needs, and mediating conflict in the interest of political stability – these are all tasks that are essential to promoting economic and political development and they are ones traditionally assumed by political leaders and institutions.

Based on the notion that economic and political development require capable states, this book traces the ways in which state capacity is built, destroyed, and, at times, rebuilt. It indicates how, for some countries, a decade of deep and sustained crisis also became a decade of innovations in ideas, policy directions, political coalitions, and government institutions.

CAMBRIDGE STUDIES IN COMPARATIVE POLITICS

General editor
PETER LANGE   Duke University

Associate editors
ELLEN COMISSO   Duke University
PETER HALL   Harvard University
JOEL MIGDAL   University of Washington
HELEN MILNER   Columbia University
RONALD ROGOWSKI   University of California, Los Angeles
SIDNEY TARROW   Cornell University

This series publishes comparative research that seeks to explain important, crossnational domestic political phenomena. Based on a broad conception of comparative politics, it hopes to promote critical dialogue among different approaches. While encouraging contributions from diverse theoretical perspectives, the series will particularly emphasize work on domestic institutions and work that examines the relative roles of historical structures and constraints, of individual or organizational choice, and of strategic interaction in explaining political actions and outcomes. This focus includes an interest in the mechanisms through which historical factors impinge on contemporary political choices and outcomes.

Works on all parts of the world are welcomed, and priority will be given to studies that cross traditional area boundaries and that treat the United States in comparative perspective. Many of the books in the series are expected to be comparative, drawing on material from more than one national case, but studies devoted to single countries will also be considered, especially those that pose their problem and analysis in such a way that they make a direct contribution to comparative analysis and theory.

OTHER BOOKS IN THE SERIES

Catherine Boone, *Merchant Capital and the Roots of State Power in Senegal, 1930–1985*
Donatella della Porta, *Social Movements, Political Violence, and the State*
Roberto Franzosi, *The Puzzle of Strikes: Class and State Strategies in Postwar Italy*
Ellen Immergut *Health Politics: Interests and Institutions in Western Europe*
Thomas Janoski and Alexander M. Hicks, eds., *The Comparative Political Economy of the Welfare State*
Robert O. Keohare and Helen V. Milner, *Internationalization and Domestic Politics*
David Knoke, Franz Urban Pappi, Jeffrey Broadbent, and Yutaka Tsujinaka, eds., *Comparing Policy Networks*
Allan Kornberg and Harold D. Clark, *Citizens and Community: Political Support in a Representative Democracy*
David D. Laitin, *Language Repertories and State Construction in Africa*
Doug McAdam, John McCarthy, and Mayer Zald, *Comparative Perspectives on Social Movements*
Joel S. Migdal, Atul Kohli, and Vivienne Shue, *State Power and Social Forces: Domination and Transformation in the Third World*
Paul Pierson, *Dismantling the Welfare State: Reagan, Thatcher and the Politics of Retrenchment*

CHALLENGING THE STATE

CRISIS AND INNOVATION IN LATIN AMERICA AND AFRICA

MERILEE S. GRINDLE

Harvard University

CAMBRIDGE
UNIVERSITY PRESS

Published by the Press Syndicate of the University of Cambridge
The Pitt Building, Trumpington Street, Cambridge CB2 1RP
40 West 20th Street, New York, NY 10011–4211, USA
10 Stamford Road, Oakleigh, Victoria 3166, Australia

First published 1996

Printed in Great Britain at the University Press, Cambridge

A catalogue record for this book is available from the British Library

Library of Congress cataloguing in publication data

Grindle, Merilee Serrill.
Challenging the state: crisis and innovation in Latin America and
Africa / Merilee S. Grindle.
p.   cm. – (Cambridge studies in comparative politics)
Includes bibliographical references.
ISBN 0 521 55106 4 (hc). – ISBN 0 521 55919 7 (pb)
1. Latin America – Politics and government – 1948–   2. Latin
America – Economic policy.   3. Africa – Politics and government – 1960–
4. Africa – Economic policy.   5. Mexico – Politics and
government – 1970–1988.   6. Mexico – Politics and government – 1988–
7. Mexico – Economic policy – 1970–   8. Kenya – Politics and
government – 1978–   9. Kenya – Economic policy.   I. Title.
II. Series.
JL958.G75 1996
320.9172′4–dc20   95–17916 CIP

ISBN 0 521 55106 4 hardback
ISBN 0 521 55919 7 paperback

Contents

Figures

Tables

Acknowledgments

Writing a book is often a solitary enterprise. Just as frequently, however, it is a joint venture of many who offer support, insights, and access to research materials. I have benefited greatly from the willingness of many to assist in the joint venture that has resulted in this book.

Above all, I am grateful to the numerous officials and concerned citizens in Mexico and Kenya who, with generosity of time and effort, helped me develop insights into processes of continuity and change that affect the state and public policy in their countries. I was deeply impressed by their intelligence and concern for the future development of their countries. Their willingness to share professional experiences and perspectives was a critical factor in allowing me to understand the history and contemporary realities of two important countries; I hope I have done justice to their values and insights in this book.

I have been very fortunate to work with colleagues who encouraged my research interests. At the Harvard Institute for International Development (HIID), John Cohen was extremely generous in providing me with valuable suggestions, data, and references on Kenya. Michael Roemer provided excellent advice and Richard Goldman also shared his extensive experience in Kenya with me. Dwight Perkins and Richard Pagett facilitated the research with ongoing support. I am also grateful to Jennifer Widner of Harvard University for her encouragement. Ellen Pigott proved an able assistant with a keen eye for misspellings and poor syntax. Her patience and editorial skills are greatly appreciated.

I have also been fortunate in having access to talented research assistants. In particular, Adrienne Taptich and Mary Kay Gugerty undertook work in Mexico and Kenya that advanced the objectives of the research. They also carried out extensive data collection and analysis in Cambridge. Andrew Astley, Allison Barrows, Suzanne Goldstein, and Mia MacDonald also assisted in the project with intelligence, good humor, and hard work. Their combined efforts in the library and at the computer made it possible for me to complete the manuscript without having to abandon my teaching, advising, and project responsibilities. Had I done so, I would have missed the continuing insights and intellectual challenges that I receive from teaching courses at the Kennedy School of Government at Harvard. Many of my students are public officials from developing countries; their lively presence is a constant incentive to think about the implications of theory and analysis for the very

x

real dilemmas confronting officials and citizens in these countries. I am much in their debt for this stimulus.

I benefited also from the generous support of several institutions. HIID provided funding for research assistance when I first began to collect data. I was able to initiate research in Mexico with a grant from Fundación México en Harvard. The Social Science Research Council supported most of the field work in Mexico and the analysis of data from Latin America. The Swedish International Development Agency funded the Africa research. I am extremely grateful to these organizations for their support, and also to Mary Schneider Enríquez, Eric Hershberg, Borje Ljunggren, and Anders Ostman for their encouragement. I hope they will find the resulting study interesting and useful.

As always, Steven, Alexandra, and Stefanie Grindle accepted my travel schedule with good grace and pretended not to notice when I was at home but distracted by research. Collectively, they provided a constant reminder not to take myself too seriously.

1

Challenging the state: a decade of crisis

The 1980s and 1990s posed great challenges to governments in Latin America and Africa. Deep economic crisis and significantly heightened pressure for political reform severely taxed their capacity to manage economic and political tasks. In fact, the era was a critical moment in which existing state–economy and state–society relations were challenged and, at times, redefined. This book is about the significance of these challenges and redefinitions for the capacities – institutional, technical, administrative, and political – that states in Latin America and Africa require if they are to encourage economic development and provide effective governance for their societies. It explores the roles that political leaders and institutions played in a decade-long drama of crisis and change.

There is little question that this period will be remembered as an era of crisis for countries in Latin America and Africa. An economic crisis, often rooted in development policies adopted in prior decades and greatly increased prices for oil in the 1970s, was precipitated in the early 1980s by a series of external shocks, principal among which were a sharp rise in real interest rates, a rapid decline in the availability of international credit, and a sharp fall in international commodity prices. As a consequence, external terms of trade became highly unfavorable for many developing countries, budget deficits escalated, and foreign debt burdens became unmanageable. International conditions as well as domestic policies explain these problems.

The impact of such conditions on developing country economies was extensive and often extreme. Per capita growth rates in GDP for all developing countries declined from an annual average of 3.4 percent between 1965 and 1980 to one of 2.3 percent between 1980 and 1989. For Latin American countries, per capita GDP growth averaged −0.6 percent for the decade and, for sub-Saharan Africa, it was −2.2 percent.[1] Economic stagnation and decline in real per capita income affected most countries in both regions. In many of them, the 1980s were referred to as the "lost decade."

This economic crisis had major implications for the relationship between state and economy in large numbers of countries. Whether by choice or necessity, state leadership in the process of economic development was significantly reduced. Severe budget deficits and massive debt burdens led many governments to restrain or even halt public sector investments, cut operational budgets to the minimum, and reduce the size of national, regional, and local bureaucracies. At the same time, state-led development strategies, which had been dominant in some countries as far back as the 1930s, gradually yielded to strategies that placed greater emphasis on market forces to generate economic growth. Such strategies implied efforts to liberalize trade and privatize a plethora of state-owned enterprises and public functions. While in most countries the state continued to be active and interventionist, its former ability to dominate the economy was sharply reduced.

Political crisis also characterized this era. Public protests, demands for greater democratic responsiveness, and regime transitions occurred throughout Latin America, Africa, Eastern Europe, Asia, and elsewhere. In Latin America and Africa, some twenty-four countries experienced at least one change of regime between 1980 and 1990. In Latin America, all such changes were transitions to democratic regimes. In Africa, the 1980s witnessed a succession of military coups, but by the early 1990s, there was an equally impressive spate of transitions to competitive electoral regimes.[2] In almost all countries in both regions, an invigorated civic society pressed for greater presence in political arenas and policy discussions. Increasingly, civic society was characterized by the burgeoning of opposition parties, community level movements, and voluntary associations, as well as by an increase in public debates, media criticism of government, and competitive elections. This heightened political mobilization, debate, and electoral activity expanded public contestation over issues of policy and governance.

These political challenges, coupled with the impact of economic crisis, had clear implications for the relationship between state and civic society. In particular, this was a period of increased vulnerability for political leaders and entrenched political institutions. Often, economic stagnation or decline went hand in hand with widespread questioning of regimes in power and a generalized delegitimation of the state as an agent of economic growth. Many political leaders saw their coalitions of support fall apart or become seriously fragmented under the resulting strains. Moreover, the policies adopted to respond to the economic crisis meant that governments became less frequently the providers of investment capital, services, and benefits and more often the enforcers of unpopular stabilization and structural adjustment measures.

Economic adjustment policies diminished the political centrality of the state by encouraging the privatization of publicly managed activities, liberalization of economic interactions, and curtailment of other traditional state functions. Austerity, privatization, and liberalization, in addition to the increased power of international financial agencies to monitor government performance, meant that political leaders had fewer material resources with which to reward supporters and maintain coalitions. Many policy interventions of the decade also imposed at least short-term hardship on broad sectors of the population; countries varied greatly in public tolerance for such measures, but disenchantment with government in general and political leaders in particular was widespread.

Thus, a decade or more of profound economic and political crisis in Latin America and Africa had an equally profound impact on the nature of state involvement in economic development and on the power of the state directly to shape modes of collective and individual political behavior. In this regard, the period is similar to development crises of the 1930s and 1940s in Latin America and the 1950s and 1960s in African countries. Just as in those earlier periods, more recent crises encouraged disarray among existing economic and political forces and simultaneously opened up space for new definitions of the role of the state in development, new policy departures, new political coalitions, and new scope for political leadership and institutional innovation. And, just as the crises of earlier periods are important in explaining the economic and political relationships that emerged and characterized the next several decades, so responses to this new era of crisis are the basis on which state–economy and state–society relations in many countries will be constructed for the next several decades.[3]

STATES AND STATE CAPACITIES: DEFINITIONS AND ISSUES IN THE LITERATURE

In this book, I am concerned with how economic and political crises in Latin America and Africa affected dimensions of state capacity that are important in defining relationships among state, economy, and society. This question, explored at a general level for eight Latin American and eight African countries, is assessed in greater depth through the specific experiences of Mexico and Kenya. For these two countries, I expand the analysis to consider how state leaders and political institutions influenced and responded to the pressures that altered the ability to regulate the economy and respond to civic society. The experiences of Mexico and Kenya shed considerable light on how state–economy and state–society relationships are contested, negotiated, and reconstituted at critical historical moments.

In this analysis, I understand the state to be a set of ongoing institutions for social control and authoritative decision making and implementation.[4] The state is conceptually distinct from both economy and society, with inherent interests in expanding its scope for autonomous action, asserting control over economic and social interactions, and structuring economic and social relationships. These interests derive primarily from the state's concern to establish and maintain internal and external security, to generate revenue, and to achieve hegemony over alternative forms of social organization.[5] The ability to achieve security, raise revenue, and assert autonomy and control, however, is profoundly influenced by economic conditions and degrees of social mobilization, as well as by the legitimacy and internal cohesion of the state itself. States are therefore frequently engaged in contesting the right and capacity to make and implement authoritative decisions that structure economic and social interactions. In this regard, the state is a moving target, "defined by contention along its boundaries and among politicians and bureaucrats who, in competing for office and influence, rework social and economic conflict into political terms."[6] States are not monolithic and contention along boundaries is often combined with contention among branches and levels of government, agencies, and diverse bureaucratic interests.

States assume empirical reality through regimes that attempt to establish political order, set terms for political interaction, allocate leadership positions and power resources, and determine the representation of interests within decision-making contexts.[7] Regimes attempt to negotiate and impose formal and informal rules about how the state will relate to the economy and to the society; durable and legitimate regimes have greater capacity to achieve these goals than do those that are less institutionalized. Within the context of regime structures, political leaders create or maintain coalitions of support to achieve particular policy goals and may seek to use them to expand the scope of autonomous action for the state. In turn, political institutions allocate position and power resources that affect the ability of such leaders to act on their preferences and achieve their goals. These institutions are also subject to contestation over their structures and roles and can change over time to reflect different degrees of autonomy and strength.

As already indicated, economic and political crises had a destabilizing effect on existing state–economy and state–society relations throughout Latin America and Africa, and in many ways, the capacity of states to encourage economic development and maintain social stability was severely undermined. Nevertheless, these crises opened up increased space for deliberate efforts to craft new relationships between state and economy and to redefine relationships of power and accountability with society. They provided opportunities for state elites to mobilize support for new strategies of national 'development and strengthen the state's capacity to assume newly defined roles.[8] In considering the cases of Mexico and Kenya, the influence of specific political leaders with particular economic and political goals looms large in the explanations of crisis and change. So, too, do the ways in which institutions structure power relationships and allocate political resources that can be used to shape both economic and social agendas. The 1980s and 1990s presented governments with difficult challenges, but this book indicates the extent to which they also provided expanded scope for innovation.

The concept of state capacity provides the organizing theme for this analysis. In recent years, considerable scholarly attention focused on the state as political scientists, economists, and political economists debated its definition, assessed its strength and relative autonomy from groups and interests in national and international arenas, and discussed the role it should play in development.[9] Inevitably, these discussions, along with heightened concern about the causes and consequences of economic and political crisis, fostered questions about state capacity; considerable evidence accumulated during the 1980s to suggest that states varied widely in their ability to set the terms for economic and political interactions and to carry out the functions assigned to them.[10] The notion of state capacity, long assumed to be an inherent characteristic of "state-ness," became more frequently a matter of theoretical concern and empirical assessment.[11]

Growing theoretical interest in state capacity was encouraged by shifting paradigms in development economics. This field, which in the 1950s and 1960s pioneered work on market failures and the rationale for state intervention in developing country economies, began by the mid-1970s to focus on government failures, that is, the ways in which public action can distort markets and create disincentives for productive investment and behavior.[12] State intervention in the economy through regulatory mechanisms, investment, marketing boards, and parastatal industries soon became central in explaining the economic stagnation and imbalances experienced by a wide range of countries. A prominent view among neoclassical economists and political economists pointed to the state as the single most important impediment to economic development – an "invisible foot" corresponding to the "invisible hand" of the market, an economic predator, and an arena for encouraging directly unproductive activities (DUPs).[13]

Indeed, a new orthodoxy of market liberalism emerged in development economics and was widely subscribed to by academics and practitioners in the 1980s. Embedded in the new consensus, at least initially, was a strong strain of anti-statism, a theme also emphasized in political science by public choice analysts.[14] Extensive state intervention in the market and a series of government failures were shown to be a logical consequence of a close alliance between rent-seeking public officials and rent-seeking economic interests. In turn, radically diminishing the size and scope of state intervention was the clearest way to end rent seeking and to encourage more dynamic economies. At an operational level, this perspective implied the need to disband marketing boards and parastatal organizations, diminish regulatory constraints, and strengthen the role of the private sector in investment decision making. For many economists, the notion of a minimalist state replaced that of the developmentalist state of prior decades.

The vehemence of the neoclassical attack on the state cooled somewhat by the late 1980s, however. Thoughtful observers noted that state minimalism could be carried too far.[15] While the general tone of the attack on the state by development economists remained negative – and considerable empirical evidence accumulated to support their views – literature in economics and political economy raised increasingly insistent questions about the appropriate role for the state in economic development. States were important in the process of development, analysts argued, because states alone could provide a set of conditions essential to economic development – law, order, effective macroeconomic policy, infrastructure development, investment in human capital, enhancement of equity.[16] Renewed interest in state capacity and the relationship between state and economy also encouraged scholars to pay greater attention to institutional structures and how such institutions affect the course of economic development. The research of "new institutional economists," for example, suggested that western capitalist economies developed in the wake of institutional innovations to ensure the rights of private accumulation and the sanctity of contracts among economic agents.[17]

Increasingly, analysts emphasized the importance of the type and quality of state intervention rather than its quantity, the capacity of the state rather than its size. Thus, a number of researchers who sought to uncover the secret of the East Asian "success stories" found significant evidence that the actions and policies of development-oriented states were central to generating high and sustained growth rates.[18] In several of these countries, strong, centralized, interventionist, and authoritarian states were specifically credited with engineering economic growth through state policies for investment, trade, and social control. State capacity to set institutional structures conducive to economic growth, to manage macroeconomic policy, and to carry out basic public functions thus became important in explaining the differential history of states that developed and states that stagnated economically.[19]

Scholarly attention also focused on changes occurring in civic society. Empirically, analysts noted that an often weakened, less pervasive, and at times delegitimized state opened up considerable room for redefining and renegotiating traditional forms of state–society relations. This space was increasingly occupied by varieties of civic associations pressing demands on the state or seeking greater autonomy to find solutions to collective problems without the threat of state intervention and control.[20] In Latin America and Africa, the decade witnessed the emergence and strengthening of groups pressing for democratic structures of government and more equitable and participatory forms of decision making. At times, local communities and non-governmental organizations responded to an apparent loss of state presence by attempting to find grassroots solutions to economic and social problems as well as by making collective demands on government at local, regional, and national levels.[21] Responding to the liberalization of economic activities, some private sector groups began to eschew traditional corporatist or clientelist relationships with the state and became more insistent as pressure groups and lobbyists in policy making.

Several currents in social science literature attempted to define the nature of these efforts to establish new political relationships between state and civic society.[22] For example, literature on redemocratization and authoritarian transitions focused attention on the emergence or reemergence of political parties, labor unions, and economic groups that characteristically form the basis for political mobilization in democratic societies.[23] Related work on regime transitions pointed to concerted efforts among politically relevant actors to form pacts around agreements about the rules of the game for political and policy contestation.[24] Still other scholars focused on "new social movements" in which citizens identified common interests that transcended traditional categories of class, interest, or clientelism, coalescing around alternative identities such as community membership, ethnicity, greenness, or gender.[25]

This literature posed several possible outcomes of renewed political vigor in civic society. For example, a significant body of research pointed to the role of civic associations in opposing the state, particularly in non-democratic settings.[26] Common to much of this literature was the emphasis on protest and contestation. In this regard, civic society was credited with a range of efforts to oppose and transform authoritarian regimes, to lay the basis for multiparty systems where no-party or one-party regimes held power, and to open up policy-making processes to public input. The importance of contestation was less evident in literature that defined the ends of state–society interaction as that of negotiation and bargaining. This literature emphasized the formation of horizontally based interactions with representatives of the state and pointed to efforts to use negotiation rather than petitioning as a form of extracting resources. The movement toward a political culture of citizenship, stressing rights and obligations, as opposed to one based on clientelism, stressing dependent relationships, was identified in this literature.[27]

Interest in the social impact of economic stagnation and fiscal austerity led other scholars to concentrate on efforts of various civic groups to substitute for the state. Many analysts of African political economy focused on the widespread corruption, exploitation, and brutality of some regimes and explored how those most vulnerable to economic and physical exploitation responded to such conditions. They identified a common pattern of disengagement from the state whereby individuals, households, and groups withdrew or tried to avoid contact with officials and organizations representing it.[28] The emergence of parallel markets, black markets, and the informal economy were widely documented forms in which disengagement characterized economic interactions.[29] Less well-documented but increasingly noted were forms of political disengagement such as the emergence of "parallel governments" in which local communities, at times abandoned by state institutions that had formerly provided social welfare services, sought to provide these services for themselves.[30] This literature pointed to the creativity and vitality of efforts at collective problem solving among communities, ethnic groups, and religious or voluntary associations, providing a positive view of the capacity for grassroots organization and supporting a growing literature on the importance of grassroots democracy, self-government, and autonomy.[31]

Literature on contesting, negotiating with, or substituting for the state focused attention on the ways in which citizens attempted to increase their power and autonomy relative to the state. As part of this larger critique of authoritarian modes of political organization and research on emerging forms of political organization, the concept of state capacity was broadened to include characteristics of political representation, conflict resolution, and administrative openness and fairness. Political scientists and others argued that capable states had to be responsive to the demands and pressures of societal groups and to be able to mediate social demands and maintain institutions that were effective in resolving conflict. The concept of governance, referring in part to the political and institutional development of a country and its capacity to achieve and maintain good government, was increasingly used to denote a state's capacity to tolerate and even invite political pluralism.[32]

As suggested in the foregoing paragraphs, diverse literatures converged on the notion that states must have certain kinds of capacities if they are to be effective in managing tasks of economic and political development. The first column in Table 1.1 presents a set of characteristics widely asserted to be those that capable states ought to have. A capable state is one that exhibits the ability to establish and maintain effective institutional, technical, administrative, and political functions, as these characteristics are defined in the table. Theoretically, states that exhibit these characteristics should be well-equipped to manage tasks essential to economic and political development.

Table 1.1 *State capacity: theory and predictions*

Theory	Predictions
Capable states ought to have:	Hypothesized condition after a decade of economic and political crisis:

Institutional capacity

Authoritative and effective "rules of the game" to regulate economic and political interactions. Ability to assert the primacy of national policies, legal conventions, and norms of social and political behavior over those of other groupings.	Decreased authority and legitimacy of government. Weakened ability of states to set authoritative standards for individual and group behavior. Increased conflict over "rules of the game" for economic and political interactions.

Technical capacity

The ability to set and manage effective macroeconomic policies. A cadre of well-trained economic analysts and managers. Well-staffed and appropriately placed units for policy analysis. Important role for technical input and information in decision making.	Increased numbers, visibility, and influence of economic technocrats, economic ministries, and policy analysis units. Increased presence of international technocrats in national policy making. Tension between technocratic and participatory policy making.

Administrative capacity

Effective administration of basic physical and social infrastructure. Ability to perform basic administrative functions essential to economic development and social welfare.	Weakened administrative ability to deliver basic services and carry out normal functions of government. Decreased ability to mediate social and economic demands within administrative contexts.

Political capacity

Effective and legitimate channels for societal demand making, representation, and conflict resolution. Responsive political leaders and administrators. Societal participation in decision making.	Increased vitality of civic society and lessened responsive capacity of state leaders and managers. Decreased capacity of state elites and political institutions to mediate conflict. Tension between increased technocratic decision making and responsiveness to societal demands and participation.

STATE CAPACITY: HYPOTHESES AFTER A DECADE OF CRISIS

Much of the analysis that produced a multidimensional definition of state capacity centered on what states ought to do to manage dynamic and sustained economic development and what political characteristics ought to define good government.[33] Rarely did issues of how more capable states emerge or change over time get addressed, resulting in considerable gaps between concerns about "what ought to be" and "what is" in a realistic appraisal of state capacity. In fact, persistent crises of the kind that characterized many Latin American and African countries in the 1980s and 1990s could significantly affect existing abilities to set the terms for economic and political development. In the second column of Table 1.1, I summarize a series of general hypotheses about how crisis can affect institutional, technical, administrative, and political capacities.

The first set of hypotheses relates to the impact of crisis on the institutional capacity of states, that is, the ability of states to set and enforce the broad sets of rules that govern economic and political interactions. Of concern here are institutions such as legal norms governing relationships among economic agents, constitutional and administrative rules setting standards for the behavior of public servants, constitutional dictums governing relationships among state organizations, and electoral systems and procedures for holding public officials accountable for their actions. Similarly important is the ability to ensure the primacy of national policies, legal codes, and norms of social and political behavior over those adhered to by sub-national groupings.[34] To what extent have the convergence of economic and political crises undermined existing capacity to set and enforce such rules and to ensure the stable functioning of authoritative institutions?

At a general level, I hypothesize that economic crisis combined with increased political challenges to existing regimes weakened the legitimacy and coercive capacity of state institutions and laid bare the inadequacy of systems for regulating property rights, enforcing contracts, controlling official corruption, setting boundaries on the use of coercion, and other basic institutional functions. In many countries, then, contention over policy issues frequently incorporated more basic disagreements about the rules of the game for resolving economic and political conflict. Of course, many states lacked effective rules and coercive capacity in the pre-crisis period, but the dual impact of economic and political crises raised the visibility of the need for authoritative institutional structures at the same time that it weakened the capacity of many states to provide them.

A second set of generalizations relates to changes in the technical capacity of states, defined here as the ability to manage macroeconomic policy and analyze economic policy options more generally. I hypothesize that, for many countries, the pressures of economic crisis and the need to negotiate more effectively with international financial agencies during the 1980s and 1990s increased technical capacity in macroeconomic analysis and management. Ministries of finance, central banks, and national planning institutes often became more powerful players in setting economic policies and negotiating agreements with multilateral and bilateral agencies and domestic economic groups. Policy analysis units also became more widespread and influential in government. Similarly, technocrats and policy analysts increased in number and became more visible in decision-making arenas; at times they were able to use their access to data and analysis to increase their power vis-à-vis domestic economic interests opposed to policy change. Equally important was the increased presence of international technocrats in national policy discussion. Such changes can alter how policy decisions are made and who participates in decision-making processes. In some cases, for example, technocratic decision-making styles were noted to conflict with the more open, participatory styles pressed for by politically mobilized groups.[35]

A third set of issues concerns the administrative capacity of states and how it was affected by deep budgetary and personnel cuts that resulted from stabilization efforts. Administrative capacity refers to the ability of states to deliver goods and services such as public health and education, provide physical infrastructure, and carry out the normal administrative functions of government, such as revenue collection, necessary economic regulation, and information management. This is a critical capacity for governments because it affects the ability of private economic agents to achieve their goals and the ability of government to satisfy basic needs demanded by civic society. I hypothesize, however, that the administrative capacity of many states declined due to austerity budgets, declining civil service performance, and heightened political conflict. Thus, after a decade of crisis, many governments may have increased their abilities in macroeconomic management while losing valuable capacity to respond to public needs, develop human resources, maintain investment, and provide essential sectoral and infrastructural services.

A fourth set of issues relates to the impact of greater political pluralism on state capacity. Political capacity, as used here, refers to the ability of states to respond to societal demands, allow for channels to represent societal interests, and incorporate societal participation in decision making and conflict resolution. It refers to the effectiveness of everyday interactions between government and citizens, rather than to the broader rules of the game that comprise institutional capacity. How effective are governments on a day-to-day basis, in response to conflict, demand making, and opposition? How good are they at problem solving? Many states moving from authoritarian modes of political control to more open ones lacked channels of access for more pluralistic demand making and representation and the means for negotiating and resolving conflict with an invigorated civic society. As suggested earlier, the confluence of economic and political crisis diminished the capacity of state leaders to command adherence to traditional norms of civic behavior or to purchase allegiance through beneficial policies or clientelistic distribution of public resources. Demands for policy responsiveness nevertheless increased. States were thus under heightened pressure to respond to diverse interests and mediate overt societal conflict, but their capacity to do so may have diminished.

These sets of interrelated questions about the impact of economic and political change on the institutional, technical, administrative, and political capacity of states are broad. Nevertheless, the impact of crisis on state capacity is only part of the task undertaken in this book. As suggested earlier, how states respond to the challenges of crisis and its implications for various dimensions of state capacity is critical to understanding how state–economy and state–society relations can be reformulated at critical historical junctures.

RESPONDING TO CRISIS

Crises of the kind experienced in many developing countries in the 1980s and 1990s opened up increased space for redefining existing relationships between the state and the economy and society. But states do not respond in disembodied ways to the challenge of crisis. Instead, those who hold political power and have access to political resources must use the conditions created by crisis to mobilize coalitions of support, promote new visions of economic and political development, and alter the constraints they face in achieving these visions. Political leaders differ significantly in their interest in promoting economic and political change as well as in the skills they bring to these tasks. They also differ in access to resources enabling them to spearhead change. These factors are important in explaining divergent outcomes in the state's response to economic and political crises.

Concrete actions of state leaders to alter existing economic and political relationships are supported or hindered by political institutions that determine the availability of strategic resources, coalitions of support, and capacity to exert power over other actors and institutions. The presidency as an institution, for example, can have considerable influence on the ability of incumbent leaders to act on their preferences because the position itself provides more or fewer strategic advantages and greater or lesser legitimacy. In the case studies of Mexico and Kenya to be explored later in this book, for example, the institution of the presidency provided a range of advantages to incumbents that allowed them to centralize great power for the pursuit of their economic and political goals. Similarly, the bureaucracy as an institution can allow for greater or lesser degrees of social control and more or less responsiveness to policy pronounce-ments. Both Mexico and Kenya had relatively well-institutionalized public bureaucracies that increased the capacity of state leaders to set the terms for policy making and implementation. In addition, political parties, as institutions that act at the boundaries between state and society, can enhance or diminish the capacity of the state to redefine critical economic and social relationships. Dominant parties in Mexico and Kenya expanded state power to control the extent of social mobilization.

Clearly, then, the ability of states to respond to the heightened space – and risk – created by crisis conditions is likely to vary widely. It will depend on economic exigencies and constraints, the strength of pressures for economic and political change from domestic groups and international actors, legacies of a variety of historical and policy experiences, the legitimacy, coherence, and strength of state institutions, and the goals and skills of state leaders.[36] In terms of the dimensions of state capacity that are of interest here, a series of questions focus attention on the degree to which political leaders and institutions take advantage of the increased space created by crisis to pursue changes in state–economy and state–society relationships.

To what extent, for example, were there efforts by state elites and political institutions:

- To reassert *institutional capacity* by defining and negotiating new rules to govern economic and political behavior and forging new institutional structures and asserting their predominance over prior rules of behavior?
- To take advantage of increased *technical capacity* by developing and implementing alternative strategies for economic development, increasing the insulation of economic policy making from domestic rent seekers, or altering the policies that shape the behavior of economic interests in society?
- To compensate for weakened *administrative capacity* by experimenting with alternative production and service delivery mechanisms, introducing effective programs to compensate for the social costs of adjustment, or increasing public sector efficiency?
- To increase *political capacity* to mediate and resolve conflict and respond to societal demands by enhancing the problem-solving skills of government, incorporating new groups into decision making, allowing for increased political participation and local level problem-solving, and finding ways to increase technical input into decision making without compromising opportunities for wider participation?

Such activities significantly influence the performance of national economies and the political integration of society by encouraging the adoption of new definitions of the role of the state, altering opportunities available to private economic agents, and affecting the ways in which citizens relate to government and engage in efforts to influence policy outcomes. They also affect the extent to which new definitions of state–economy and state–society relations become embedded as enduring patterns for pursuing economic development and distributing political power.

CHALLENGE AND RESPONSE: THE SCOPE OF RESEARCH

In preceding pages I outlined a series of hypotheses about dimensions of state capacity and how they were affected by economic and political crisis. In Chapter 2, I begin to assess these hypotheses using data from sixteen countries in Latin America and Africa. The chapter describes the nature of the crises and provides a general analysis of their causes. It assesses the origins of these crises in international and domestic contexts. It considers the impact of crisis on four dimensions of state capacity for the same set of sixteen countries, exploring the extent to which the hypotheses present a useful analysis of the institutional, technical, administrative, and political capacities of states during a decade or more of economic stagnation and political turmoil. The chapter indicates the extent to which long-entrenched relationships among state, economy, and society were torn asunder by the depth and duration of economic decline and political upheaval.

Chapters 3 through 7 present an analysis of one country from each region to consider not only the nature of economic and political crises and their impact on state capacity but also the ways in which political leaders and institutions shaped responses and influenced how state–economy and state–society relations were redefined. The case study countries, Mexico and Kenya, are not compared directly. Their colonial histories are distinct and struggles for independence marked them in different ways. The conditions and timing of economic and political development diverge. Kenya's economy is more agrarian and rural than Mexico's and its political history as an independent state is much shorter. The international contexts of the two countries also differ significantly, as does the size of their economies, territories, and populations.

Despite such significant differences, they were selected as case studies because, in relation to their own regions, they shared some important characteristics that enhanced their utility for analysis. First, they each presented relatively successful examples of sustained economic growth. Prior to the 1980s, Mexico stood out among Latin American countries for having achieved a relatively strong record of economic growth that was sustained over several decades. In Africa, Kenya had achieved a similar distinction for sustained growth. They had each adopted a development model based on state capitalism and import substitution. Expanding industrial, agricultural, and commercial sectors and considerable foreign investment also characterized the economic development of the two countries. In considering the impact of economic crisis, then, I am able to consider the extent to which sustained crisis can undermine even relatively effective state–economy interactions.

Second, both Mexico and Kenya developed relatively strong and effective states in their respective regions and experienced sustained political stability. In continents wracked by political upheaval, regime changes, and polarizing tendencies, both countries achieved centralized political and administrative control in prior decades and a generally legitimized set of institutions to manage conflict resolution. Civilian authoritarian regimes characterized each country. In considering the impact of political crisis, these similarities facilitate description and analysis. Moreover, their relatively strong state structures provide greater scope for assessing the impact of crisis on dimensions of state capacity than would be the case in countries with states that had failed to develop effective control over their domestic economies and societies. States that were initially stronger and more institutionalized are also in a better position to influence the restructuring of state–economy and state–society relations than would be the case with historically weak and unstable states.

Third, political institutions in these two countries provided state leaders with a wide range of resources should they attempt to influence the restructuring of state–economy and state–society relations. In each case there was an established tradition of a strong presidency with both constitutional and charismatic authority. Mexico and Kenya also had relatively strong bureaucratic institutions for policy development and management, providing state leaders with considerable ability to intervene in the market and in society.[37] Similarly, both countries had multiclass, integrative, and clientelistic political parties that were used as instruments of political control. In Mexico, of course, the Instutitional Revolutionary Party (PRI) was the dominant party among several, while the Kenya African National Union (KANU) in Kenya was the only legal party from 1982 through late 1991. Nevertheless, political control and mechanisms for distributing government largesse were effectively institutiona-lized through the clientelist networks of a dominant party in each country. The presidency, the bureaucracy, and the parties in Mexico and Kenya were affected significantly by the economic and political challenges of the 1980s and 1990s and their strength and legitimacy dropped to historically low levels. However, the resources available to presidents in both countries remained considerable, their state bureaucracies did not collapse as did those in some other countries, and the political machinery of the party organizations remained significantly intact.

Like other countries in their regions, Mexico and Kenya faced major economic problems in the 1980s. Mexico's was by far the most dramatic and painful. In 1982, the announcement that the country could no longer service its international debt triggered an era of debt crisis that had reverberations around the world. Its efforts to adjust were therefore apparent earlier than Kenya's and the extent to which it embarked on a sustained commitment to stabilization and structural adjustment was much more marked. Kenya's economic crisis was slower to emerge and was taken less seriously by its leaders, despite increasing pressure from international financial institutions. Chapter 3 presents an overview of the economic problems of these two countries.

Pressures for political liberalization that confronted these two relatively strong states are also assessed in Chapter 3. By the mid-1980s, many analysts of Mexico's development were predicting the demise of the PRI-dominated political system under the strain of increased civic activism and much heightened criticism of government. In Kenya, the late 1980s witnessed an extensive mobilization of opposition to government and a national struggle to force the introduction of multiparty elections. In both countries, the mobilization of civic associations was vibrant.[38] These organizations were simultaneously seeking newly defined space in which to contest political and economic issues, demanding greater responsiveness from the state, seeking ways to negotiate with state agencies, and, at times, withdrawing from interaction with the state. In each case, the challenge to the authority, legitimacy, and problem-solving capacity of the state was clear. By 1988 in Mexico and 1993 in Kenya, long-established relationships between the state and economy and the state and society had ceased to define the realities of economics and politics.

Against this overview of the challenges to the state created by economic and political crises, Chapter 4 initiates the analysis of state capacity in Mexico and Kenya. The chapter focuses on institutional capacity; it assesses the extent to which the authoritative role of the state in setting and enforcing the rules of the game for economic and political interactions was altered as a result of crisis. It assesses rules to regulate interactions among economic agents such as property rights and contracts and those that relate to the power of civic society and the accountability of public officials such as electoral and representational systems. In periods prior to the 1980s, Mexico and Kenya had developed relatively strong institutional capacity. But the history of these two countries underscores the extent to which such capacity can wax and wane over time; authority and legitimacy can be contested and undermined as well as developed. The chapter also indicates the extent to which the actions of political leaders and institutions affect the timing and content of efforts to redefine important rules for economic and political interactions. Ultimately, however, new rules must be accepted as appropriate and legitimate by those who will be subject to them. Strengthening institutional capacity, therefore, requires creating the basis for social consensus and consent.

In Mexico, economic deregulation, changes in property rights in the countryside, and the reassertion of presidential power are cases in formal and informal rule redefinition considered in Chapter 4. In each of these areas, political leaders and institutions were principal protagonists. The experience of Mexico reaffirms the extent to which crisis can diminish the institutional capacity of the state but also open up opportunities for developing alternative rules that restore its authority. In Kenya, the authority and legitimacy of the state reached perilously low levels in the early 1990s and the redefinition of rules was hotly contested. The chapter explores changes to the constitution, the extent of presidential power, economic liberalization, and privatization as arenas of contention over who would determine the rules and how they would be enforced. In the cases of Mexico and Kenya, the preferences and strategies of political leaders, as well as the resources available to the presidency, the bureaucracy, and the party, affected the outcome of contestation, but the degree of acceptance of new rules was only partly determined by these actors and institutions.

Chapter 5 assesses changes in the technical capacity of the two governments and the implication of these changes for developing and managing economic development policies. More specifically, the chapter focuses on central economic ministries and agencies in Mexico and Kenya and asks to what extent the technical capacity of these organizations was altered through crisis and affected by the actions of political leaders. Data on change and its consequence are derived primarily from organizational histories, the changing relationships of technical units and technical advisors to high level decision makers, the emergence of technocrats in positions of influence, and changes in the structure of presidential advisory units, staffs, and cabinets.

This chapter details the extent to which technical capacity changed and the extent to which state leaders encouraged technical input into decision making. Mexico provides a clear-cut case of increased technical capacity and use of that capacity in policy making. In Kenya, on the other hand, the state lost technical capacity. Policy making about the economy became more capricious and less informed by technical analysis. In explaining these divergent experiences, the goals and strategies of political leaders are critical. The chapter indicates clearly that technocratic influence is derivative of political power. Mexico's leaders empowered technical experts in policy arenas; Kenya's did not.

The administrative capacity of the state in Mexico and Kenya is explored in Chapter 6, primarily through an assessment of public expenditures for health, education, and public works and changing priorities within ministries responsible for social and physical infrastructure. In both countries, budgets for health and roads suffered serious declines; education budgets were expanded in Kenya but slashed in Mexico. More generally, conditions for public sector workers declined significantly, particularly in Kenya, and the capacity to carry out normal functions of government suffered.

Within this context of weakened administrative capacity, a number of experiments were undertaken to test the potential for doing "more with less." There were, for example, efforts to increase efficiency and to reallocate resources within sectors to protect the most vulnerable. In addition, in Mexico, decentralization in health and education, community-based services, and contracting out of physical infrastructure development and maintenance were important efforts to deal with the impact of crisis and the implications of austerity for the ability to deliver basic services. These innovations are assessed in the chapter. In Kenya, user fees in health and education, a reorganized education structure, and reallocation of resources for roads are also considered. New modes for delivering basic services became more acceptable in both countries. Nevertheless, the administrative capacity of the state remained low. Despite innovation, poorly funded and badly managed ministries remained impediments to the more effective delivery of social and physical infrastructure. In fact, in this area, the impact of the goals and strategies of political leaders and the resources available to political institutions were less influential than for other dimensions of state capacity. Implementation remained the weakest link in state-sponsored efforts to alter state–economy and state-society relations.

Chapter 7 addresses the issue of the changing capacity of state elites and institutions in Mexico and Kenya to respond to increased demands for responsiveness, representation, and participation. Traditionally, the state in both countries had been effective in channeling and controlling political behavior. On a day-to-day basis, political conflict was managed through the distribution of state resources and patronage and through elaborate systems of cooptation and control. But economic crisis robbed political leaders and institutions in both countries of the resources formerly used to cement relationships between state and civic society.

This chapter addresses the relationship between diminished political capacity and more open and pluralistic practices of governance. The ability of new voices and new demands to be heard, of political parties to represent interests in society, and of citizens to participate in meaningful elections are among the issues considered. The case studies suggest that, in contrast to other dimensions of state capacity, political capacity does not respond directly to the actions of political leaders and institutions. Rather, such capacity is a result of contestation between state and civic society within specific arenas and over specific issues. I assess how political institutions – primarily the presidency and the political parties – responded to changes in the nature and extent of political mobilization and the degree to which they were forced to accommodate new voices, new demands, and new forms of participation. These experiences indicate the extent to which the political capacity of the state is dependent on the political capacity of civic society.

The question of the extent to which governments in Mexico and Kenya were able to respond to the challenges of crisis is considered more broadly in Chapter 8. In these two countries, and in a large number of others in Latin America and Africa, deep and sustained economic and political crises clearly challenged the state to strengthen, reform, or reinvent itself. Their leaders and institutions were challenged to assume formative roles in establishing new ways for the state to interact with the economy and society. In assessing how state leaders and political institutions in Mexico and Kenya managed and at times reinterpreted the institutional, technical, administrative, and political tasks of government, this chapter suggests the nature and range of opportunities available for political leadership in moments of crisis. It also provides insight into the constraints set by leadership goals and existing economic and political structures on the potential for innovation. The divergent experiences of Mexico and Kenya suggest that political leadership and structures of political control can be simultaneously part of the problem and part of the solution to building more efficient, effective, and responsive states.

Chapter 8 also explores the role of ideas in reshaping state-economy and state-society relations. The importance of ideas – and the use of those ideas in providing strategic vision and creating new coalitions of support – about the role of the state in development and the relationship between government and citizen is central to explaining outcomes in Mexico and Kenya. Chapter 8 builds on the country case studies to provide a series of generalizations about political and institutional leadership and "the power of public ideas" in economic and political reform.[39] In addition, the cases of Mexico and Kenya raise important issues about the relative merits of authoritarian and democratic systems in establishing the bases for efficient, effective, and responsive states. The case of Mexico provides evidence of the extent to which concentrated resources of power can speed the introduction of change, but the case of Kenya is a powerful reminder of the equally great extent to which power can be abused in authoritarian systems. Indeed, the changes that occurred in Mexico were often introduced with little concern for the participation and representation of societal interests and carried out in ways that limited the capacity of citizens to hold public officials accountable for their actions. In concluding this book, I suggest that while change may be more difficult to introduce in democratic contexts, it may ultimately result in states with greater legitimacy, accountability, and responsiveness.

2
Crisis and the state: evidence from Latin America and Africa

The 1980s and 1990s witnessed economic and political crises of historic significance in Latin America and Africa. Throughout both regions, economies that were already fragile were almost destroyed by debt, inflation, low commodity prices, high interest rates, and devastating natural disasters. Political systems faced grave challenges to their right to govern societies that were themselves torn by division and unrest. Regime changes, civil wars, civic protest, and demands for human rights and accountable public officials characterized the political history of this era. The evidence is extensive and unambiguous: economic and political distress were hallmarks of an unsettled and unsettling era. Repeatedly, crisis exposed the weakness of existing state capacities to manage economic and political relationships.

This chapter uses data from sixteen countries in Latin America and Africa to explore the scope, nature, and implications of economic and political crisis.[1] It addresses four questions. First, what was the scope of the dual crises of economic and political development facing countries in these regions? Second, what factors explain the nature of the problems that confronted a wide range of governments? Third, what impact did economic and political collapse or near collapse have on various dimensions of state capacity? Finally, what consequences did crisis have for state–economy and state–society relationships? Subsequent chapters deal in greater detail with the same issues in Mexico and Kenya; this chapter indicates the extent to which these two countries shared in region-wide political and economic trends.

THE SCOPE OF CRISIS

Many Latin American and African countries were significantly less well off at the end of the 1980s than they had been at the beginning of the decade. Tables 2.1 and 2.2 provide an overview of economic growth and decline in both regions between 1970 and 1990. In Latin America, these data indicate that the 1970s were a period of relatively robust economic expansion; GDP growth averaged 5.5 percent annually, with rates varying between 3.1 and 8.5 percent per year. Per capita GDP growth rates were of course more modest, but they remained generally positive. As indicated in Table 2.2, the relatively stronger performance of Brazil, Colombia, Ecuador, and

18

Mexico was countered by weaker per capita growth in Argentina, Bolivia, Chile until 1976, and Peru. Latin America's strong 1970s performance altered in the 1980s, however. Average per capita growth rates in the eight countries became negative in 1982 and remained low throughout most of the decade, with the exception of Chile, which demonstrated sustained growth after 1984.

GDP growth rates in Africa averaged 4.0 percent for the 1970s. They varied between no growth and 7.7 percent, demonstrating greater annual fluctuations than was true for Latin America. On a per capita basis, 1970s' growth rates were modest and, for many countries, as frequently negative as positive, with the same pattern of extreme annual fluctuations reflecting the less diversified nature of the region's economies. Table 2.2 indicates that, on a per capita basis, economies in Ethiopia, Ghana, and Zambia experienced stagnation and decline for much of that decade. Economic decline increased in the 1980s, with negative or almost static per capita growth rates characterizing much of the region. Cameroon, Côte d'Ivoire, Ethiopia, and Zambia had the most crisis-prone economies. The long-term impact of these economic conditions was emphasized when Zambia was recategorized by the World Bank from a middle-income to a low-income country in 1981; a similar fate befell Ghana in 1983 and Nigeria in 1990.

The impact of economic decline and instability at the individual and household level was severe. The World Bank estimates that the percentage of populations living below the poverty line in Latin America and sub-Saharan Africa increased in the 1980s. In absolute terms, 87 million people in Latin America lived in poverty in 1985, compared to 108 million in 1990; in Africa, the number increased from 184 to 216 million in the same period.[2] In many Latin American countries, wage earners in urban areas received 20 to 40 percent less wage income in 1990 than they had in 1980.[3] For Africa, average per capita income dropped to levels found in the early 1960s.[4]

In both regions, there was dramatic evidence of economic distress. As industrial production dropped and public sector employment and wages were reduced, the number of workers in the informal sector increased. In Latin America by 1989, an estimated 30 million people earned incomes in the informal economy. Between 1980 and 1985, the number of people in this sector increased by 39 percent, a trend accompanied by a significant drop in average income.[5] Country studies confirm these overall trends. In Chile, unemployment increased markedly, particularly among the lowest income group, and real wages fell by 20 percent over the course of the five-year period.[6] In Quito, Ecuador, estimates indicated a decrease of 53 percent in real wages between 1980 and 1989.[7] Real minimum wages fell 47 percent in Mexico between 1980 and 1989 and by 32 percent in Argentina, 31 percent in Chile, 37 percent in Colombia, and 77 percent in Peru in the same period.[8]

Conditions in Africa were, if anything, more difficult. In Côte d'Ivoire, formal sector employment dropped almost 30 percent between 1981 and 1985 and estimates indicate that real per capita income declined an average of 2.6 percent annually.[9] In 1985, a study in Zambia indicated that 80 percent of manufacturing jobs were in the informal sector.[10] Cuts in public sector employment opportunities and wages were

Table 2.1 *Real GDP growth in Latin America and Africa, 1971–1992 (percent)*

	Latin America and Caribbean[a]	Sub-Saharan Africa[b]
1971	6.5	0.6
1972	6.9	2.7
1973	8.5	2.9
1974	6.3	7.7
1975	3.1	1.4
1976	5.8	7.7
1977	4.9	4.7
1978	3.6	0.0
1979	6.1	2.9
1980	5.7	3.8
1981	−0.1	0.1
1982	−1.5	2.5
1983	−2.6	−0.4
1984	3.9	−0.1
1985	3.3	2.9
1986	4.5	3.8
1987	3.2	0.8
1988	0.6	3.7
1989	1.3	3.1
1990	−0.1	2.0
1991	3.1	1.8
1992	2.2	2.4
Annual average		
1971–1980	5.5	4.0
1980–1991	1.7	2.1

[a] Includes twenty-seven countries.
[b] Includes forty-two countries.
Sources: World Bank, *World Tables* (1993:22–25); World Bank (1993:241).

extensive. In addition, inflation cut deeply into the earning capacity of the population in a large number of countries. This was particularly true in Latin America, where five of the eight countries had average annual inflation rates of 50 percent or more (see Table 2.3).

Political data are equally evocative. Table 2.4 tabulates the incidence of several types of political events, culled from reports in major news sources between 1980 and 1992 for sixteen countries. During this period, fifty riots were reported, with Nigeria, Kenya, and Zambia leading the list for frequency of such events.[11] Fifty-one strikes were reported in the same news sources, with Argentina, Bolivia, Brazil, and Peru accounting for 63 percent of the total. During this same period, twenty-seven coups or coup attempts were reported. Bolivia accounted for six of these, and Argentina, Ethiopia, Ghana, and Nigeria each accounted for four coups or attempted coups. Eleven of the sixteen countries experienced at least one regime

Table 2.2 Real GDP per capita growth in Latin America and Africa, 1973–1991 (percent)

	1973	1974	1975	1976	1977	1978	1979	1980	1981	1982	1983	1984	1985	1986	1987	1988	1989	1990	1991[a]
Argentina	2.0	3.7	-2.2	-1.9	4.8	-4.9	5.5	0.4	-8.3	-6.9	1.4	0.8	-6.1	4.6	1.1	-4.2	-5.3	-1.7	3.8
Bolivia	2.7	2.5	3.9	3.4	1.5	0.6	-2.6	-3.5	-1.7	-6.8	-6.9	-1.5	-3.2	-5.6	0.1	1.3	0.4	0.0	1.7
Brazil	11.1	6.5	2.8	7.2	2.2	0.9	4.3	6.6	-6.5	-1.7	-5.5	3.1	5.6	5.7	1.2	-2.3	2.2	-6.2	-0.1
Chile	-7.1	-0.7	-14.3	2.0	8.3	6.7	6.7	6.1	3.9	-15.5	-2.4	4.5	0.7	3.9	4.0	5.6	8.2	0.5	4.3
Colombia	4.6	3.6	0.0	2.5	1.8	6.1	3.1	1.9	-0.1	-1.2	-0.5	1.4	1.2	4.1	3.4	2.2	1.6	2.2	0.4
Ecuador	24.6	2.8	2.2	6.5	3.3	4.0	2.5	1.7	1.2	-1.6	-4.7	1.4	1.6	0.4	-10.8	8.3	-2.2	4.5	4.3
Mexico	4.8	2.8	2.6	1.3	0.5	5.5	6.4	6.0	6.2	-2.9	-6.3	1.5	0.7	-5.6	0.0	-0.5	1.6	2.7	1.6
Peru	2.4	6.2	0.8	-0.9	-2.3	-2.4	3.1	0.5	4.7	-3.7	-14.3	4.4	-0.2	5.4	7.6	-10.1	-13.7	-6.2	0.5
Average of eight Latin American countries	5.7	3.4	-0.5	2.5	2.5	2.0	3.6	2.5	-0.1	-5.0	-4.9	2.0	0.1	1.6	0.8	0.0	-0.9	-0.5	2.1
Cameroon	2.7	7.7	-3.6	1.2	5.0	11.6	9.2	12.2	9.7	-0.2	4.9	3.1	4.9	5.1	-9.1	-10.4	-6.2	-5.4	-8.2
Côte d'Ivoire	1.7	-0.7	4.3	7.8	2.4	7.1	-1.2	-0.3	-5.0	-2.3	-6.4	-9.1	-2.2	-0.4	-8.2	-4.3	-6.7	-7.1	-4.2
Ethiopia	0.6	-1.4	-2.5	0.0	0.0	-3.7	3.6	1.6	-0.6	-1.1	2.3	-4.8	-9.5	3.1	5.8	-1.4	-1.8	-4.8	-3.6
Ghana	0.2	4.7	-15.2	-5.3	0.3	8.3	-3.3	-1.7	-5.5	-9.3	-7.5	5.0	1.3	1.5	1.1	2.1	1.7	-0.1	1.8
Kenya	2.1	-0.1	-2.3	-1.5	5.3	2.8	3.4	1.3	0.0	-2.1	-2.5	-2.2	0.5	3.3	2.1	2.5	1.1	0.8	-1.8
Nigeria	4.7	8.1	-6.0	6.1	3.0	-8.5	3.6	0.8	-12.0	-3.9	-9.5	-7.2	6.0	-1.3	-3.1	6.6	3.7	2.6	2.1
Senegal	-8.0	1.1	4.6	5.7	-4.2	-8.5	5.6	-4.7	-4.4	12.0	-0.7	-6.9	0.9	1.5	0.9	1.9	-3.4	1.5	1.2
Zambia	-3.3	3.5	-5.1	3.0	-7.5	-2.3	-6.2	-0.3	2.5	-6.1	-5.5	-4.4	-2.1	-3.4	-0.5	1.9	-4.3	-2.8	-5.7
Average of eight African countries	0.1	2.9	-3.2	2.1	0.6	0.9	1.8	1.1	-1.9	-1.6	-3.1	-3.3	0.0	1.2	-1.4	-0.1	-2.0	-1.9	-2.3

[a] 1991 data are calculated from estimates of GDP.

Source: calculated from constant local price GDP and population. World Bank, *World Tables* (1993).

Table 2.3 *Average annual inflation rates in Latin America and Africa, 1980–1991 (percent)*

	1980–1991
Argentina	416.8
Bolivia	363.8
Brazil	327.7
Chile	20.5
Colombia	25.0
Ecuador	38.1
Mexico	18.2
Peru	287.4
Cameroon	4.5
Côte d'Ivoire	3.9
Ethiopia	2.4
Ghana	40.2
Kenya	9.3
Nigeria	66.5
Senegal	5.9
Zambia	42.3[a]

[a] For 1980–1990, World Bank (1992).
Source: World Bank (1993: 262–263).

Table 2.4 *Protest and instability in Latin America and Africa, 1980–1992*

	Riots	Strikes	Military coups or coup attempts
Argentina	3	12	4
Bolivia	1	6	6
Brazil	4	9	1
Chile	0	4	0
Colombia	1	4	0
Ecuador	2	2	0
Mexico	1	4	0
Peru	3	5	1
Cameroon	0	1	1
Côte d'Ivoire	1	0	0
Ethiopia	0	0	4
Ghana	1	1	4
Kenya	8	2	1
Nigeria	15	1	4
Senegal	3	0	0
Zambia	7	0	1

Sources: BBC, *Christian Science Monitor, Los Angeles Times, New York Times, Wall Street Journal, Washington Post.*

change between 1980 and 1992. In sub-Saharan Africa in 1980, fourteen of forty-five countries had military governments (31 percent); in 1992, there were sixteen such governments (36 percent).

These events indicate the widespread existence of political dissent and regime vulnerability – extensive mobilization of students, urban workers, and professionals, and the emergence or reemergence of activism among political parties, labor unions, and civic associations of all kinds.[12] Hidden behind such events were other factors – evidence of the ineffectiveness of national police and security forces, weakened by corruption, abuses of authority, austerity budgets, low pay, and declining morale.[13] Conditions were most severe in Africa. Some 7 million lives were lost through war in sub-Saharan Africa between 1960 and 1990.[14] Countless others died from violence and the massive population movements and famines spawned by war and political discord. By the end of the decade of the 1980s, there were an estimated 16 million refugees from war, internal disorder, and famine in that region.[15] Violence and strife reached such levels in Angola, Chad, Ethiopia, Liberia, Mozambique, Rwanda, Somalia, Sudan, and Uganda that evidence of civic order and government virtually disappeared for extended periods of time.

Political dissent and upheaval had other, more positive consequences, however. Overall, the decade witnessed the widely celebrated resurgence of democratic systems and, in Latin America, the return of the military to the barracks, at least for the moment. At the outset of the decade of the 1980s, ten of nineteen Latin American countries were ruled by the military (53 percent); in 1992, there remained only one such country (5 percent), although the military continued to have significant informal political influence in at least eight others.[16] In 1992, there were at least eleven genuine multiparty political systems with competitive and periodic elections in the region. In Africa, while military presence increased over the course of the decade, there was a more salutary movement of civilian one-party regimes toward multiparty systems. Among thirty-one regimes with civilian leadership in 1980, only six allowed multiparty competition (19 percent).[17] Of twenty-nine civilian regimes in 1992, eleven were categorized as having multiparty competitive systems (38 percent) and at least one other country was moving toward a multiparty electoral system.[18]

THE NATURE OF CRISIS

Domestic policies for economic development created a basis for stagnation and decline in many countries in Latin America and Africa, and an altered international environment contributed to the depth of crisis and made recovery a distant prospect for most.[19] For most countries, separating domestic and international causes of the crisis is difficult. Domestic policies often had their origin in approaches to development espoused by international agencies, advisors, or intellectual trends. They were also frequently adopted to deal with the potentially negative impact of international economic conditions, or to respond to a desire to lessen dependency on former colonial centers. International conditions discouraged the development potential of many countries. In the 1970s, rising fuel costs, and then an international liquidity crisis, rising interest rates, and falling commodity prices in the 1980s were significant factors that laid bare deficiencies in national development policies. Conditions linked to "cascading monetarism" exposed problems created by extensive state intervention within contexts characterized by poor economic planning, inefficient agricultural and industrial sectors, weak economic institutions, low savings rates, restrictive trade policies, and ineffective public bureaucracies.

In Latin America, import substitution policies, which had fueled significant growth in the 1960s and into the 1970s in many countries, began to suffer from a series of limitations. In some cases, domestic markets were saturated with domestically produced goods that could not be marketed internationally because of high production costs and poor quality. Protectionism and a wide variety of subsidies to both capital and labor encouraged inefficient industries. Moreover, import substitution actually increased demand for imports and foreign exchange to stimulate the industrialization process.[20] At the same time, incentives to the agricultural sector were repressed through policies to hold domestic food prices low to stimulate industrialization.[21] With agricultural exports discouraged through overvalued exchange rates and domestic manufactures uncompetitive internationally, foreign exchange crises were inevitable. This, combined with excess demand for consumption goods from urban sectors, encouraged high rates of inflation. Together, these factors contributed to an increasing consensus that import substitution as a development strategy for Latin America had become exhausted.[22]

In Africa, post-colonial initiatives to spur economic growth encouraged highly centralized economic management, despite institutions and human resources that were poorly prepared for the management tasks this implied. Equally important was the burgeoning of the parastatal sector that quickly became populated by large, inefficient, deficit-prone, and highly subsidized enterprises. The agricultural sector was affected negatively by policies to hold food prices low and state trading companies that taxed export agriculture heavily in the name of modernization and industrialization.[23] In addition to these policy-induced problems, many countries in Africa experienced severe and sustained drought during the 1980s. High rates of population growth and war added to the causes of economic stagnation in the region.

Table 2.5, which compares growth in productivity between 1965–1980 and 1980–1991 in the sixteen countries, indicates a consistent pattern of slower average annual GDP growth rates for the latter period compared with the former, with the exceptions of Chile and Ghana. With very few exceptions, this pattern is consistent across all sectors of the economies of these countries.

The rapid rise in fuel prices in 1973–1974 and again in 1979–1980 had a significant impact on economies whose industrial and institutional underpinnings were weak. Government budget deficits, which were already significant for many countries in the 1970s, particularly in Africa, continued to be a major problem in the 1980s (see Table 2.6). In the 1970s and early 1980s, many countries responded to rising energy

Table 2.5 *Average annual growth rate of production in Latin America and Africa, 1965–1991 (percent)*

	GDP		Agriculture		Industry		Services	
	1965–1980	1980–1991	1965–1980	1980–1991	1965–1980	1980–1991	1965–1980	1980–1991
Argentina	3.4	−0.4	1.4	1.5	3.3	−1.4	4.1	0.1
Bolivia	4.4	0.3	3.8	1.8	3.7	−0.8	5.6	−0.1
Brazil	9.0	2.5	3.8	2.6	10.1	1.7	9.4	3.2
Chile	1.9	3.6	1.6	4.1	0.8	3.6	2.7	3.4
Colombia	5.7	3.7	4.5	3.2	5.7	4.8	6.3	3.1
Ecuador	8.8	2.1	3.4	4.4	13.7	1.1	7.6	2.1
Mexico	6.5	1.2	3.2	0.5	7.6	1.3	6.5	1.3
Peru	3.9	−0.4	1.0	2.2	4.4	−1.1	4.2	−0.9
Cameroon	5.1	1.4	4.2	1.1	7.8	2.2	4.8	1.1
Côte d'Ivoire	6.8	−0.5	3.3	−1.2	10.4	−1.6	11.8	0.8
Ethiopia	2.7	1.6	1.2	0.3	3.5	1.8	5.2	3.1
Ghana	1.3	3.2	1.6	1.2	1.4	3.7	1.1	6.6
Kenya	6.8	4.2	5.0	3.2	9.7	4.0	7.2	4.9
Nigeria	6.0	1.9	1.7	3.5	13.1	−0.4	5.9	3.1
Senegal	2.3	3.1	1.4	2.7	5.5	3.8	1.9	3.0
Zambia	2.0	0.8	2.2	3.3	2.1	0.9	1.8	0.0

Sources: World Bank (1992: 220–221, 1993: 240–241).

prices, decreased industrial and agricultural productivity, and increased demands for public sector investment by borrowing heavily abroad, an activity made extraordinarily attractive by an excess of international liquidity and low interest rates.[24] In fact, for a large number of countries, deficits were increasingly financed by external borrowing. The external debt for the eight Latin American countries grew by 26 percent between 1976 and 1980 and by 19.1 percent between 1980 and 1982. In the eight African countries, external debt grew by 40.4 and 12.8 percent in the same periods.[25]

In the early 1980s, tightened credit supplies and rapidly rising interest rates brought a sudden drop in international liquidity that triggered a debt crisis throughout Latin America and Africa. When Mexico announced it was not able to service its 62 billion dollar debt in August 1982, few countries were in a position to avoid the negative consequences of a new and harsher international economic environment. Table 2.7 shows external debt as a percentage of GDP rising rapidly after 1980. It reached 344 percent in Zambia in 1986. Total and per capita debt burdens doubled and even tripled in many countries between 1980 and 1991 (see Table 2.8). Interest payments accounted for over 50 percent of government expenditures in Brazil, Mexico, Peru, and Zambia in 1991. The decade was littered with intense negotiations with international financial institutions to reschedule this debt.

The burden of high levels of indebtedness was increased by a decade of low commodity export prices.[26] Between early 1981 and early 1983, the price of oil from

Table 2.6 *Government budget surplus/deficit[a] as a percentage of GDP in Latin America and Africa, 1975–1990*

	1975	1976	1977	1978	1979	1980	1981	1982	1983	1984	1985	1986	1987	1988	1989	1990
Argentina	10.49	7.11	2.77	3.21	2.60	3.53	9.13	7.45	12.74	5.06	7.39	2.64	3.77	2.66	—	—
Bolivia										29.67		0.06	[0.66]	0.64	1.24	1.48
Brazil	0.50	1.80	0.84	2.76	—	2.38	2.44	2.57	4.09	4.87	11.16	13.34	12.08	15.33	16.14	—
Chile	[0.14]	[1.37]	1.11	0.11	[4.82]	[5.41]	[2.59]	0.98	2.63	2.97	2.36	0.97	[0.48]	0.23	—	—
Colombia	0.22	[1.00]	[0.63]	[0.68]	0.77	1.76	3.05	4.73	4.19	4.32	-3.19	1.58	0.69	1.34	1.89	—
Ecuador	—				—			—					—			
Mexico	4.91	4.67	3.30	2.70	3.33	3.13	6.67	15.44	7.95	7.29	8.73	13.10	13.56	10.19	5.36	—
Peru	3.27	4.19	3.21	5.07	0.54	2.37	3.98	3.20	7.46	4.38	2.19	3.67	5.69	2.78	4.16	0.48
Cameroon	2.24	2.41	0.38	[0.42]	[2.77]	[0.51]	3.26	2.54	[1.29]	—	—	—	3.41	—	—	—
Côte d'Ivoire					8.65	10.85				3.01						
Ethiopia	4.10	5.41	3.41	5.81	3.19	4.48	3.83	5.46	13.86	6.32	8.76	7.46	6.62	—	—	—
Ghana	8.07	12.47	11.95	11.80	7.32	5.09	8.16	6.10	2.68	1.79	2.21	[0.06]	[0.54]	[0.37]	—	—
Kenya	5.21	6.46	4.00	4.15	6.96	4.91	7.08	8.32	5.21	5.21	6.63	4.71	6.69	4.42	6.92	—
Nigeria	—	—		—	—					4.56	2.76	3.80	8.91	—		
Senegal	0.58	—	3.19	[0.30]	0.79	[0.90]	3.49	6.91	6.27	8.50	—	—	—	—	—	—
Zambia	21.52	14.24	13.16	14.42	9.06	18.52	12.90	18.59	7.83	8.39	15.17	21.63	12.98	15.41	—	—

[a] Surpluses are bracketed.
Source: IMF (1992: 142–143).

Table 2.7 *External debt as a percentage of GDP in Latin America and Africa, 1980–1991*

	1980	1981	1982	1983	1984	1985	1986	1987	1988	1989	1990	1991
Argentina	17.6	28.7	76.6	70.8	62.6	77.4	66.6	72.6	62.6	107.6	58.7	49.4
Bolivia	53.9	46.3	56.9	69.4	67.8	93.9	143.6	135.4	110.8	91.7	94.9	76.1
Brazil	29.8	30.7	33.0	48.4	50.5	47.6	42.4	42.1	35.2	24.9	24.6	28.0
Chile	43.8	48.0	71.1	90.7	102.8	127.4	125.7	113.4	88.7	71.1	68.8	57.2
Colombia	20.8	24.0	26.4	29.5	31.5	40.8	44.0	46.8	43.3	42.7	42.8	41.7
Ecuador	51.1	55.0	61.9	71.7	81.2	71.7	82.9	99.5	107.3	115.2	113.9	107.5
Mexico	29.5	31.3	49.5	62.4	54.0	52.5	77.9	78.2	58.9	46.6	40.3	36.0
Peru	45.1	34.5	43.2	59.4	61.3	79.8	63.9	63.0	6.2	75.3	82.3	85.2
Cameroon	33.5	30.3	35.0	34.9	34.1	36.1	34.4	32.4	33.3	46.5	54.7	53.8
Côte d'Ivoire	55.6	78.9	103.9	115.4	123.5	139.5	118.3	130.7	135.9	169.7	181.9	197.9
Ethiopia	19.6	26.5	28.0	28.6	31.5	39.2	42.5	49.3	52.1	50.5	54.3	52.6
Ghana	9.0	5.9	4.7	7.9	25.8	35.3	47.6	67.2	58.7	62.8	64.5	65.6
Kenya	47.5	48.3	53.6	62.1	57.7	68.2	64.5	71.9	67.7	68.8	80.8	78.7
Nigeria	9.6	14.8	16.8	23.5	22.3	24.1	56.4	113.1	97.6	102.3	97.5	101.1
Senegal	48.8	67.4	72.0	83.8	94.2	99.4	85.7	87.7	78.2	70.6	64.0	61.0
Zambia	84.0	90.3	95.3	113.9	139.5	205.0	344.4	318.6	188.3	154.6	196.0	190.0

Source: calculated from World Bank, *World Tables* (1993).

Table 2.8 *Debt burdens for Latin American and African countries, 1980 and 1991*

	Total external debt (millions of dollars)		Per capita debt (dollars)	
	1980	1991	1980	1991
Argentina	10,285	16,774	371	513
Bolivia	2,124	4,075	379	558
Brazil	37,824	57,500	319	380
Chile	4,885	9,399	440	701
Colombia	4,090	17,369	153	530
Ecuador	2,655	12,469	332	1,155
Mexico	33,490	41,215	480	495
Peru	6,204	20,709	357	946
Cameroon	2,002	6,278	238	528
Côte d'Ivoire	4,265	18,847	514	1,520
Ethiopia	728	3,475	23	66
Ghana	1,011	4,209	86	275
Kenya	1,745	7,014	110	281
Nigeria	4,997	34,497	59	348
Senegal	906	3,522	159	463
Zambia	1,815	7,279	313	877

Source: World Bank (1993: 238, 278).

Mexico dropped from 33.2 dollars to 29 dollars a barrel before plunging to 12 dollars in 1986. Nigeria's oil stood at 40 dollars a barrel in 1981, dropped to 30 dollars in 1983, and then to 19 dollars in 1987. Bolivia's tin, which had earned 760.36 cents a pound in 1980, sold for 253.36 cents in 1991. Zambia and Chile's copper, which had sold at 99.12 cents a pound in 1980, declined to 62.13 cents a pound in 1986 before beginning to rise again. Colombia's coffee, which reached a high of 216.69 cents a pound in 1977, declined to 83.92 cents a pound in 1991. Brazil's cocoa beans sold at 183.53 cents a pound in 1977 and declined to 49.06 cents by 1990. Nigeria's groundnuts earned 623 dollars a metric ton in 1981, 383 dollars a ton in 1982, and then continued to decline to 350 dollars a ton until prices recovered in 1986. Similarly, its palm kernel exports reached 500 dollars a metric ton in 1979 and declined to 181 dollars by 1987.

Domestic policy adjustments to the crisis were widespread, as was the need to negotiate with the International Monetary Fund (IMF) for emergency assistance to meet international obligations and stave off national bankruptcy. Devaluations, long resisted by domestic policy elites for their politically destabilizing impact, became a common phenomenon throughout the decade, as did efforts to impose austerity budgets, lower inflationary pressures, and cut back on a wide variety of subsidies to industrial and agricultural producers and consumers. Almost all countries in both regions introduced at least one major economic reform package. Among the most well known were the adjustment programs introduced in 1983 in Ghana, 1985 in Bolivia, 1986 in Nigeria, and 1987 in Mexico. Also well known was Chile's adjustment program of the mid-1970s and its subsequent policy package of 1982–1983. The IMF concluded numerous stand-by agreements with Latin American and African countries over the decade between 1982 and 1992, and the World Bank was equally busy negotiating structural adjustment loans with them. Along with these agreements came strong pressure to adopt market-oriented development strategies.

These and other efforts to alter domestic policies often revealed underlying political weaknesses. Frequently, histories of fragile political legitimacy left governments with little ability – or desire – to introduce new economic measures, particularly ones that would have negative implications for large or politically powerful groups. In fact, initiatives to carry out economic reforms frequently met with political protests that weakly legitimized regimes were unable to withstand, further increasing political instability. Some reform efforts, even when introduced, were ineffective in the face of widespread resistance and weak enforcement capacity.[27] Economic grievances lay behind the riots that met efforts to diminish or end subsidies on corn meal in Zambia in 1986 and 1990. Student and police strikes occurred in 1987 in Senegal and riots broke out in 1988. Nigeria experienced student riots in 1989 to protest the negative impact of structural adjustment policies; Brazil witnessed protest strikes in 1989 and 1991. Students protested against bus fare increases in Bolivia in 1980 and riots broke out in Ecuador and Brazil in 1983. There were food riots in Argentina and Venezuela in 1989 and again in 1990.

But political unrest was not a simple response to economic hardship and the bite of policy change. It was often deeply political also. In large numbers of countries, authoritarian systems that had held power for many years were confronted by demands of diverse groups of citizens to participate more fully in public debate and decision making. This was particularly true in the late 1970s and early 1980s in Latin America. In earlier periods, claims that strong authoritarian governments were required to impose economic and political order conducive to economic growth and that civilian governments had proved themselves ineffective and corrupt in this task were made by militarists seizing power in Argentina, Brazil, Chile, Peru, and Uruguay. With this rationale called into question by the reality of the economic situation, the extraconstitutional nature of military regime authority was also widely exposed.[28]

Elite groups, in addition to traditional political parties, mobilized to protest the continuation of authoritarian rule and to negotiate the military back to the barracks. Throughout the region, civilian elites – often representing the political parties and unions that had been suppressed by the military – met to negotiate "pacts" that would ease the transition to civilian and democratic regimes.[29] Pact making generally involved not only coming to agreement about the rules of the game for political competition and policy decision making, but also overcoming long-standing animosities and policy divisions among diverse groups of politicians and economic interests. Rank and file party and union members were publicly engaged in such efforts, organizing protest marches and strikes against the authoritarian regimes.[30] And from local communities came pressure from religious organizations, women's groups, and others demanding democratic reforms and greater responsiveness from government.[31]

In Africa, protest also focused on economic and political grievances. The economic crisis helped undermine the legitimacy of regimes that, over the decades since independence, had been increasingly held together only by clientelism, cronyism, and corruption. These neo-patrimonial regimes, most clearly in evidence in Zaire, were characterized by the personal rule of strongmen with personally loyal militaries. In such systems, patronage networks radiating from the strongman throughout the political system were established and kept in place through the distribution of jobs and other economic benefits.[32] With ongoing economic crisis, which severely limited the spoils that could be used to shore up loyalty to the regime, such systems became increasingly weak, ineffective, and vulnerable, as well as more likely to use coercion and violence as a means of staying in power. Through this dynamic, some regimes could self-destruct, as was the experience of Ethiopia, Liberia, Somalia, and Sudan.

More broadly, the deterioration of cohesiveness within elite coalitions that had helped maintain political systems in power was widespread. Elite defection from long-standing support coalitions weakened existing regimes, encouraged movements toward political opening, and generated significant international interest in such movements.[33] To the extent that the cohesion of political coalitions depended strictly on rents, the loss of the capacity to provide them was a significant factor fueling elite defections and political opposition.[34]

In the face of increasingly limited opportunities to participate in decision making, citizens in many African countries began to agitate for democratic elections and greater freedom to organize political parties and contest elections.[35] In some countries, political elites sought to engender political openings, as in Côte d'Ivoire and Gabon, while in others, opposition groups coalesced in national conferences to negotiate new rules of the game among themselves. These conferences, similar to a number of pact-making initiatives in Latin America, were important events in the movement toward political opening in Benin, Congo, Mali, and Togo.[36] In some cases – Kenya and Ethiopia are good examples – the breakdown of the effectiveness of one-party or no-party regimes was accompanied by the politicization of claims for ethnic and regional diversity or even separation.

As in Latin America, political dissent and civic activism were not restricted to political and economic elites. In particular, local and national civic mobilization was evident in the burgeoning of non-governmental organizations, religious associations, and grassroots self-help groups that took development "into their own hands" and provided a base for resistance to regimes in power.[37] According to one observer, "The expansion of nonformal participation in autonomous, voluntary associations has become a major means for the limitation of state power and the creation from below of an informed, efficacious, vigilant citizenry."[38] Civic and religious organizations were the site of political mobilization and protest because, in many countries, explicitly political organization of opposition was barred or repressed.

While some have argued that Africa's domestic political mobilization was spurred by earlier examples from Latin America, destruction of communist regimes in Eastern Europe and the former Soviet Union in the late 1980s, and pressures brought to bear by international donor agencies, the domestic roots of these democracy movements were deep.[39] Years of pent-up frustration with being unable to participate effectively in their political systems, increasingly evident corruption, brutality, and repression by entrenched and personalistic leaders, and then the impact of the economic crisis, which significantly undermined the availability of rents for maintaining political coalitions in contexts of weakly legitimized political institutions, explain far more about the timing, scope, and nature of political protests in Africa than the demonstration effect from other regions. Virtually every country in Latin America and Africa experienced political upheaval during this troubled era; international pressures and trends tell part of the story, but the far larger part of its dynamics is told by country-specific events and country-specific heroics.

THE IMPACT OF CRISIS

And what of the impact on the state of these economic and political crises? In Chapter 1, I suggested that:

- the institutional capacity to set rules of the game for economic and political interactions would be undermined;
- the technical capacity of government to manage macroeconomic policies would be strengthened;
- the administrative capacity to carry out normal functions of government would be weakened;
- and the capacity to mediate conflict and manage demands for political participation would be diminished.

As data in the following pages indicate, these hypotheses summarize the experience of many states in Latin America and Africa.

Institutional capacity

Sustained development requires relatively stable rules of the game for regulating economic and political relations. Such rules, when effectively enforced, encourage predictability in economic and political interactions and inspire individuals and groups to make current decisions in the context of longer-term expectations. Weakened institutional capacity means decreased ability to maintain the authority of government to make and implement laws and to hold both officials and citizens accountable for their actions. Concretely, loss of institutional capacity translates into inability to regulate property rights, enforce contracts, maintain law and order, and control official acts of corruption and abuses of power. Disputes over electoral processes and results, stalemates between executive and legislative branches of government, and allegations of fraud and abuses of power are other indicators of contention over basic norms for political society.

Under the impact of deep and sustained crisis, governments in Latin America and Africa lost the ability to set and enforce broad rules of the game. But loss of institutional capacity was not uniform across countries. Generally, Latin American states retained greater capacity to set and enforce authoritative rules than did African states. In large part, this was a result of the historical legacy of the relatively strong states that had emerged in this region, and the lack of such a tradition in Africa, where state building had always been challenged by the primacy of ethnic and regional identities, by the arbitrariness of colonial borders, and by the legacies of colonial rule.

In Latin America, states such as those that emerged in Argentina, Brazil, Chile, Venezuela, and Mexico had long been institutionalized in terms of their coercive and administrative infrastructure and had penetrated deep into social systems through government-sponsored programs, patronage networks, and military and police presence. Then, the emergence in the 1960s and 1970s of bureaucratic authoritarian regimes, identified particularly with Argentina, Brazil, Chile, and Uruguay, further entrenched a tradition of extensive and coercive governments.[40] Although not conforming to the bureaucratic authoritarian model, the Mexican state was also noted for its strong capacity to set the rules for economic and political interaction.[41] States in Colombia, Costa Rica, and Venezuela, while less autonomous and more penetrated by societal interests, had considerable capacity to govern authoritatively.[42] The institutional capacity of such states did not ensure equity or the effective representation of interests in national decision making, but did ensure the maintenance of order and periods of relatively stable rules of the game for economic interactions.

During the 1980s, however, state authority collapsed for extended periods in Bolivia and Peru, was severely challenged through the exposure of official corruption in Argentina, Brazil, Mexico, and Venezuela, confronted by the countervailing power of drug barons and military chieftains in Colombia and Panama, threatened by civil war in El Salvador and Nicaragua, and menaced by repeated coup attempts and officially declared states of siege in Argentina, Bolivia, and Venezuela. Disregard for laws and institutions increased almost universally among citizens and agents of the state. Regimes in El Salvador, Guatemala, Panama, and elsewhere expanded the use of coercion, even as their legitimate claims to power declined.

Although many African states were highly centralized, interventionist, and authoritarian, the 1980s exposed the fact that they were simultaneously weak and unable to coerce social conformity. Authoritarianism, centralism, and statism reflected colonial tradition and a generally misguided effort by political leaders to hold tenuous nations together.[43] Mazrui argued that many African governments became "excessively authoritarian to disguise the fact that [they were] inadequately authoritative."[44] Unable to establish either economic or political stability essential to development, many African states became "antidevelopmental" states, in which "mismanagement, inefficiency, and pervasive corruption of the public sector as well as political instability and the inability to prevent widespread evasion of laws and regulations," undermined any prospects for growth.[45]

Early in the decade, Robert Jackson and Carl Rosberg called attention to states that existed only in international arenas, so weak was their capacity to exert control and authority internally.[46] Richard Sandbrook wrote of "fictitious" states and Jackson of "quasi" states and "juridical artifacts" of such weak capacity to enforce rules of behavior and ensure the protection of society that economic development could not occur.[47] As a consequence, some countries resembled aggregations of sub-national groups pursuing strategies to cope and survive in the absence of effective state authority. Evidence suggested that in such conditions, many citizens became detached or disengaged from interaction with agents or institutions of state authority.[48] While significant numbers of governments in Africa did not reach such extreme conditions, a crisis of legitimacy was evident even in relatively strong states like Kenya.

In economics, the loss of institutional capacity in both regions was most widely evident in the burgeoning of black and informal markets, in which rules of the game were set and maintained through non-state agents and institutions.[49] In Ghana prior to policy reform initiatives in 1983, the black market was so widespread that it virtually replaced the official market; in this context, government-mandated prices were meaningless.[50] A similar situation existed in a fully "dollarized" economy in Bolivia prior to policy reforms in 1985. The loosening of the rules of the formal economy further increased the legitimacy crisis of the state. "As the black market feeds upon resources from the formal economy and undercuts prices by means of smuggling and tax evasion, economic problems worsen ... The clandestine economy cannot thrive without the evasion of regulations and taxes by the bribing of officials. However, the black market contributes in turn to the debility of the government; it not only deepens systematic corruption, but also shrinks the state's fiscal basis."[51]

The legitimacy of both political and economic rules of the game was also undermined by a crisis in judicial systems and widespread corruption in government regulatory systems; enforcement of contracts, the enforcement of laws against rule breakers, and the ability to carry on economic functions without recourse to bribery and subornation became increasingly difficult. In Angola, Bolivia, parts of Central America, Colombia, Ethiopia, Peru, Somalia, Zaire, and elsewhere, drug barons, local strongmen, and revolutionary groups were often more able to enforce rules and ensure order at local and regional levels than were national governments charged with such tasks.[52] In many such cases, and particularly in Africa, institutional capacity had never been strong; under the dual impact of economic and political crisis it was weakened further.

Governments did not necessarily remain passive in the face of the decline in institutional capacity. In fact, the 1980s and early 1990s are replete with evidence of efforts to rewrite the rules of the game for economic and political interactions.[53] In a large number of countries, efforts to introduce market-oriented economic development strategies implied initiatives to recognize more viable rules of the game. Privatization of public enterprises was undertaken in most countries, accompanied by initiatives to define the limits of public authority over private economic interactions. Similarly, deregulation efforts incorporated significant attention to rethinking the rights of property and the power of government to affect such rights. Extensive efforts to revamp judicial systems were undertaken to strengthen the rule of law and the ability of the state to enforce contracts and obligations. And, efforts to negotiate pacts and coalitions of support for transitions to democratic regimes were clear evidence of political pressure to rewrite basic rules about the relationship between the state and civic society. New constitutions were ratified in several countries as witness to these efforts to redefine roles, responsibilities, and conditions of accountability.

Technical capacity

Economic development requires that states have the ability to manage macroeconomic policy and to assess economic policy options. In analyses of the differences between the generally strong economic performance of several countries in Asia and the weak performance of many Latin American and African countries, differences in the content of their macroeconomic policies are frequently cited as centrally important.[54] And indeed, a large policy-focused literature exploring the origins of lagging industrial and agricultural productivity, debt, inflation, balance of payments crises, and budget deficits calls attention to flawed macroeconomic policies and their management in both Latin America and Africa.[55]

Despite evident limitations in macroeconomic policy making, technical capacity to establish and manage macroeconomic policy increased in many countries in both regions. In part, increased technical capacity was a response to the need to design stabilization and structural adjustment programs insisted upon by the IMF, the World Bank, and other international financial institutions as conditions for lending. These institutions became fixtures of national policy making in large numbers of countries in the 1980s and 1990s. "Policy dialogue" became a catch phrase for the insertion of such institutions in national policy-making arenas during these difficult years and, indeed, never before had they played such an extensive role in setting conditions for economic policy and institutional reform.

In Latin America, many countries had a significant supply of economic analysts; this supply increased during the decade and those trained in economics reached historically high level positions within government. Economic advisory teams and top ministerial positions were increasingly recruited from universities, think tanks, international agencies, and the private sector rather than from among party or personal loyalists.[56] Presidents of Colombia, Mexico, and Ecuador in the late 1980s and early 1990s were formally trained in economics and ministers of finance in Mexico, Argentina, Chile, Colombia, Ecuador, and Peru held PhDs in the discipline.

The influence of technocrats on high-level policy making, strategic development planning, and macroeconomic management achieved new heights under the administration of Carlos Salinas de Gortari in Mexico, where many ministerial appointees held post-graduate degrees in economics, often from departments in major US universities. Throughout his government, technocrats were placed in positions of extensive authority and technical analysis units became central to policy-making at all levels, even as traditional economic interest groups lost their easy access to the policy making process. In Chile, eighteen members of President Aylwin's team held graduate degrees.[57] In Peru, four of six top advisors in the Fujimori government held PhDs. In Argentina, Bolivia, Chile, Colombia, Ecuador, Peru, and Venezuela, technocrats assumed ministerial level positions and transformed their organizations through the introduction of computers, policy analysis units, and young, well-trained economists.

During the decade, central economic ministries, their technocratic leadership, and their technical analysis units became more important in national policy making, often to the detriment of cabinets, legislative institutions, party leaders, lobby groups, and traditional ministries such as interior, public works, and foreign affairs. Economic policy making also became more highly centralized and focused around presidents, their economic teams, and the technical units supporting these influential individuals. In a number of countries, economic cabinets formed of top policy advisors met regularly and frequently with the president. Similarly, in several cases, the minister of finance became an economic czar who, through delegated presidential authority, coordinated economic policy making and strategic planning.

Much of the economic policy change that was introduced during the 1980s and 1990s was promulgated through presidential decrees rather than as law debated and passed through legislatures, indicating the extent to which centralized economic management had come to be defined as a presidential and executive prerogative.[58] Presidents were assessed on how well they managed their economic teams and the extent to which such teams developed consensus about the broad direction of national economic policy and the instruments to be used to achieve it.[59]

In Africa, the increase in technical capacity in government was less clear and widespread than it was in Latin America.[60] Much of the impetus for increased technical skills in government came from the international financial institutions. In negotiations over the provision of economic assistance and the conditions to be set for its use, the IMF, the World Bank, and other agencies made insistent demands for data on the condition of national economies, data that were often not available. A frequent sight in ministries of finance and central banks throughout the region was the current mission from the IMF or the World Bank poring over figures, complaining about the lack of data and the unreliability of the data that existed. Equally frequent were complaints that there was "no one to negotiate with" because existing economic skills among state officials were low or even non-existent.

Over time, these demands for data and the need for "someone to negotiate with" encouraged efforts by governments and international agencies to increase technical capacity in central economic ministries.[61] The World Bank and others launched the Africa Capacity Building Foundation in the late 1980s; its purpose was to increase indigenous technical capacity. Similarly, the African Economic

Research Consortium (AERC), created in 1988 by bilateral, multilateral, and private agencies, promoted economic policy research by Africans. In Senegal, the World Bank initiated a 20 million dollar public sector management program, over 5 million of which was targeted for increasing economic and financial management capacities.[62] Regionally, the Southern African Development Coordination Conference (SADCC) and AERC initiated programs to improve economic research and analytic capacity. In Tanzania and Ghana, the World Bank, the United Nations Development Programme, the United States Agency for International Development (USAID), the African Development Bank, and others sponsored seminars, workshops, and training courses to increase knowledge of macroeconomic interactions and policies.[63]

While the supply of those with macroeconomic analytic skills remained scarce in Africa, and those trained were often attracted away from government by jobs with the international agencies or as consultants, economic cabinets met more frequently with chief executives in most countries and economic czars frequently held significant informal power. In addition, institutional changes increased the centralization of economic policy making in key ministries or in the president's office, as occurred in Botswana, Côte d'Ivoire, Ghana, Senegal, Tanzania, and Zambia.[64] New macroeconomic analysis units were established in finance ministries in Senegal and Tanzania and civil service reforms brought specialized managers to the fore, many of whom were employed through contracts based on performance indicators.[65] In Zambia, the administration of Frederick Chiluba brought new professionalism to the ministries of finance and presidency and increased influence to the minister of finance at the expense of the managers of the state-owned corporations.[66] In Côte d'Ivoire, economic policy making moved closer to top level officials as the office of the prime minister became more central than the previously influential ministry of finance and budget.[67]

Thus, many governments increased their technical capacity to set and manage macroeconomic policy during the 1980s and 1990s. Yet countries differed in the extent to which technocratic elites were insulated from the direct pressure of interest groups and political controversy and in the extent to which economic teams were able to work effectively together and agree upon the scope, nature, and priorities of stabilization and structural adjustment measures. There were also significant differences in the ability to generate and communicate a vision of what altered economic policy would bring to the country. Mexico under Salinas is the best example, but Argentina under Menem, Chile under Aylwin, and Ghana under Rawlings are cases in which this vision set the broad framework for understanding policy errors of the past, indicating remedies for these errors, explaining the need for economic hardship in the short run, and putting together coalitions of support around newly defined economic goals. In these cases, the impact of technical capabilities on the formulation and implementation of economic policy was greater because it was paired with a clear and widely disseminated vision of a new and more promising future if major economic policy changes were introduced and sustained.

Administrative capacity

The capacity of states to carry out routine administrative functions and to provide for basic services and investment in human resource development is an often overlooked aspect of economic and political development. It is a critical capacity, however, because it affects the ability of private economic agents to achieve their goals, the availability of a well-trained and healthy workforce, and the satisfaction of basic societal needs. Government budgets and budget allocations begin to suggest what impact more than a decade of economic stagnation and decline had on the administrative capacity of states in Latin America and Africa.

In large numbers of countries, austerity budgets were a clear response to expanding government deficits and inability to continue borrowing funds to finance the deficit. Even where budgets increased, government funding for national development needs often fell in relative terms as increasing proportions of government expenditures were needed to make interest payments on the debt. Table 2.9 indicates that in Bolivia, Brazil, Chile, Kenya, Mexico, and Zambia, proportions of budgets expended on education, health, and other social welfare services generally decreased from 1980 to 1991, while proportions spent on interest payments increased.[68]

Table 2.10 presents an index of per capita health expenditures in sixteen countries. Six of seven Latin American countries and two of five African countries for which data are available decreased the resources available for health care. A similar story emerges from country studies. Drastic reductions in health professionals' salaries in Mexico were documented, as were cutbacks in investment and routine maintenance of health facilities in Chile.[69] In El Salvador and Jamaica, administrative expenditures were cut and investments in preventive medicine suffered in Venezuela.[70]

These cutbacks affected Latin American and African populations at a time when economic hardship increased the number of poverty-induced diseases like malnutrition, gastro-intestinal illnesses, respiratory diseases, cholera, and tuberculosis. AIDs and AIDs-related illnesses reached epidemic proportions at the same time, particularly in Africa.[71] With growing numbers of households no longer employed in the formal sector and with a steady decrease in average wage rates, better-off households that formerly had access to private health care turned increasingly to already overburdened public health care. Everywhere, the impact of austerity budgets for health was felt most among the poor.

In education, the story is similar. Expenditures on education for eight of twelve countries declined significantly on a per capita basis for all or part of the decade, as is evident in Table 2.11.[72] Internal adjustments in sector budget allocations in Chile, Costa Rica, the Dominican Republic, and Venezuela cushioned the impact of these cuts by increasing the share of primary education in overall education expenditures; in Argentina, Colombia, and Jamaica, however, this share fell.[73] Country studies of educational services refer particularly to cuts in teacher salaries, by far the largest portion of education budgets in all countries. In the five years between 1983 and 1988, Mexico's primary school teachers' salaries decreased by 34 percent in real terms; in Costa Rica in 1991, primary teacher salaries were 66 percent of their 1980

Table 2.9 *Percentage of government expenditures for social welfare services and interest payments in Latin America and Africa, 1980 and 1991*

	Education		Health		Housing, social security, and welfare		Interest payments and misc.[a]	
	1980	1991	1980	1991	1980	1991	1980	1991
Argentina	7.3[c]	9.9[d]	1.4[c]	3.0[d]	34.2[c]	39.4[d]	27.8[c]	21.7[d]
Bolivia	24.4[c]	18.7	7.2[c]	3.3	2.7[c]	18.8	25.8[c]	29.3
Brazil	3.8[c]	3.1[d]	8.0	6.7[d]	32.0	35.5[d]	32.0	57.9[d]
Chile	14.5	10.1[e]	7.4	5.9[e]	37.1	33.9[e]	14.8	33.0[e]
Colombia	19.1[d]	—	3.9[d]	—	21.2[d]	—	22.0[d]	—
Ecuador[b]	34.7	18.2[d]	7.8	11.0[d]	1.3	2.5[d]	22.6	43.6[d]
Mexico	18.0	13.9[d]	2.4	1.9[d]	18.5	13.0[d]	27.6	55.5[d]
Peru[b]	15.6	21.2[d]	5.6	5.6[d]	0.0	0.5[d]	35.7	56.4[d]
Cameroon	12.4	12.0[d]	5.1	3.4[d]	8.0	8.7[d]	41.4	21.2[d]
Côte d'Ivoire	16.3	—	3.9	—	4.3	—	58.1	—
Ethiopia	10.1	—	3.7	—	5.4	—	57.0	—
Ghana[b]	22.0	25.7[e]	7.0	9.0[e]	6.8	11.9[e]	39.8	31.1[e]
Kenya[b]	19.6	19.9[d]	7.8	5.4[d]	5.1	3.9[d]	28.2	40.1[d]
Nigeria	—	—	—	—	—	—	—	—
Senegal	23.0	—	4.7	—	9.5	—	31.6	—
Zambia[b]	11.4	8.6[e]	6.1	7.4[e]	3.4	2.0[e]	46.6	57.2[e]

[a] Includes interest payments and expenditures not included in other categories.
[b] Data are for budgetary accounts only.
[c] For 1981.
[d] For a year other than specified, World Bank (1993).
[e] For a year other than specified, World Bank (1992).
Sources: World Bank (1984b: 268–269, 1992: 238–239, 1993: 258–259).

levels.[74] In Argentina, Bolivia, Brazil, Chile, Colombia, Costa Rica, Mexico, and Peru, expenditures on teaching materials fell during the decade.[75] In Bolivia and Costa Rica, the number of students per teacher in primary schools increased and primary enrollment rates declined in Bolivia, Chile, Costa Rica, and El Salvador.[76]

Countries in Africa, with low levels of literacy to begin with, were hard hit by this inability to fund educational services. In Mozambique, "Budget cuts in education have resulted in lower quality and efficiency as well as higher prices for books and other school materials. In areas where the education system continues to function, it is under extreme strain with high dropout rates, overcrowded classrooms, and multishift schedules."[77] In Côte d'Ivoire, sizeable cuts in per capita education expenditures were matched by a primary school enrollment rate that did not keep pace with population growth rates.[78] Capital spending in education dropped by two-thirds in Nigeria between 1979 and 1989 and primary school enrollments declined.[79] In both Latin America and Africa, rural youth suffered more than urban youth through cutbacks in educational budgets.

Table 2.10 *Index of per capita expenditure on health in Latin America and Africa, 1980–1991 (1980 = 100)*

	1980	1981	1982	1983	1984	1985	1986	1987	1988	1989	1990	1991
Argentina	100.0	84.3	57.2	78.0	79.9	74.8	105.2	114.2	74.4	85.4	—	—
Bolivia	100.0	50.7	24.3	18.0	25.2	—	11.5	51.0	51.0	48.0	19.0	27.6
Brazil	100.0	104.9	112.7	98.2	102.2	115.7	126.6	179.7	142.6	189.0	161.6	—
Chile	100.0	96.9	98.5	78.8	87.3	82.9	81.1	87.1	87.3	—	—	—
Colombia	—	—	—	—	—	—	—	—	—	—	—	—
Ecuador	100.0	113.9	106.7	92.7	94.2	97.6	102.1	140.1	118.0	65.8	—	—
Mexico	100.0	95.8	96.9	73.0	85.7	85.3	84.8	83.5	84.5	82.8	82.3	—
Peru	100.0	117.0	116.0	109.0	110.9	107.9	113.4	101.0	83.5	59.8	—	—
Cameroon	100.0	77.7	—	123.2	155.2	182.2	125.9	130.0	105.7	91.6	—	—
Côte d'Ivoire	100.0	—	—	—	93.5	—	—	—	—	—	—	—
Ethiopia	100.0	108.0	108.7	116.0	113.6	114.1	114.6	133.7	130.2	—	—	—
Ghana	100.0	84.6	71.8	—	93.0	145.3	129.2	129.4	142.9	—	—	—
Kenya	100.0	107.4	113.6	106.5	90.7	85.2	85.2	87.1	92.0	87.4	89.7	80.4
Nigeria	—	—	—	—	—	—	—	—	—	—	—	—
Senegal	100.0	103.0	105.2	122.2	105.7	—	—	—	—	—	—	—
Zambia	100.0	101.4	140.6	86.1	81.9	77.2	62.9	64.3	78.4	—	—	—

Source: calculated with data from World Bank, *World Tables* (1993).

Table 2.11 *Index of per capita expenditure on education in Latin America and Africa, 1980–1991 (1980 = 100)*

	1980	1981	1982	1983	1984	1985	1986	1987	1988	1989	1990	1991
Argentina	100.0	89.4	65.6	85.9	82.9	69.9	66.4	73.5	67.5	55.5	—	—
Bolivia	100.0	78.5	75.4	70.2	98.2	—	50.0	62.5	61.3	66.1	65.8	69.9
Brazil	100.0	106.6	128.7	97.4	83.8	103.4	135.6	175.3	191.7	270.3	147.0	—
Chile	100.0	110.8	108.5	92.4	93.6	91.4	88.9	84.0	76.3	—	—	—
Colombia	—	—	—	—	—	—	—	—	—	—	—	—
Ecuador	100.0	92.5	83.1	74.2	71.3	73.8	79.6	71.2	63.8	35.6	—	—
Mexico	100.0	124.0	129.4	89.7	92.4	94.4	81.0	79.7	75.7	84.6	79.0	—
Peru	100.0	102.2	140.5	125.1	125.0	118.5	161.0	116.9	100.5	91.2	—	—
Cameroon	100.0	87.7	—	170.0	165.4	211.7	182.4	192.4	202.2	135.3	—	—
Côte d'Ivoire	100.0	—	—	—	116.4	—	—	—	—	—	—	—
Ethiopia	100.0	108.0	123.0	128.5	132.3	134.6	132.8	147.5	149.1	—	—	—
Ghana	100.0	71.7	73.7	—	69.2	84.6	118.2	118.4	130.0	—	—	—
Kenya	100.0	108.7	121.1	116.9	108.8	101.2	105.8	123.3	131.8	132.5	133.9	120.4
Nigeria	—	—	—	—	—	—	—	—	—	—	—	—
Senegal	100.0	102.6	94.1	92.7	79.8	—	—	—	—	—	—	—
Zambia	100.0	105.9	135.4	100.7	96.5	86.5	61.1	58.2	48.4	—	—	—

Source: calculated from data in World Bank, *World Tables* (1993).

Structural adjustment programs increasingly featured quick response programs to address the anticipated short-term consequences of structural adjustment, particularly on the poor and unemployed. Generally designed to bypass traditional bureaucracies considered too weak, immobile, or corrupt to distribute resources effectively, these programs were important in providing much needed response to economic crisis and dislocation, and some were interesting as experiments in achieving poverty alleviation goals. More generally, however, programs such as the Social Emergency Fund in Bolivia, the Social Action Program in Cameroon, the Program of Actions to Mitigate the Social Costs of Adjustment and Development (PAMSCAD) in Ghana, the Social Investment Fund in Guatemala, the Social Well-Being Program in Jamaica, Solidarity in Mexico, and PAPSCA in Uganda did little to address the problems of weak administrative capacity that was pronounced in most social welfare agencies and ministries.[80]

The capacity to provide for physical infrastructure is an investment critical to economic recovery and growth, as well as a general indicator of the extent to which populations are being provided with basic services such as electricity, water, and transportation. Among the most basic investments in infrastructure is that for roads, although data on such investments are scarce. Table 2.12 indicates that of the eleven countries for which there is full or partial data, six experienced declines in expenditures on roads during all or part of the 1980s. While few studies exist that document the impact of decreasing resources, much commentary refers to roads fallen into disrepair and those that became virtually impassable due to neglect. In the case of infrastructure, much needed economic recovery was delayed as country capacity to move goods and people suffered.

The impact of economic crisis on the ability of governments to deliver basic services can also be assessed by considering what happened to public sector salaries. Universally, they dropped – in sub-Saharan Africa by more than half and in Latin America by one fifth to one half – eroded by both inflation and budget cutbacks.[81] Wage compression within the public sector was common. One study of the impact of economic crisis on the civil service in Uganda compares the salary of a new employee in the civil service at the lowest clerical or maintenance level (a messenger or a cleaner) to that of the head of the civil service. In 1988, "The monthly basic salary of a newly recruited government messenger with a family of four would permit him to purchase enough matooke [the staple food of Uganda, green bananas] to last his family only five days. The monthly salary of the head of the civil service would last 19 days."[82] In 1988 the messenger was earning about 25 percent of the value of what he had earned in 1975, while the head of the civil service was earning 3 percent of the value of his former salary.[83] Table 2.13 provides data on the decline of public sector salaries in six African countries, suggesting that other countries experienced problems similar to those in Uganda. In Côte d'Ivoire, a wage freeze beginning in 1981 severely cut into public sector salaries in mid-decade; a significant wage cut was also accompanied by a loss of access to subsidized housing.[84] Massive retrenchment, wage restraint, and hiring freezes were among measures adopted in Nigeria to implement austerity.[85] Wage compression was particularly evident in Zambia, Nigeria, Ghana, and Sudan.[86]

Table 2.12 *Index of expenditure on roads in Latin America and Africa, 1980–1991 (1980 = 100)*

	1980	1981	1982	1983	1984	1985	1986	1987	1988	1989	1990	1991
Argentina	100.0	86.9	76.7	90.8	89.0	97.6	87.8	97.8	104.0	54.4	—	—
Bolivia	—	—	—	—	—	—	—	—	—	—	—	—
Brazil	100.0	109.6	94.2	101.8	75.0	114.2	115.8	197.0	142.3	144.5	62.7	—
Chile	100.0	153.6	134.1	157.0	203.1	226.6	247.2	250.0	227.3	—	—	—
Colombia	—	—	—	—	—	—	—	—	—	—	—	—
Ecuador	100.0	90.7	88.4	69.8	96.1	136.8	129.4	120.2	—	77.0	—	—
Mexico	100.0	176.3	192.3	224.1	214.0	160.1	107.8	118.2	103.8	93.3	87.8	—
Peru	—	—	—	—	—	—	—	—	—	—	—	—
Cameroon	100.0	60.2	—	234.6	378.9	400.3	246.4	285.2	—	—	—	—
Côte d'Ivoire	—	—	—	—	—	—	—	—	—	—	—	—
Ethiopia	100.0	84.2	88.0	76.2	71.3	53.0	73.8	73.8	75.8	—	—	—
Ghana	100.0	117.0	94.6	—	151.9	301.8	125.3	130.0	125.6	—	—	—
Kenya	100.0	118.1	108.3	131.1	101.2	95.4	77.0	65.8	57.3	53.5	100.2	83.5
Nigeria	—	—	—	—	—	—	—	—	—	—	—	—
Senegal	100.0	71.0	193.4	394.0	158.7	—	—	—	—	—	—	—
Zambia	100.0	80.7	147.4	—	14.4	68.0	142.4	45.9	38.4	—	—	—

Source: calculated with data from World Bank, *World Tables* (1993).

Table 2.13 *Trends in real basic starting salaries in the public sector in selected African countries (1975 = 100 percent)*

Country	1975	1976	1983
Ghana			
Principal secretary/director, etc.	100.0	41.4	11.0
Administrative officer/chief superintendent	100.0	49.5	15.3
Manager	100.0	94.8	39.7
Malawi			
Undersecretary	100.0	84.0	64.0
University graduate	100.0	96.2	73.0
Messenger	100.0	92.2	85.2
Nigeria			
Permanent secretary	100.0	47.0	30.1
University graduate	100.0	50.1	38.1
Unskilled worker	100.0	76.5	63.8
Senegal			
With university degree	100.0[a]	106.5[b]	73.8[c]
With sec. school diploma	100.0[a]	114.3[b]	84.7[c]
No diploma	100.0[a]	126.5[b]	112.7[c]
Sudan			
Deputy undersecretary	100.0	59.6	28.7
University graduate	100.0	4.9	31.2
Sec. school graduate	100.0	6.5	32.0
Unskilled worker	100.0	72.7	35.0
Zambia			
Undersecretary	100.0	68.2	49.9
Entering university graduate	100.0	63.0	40.9
Lower salaries employee	100.0	88.7	83.0
Laborer	100.0	85.2	87.7

[a] For 1976.
[b] For 1981.
[c] For 1984.
Source: Mutahaba, Baguma, and Halfani (1993: 84).

To compensate for decline to below subsistence income, public sector employees in Uganda had recourse to more frequent claims to cash allowances provided them as part of their official perquisites as well as to extortion of kickbacks, bribes, and illegal sale of government goods.[87] Moonlighting and spending more time in private business pursuits, often in the informal sector, were common.[88] Public sector jobs were maintained, however, despite low salaries, because of the hope of future improvement and the access they provided to stable employment, connections with influential patrons, housing, and other perquisites.[89] Austerity cut deeply into the motivations and working hours of civil servants in Uganda and no doubt had similar effects elsewhere. While the public sector in many countries of Latin America and Africa had long been noted for inefficiency, lack of motivation, and high levels of corruption, these characteristics were heightened when governments lacked money to pay basic salaries of even dedicated civil servants.[90]

Political capacity

The ability to mediate conflict, respond to citizen demands, allow for the representation of interests, and provide opportunities for effective political participation at national, regional, and local levels is important to economic and political development. These capacities promote political stability and enhance the basic legitimacy of states. They also allow citizens and governments to deal with and resolve problems of everyday life. In an interesting paradox during the 1980s and early 1990s, many states lost political capacity while civic society increased its ability to make demands on political institutions. Economic hardship decreased the ability of political leaders to maintain their core constituencies of support and provide policy benefits to respond to local and national level conflicts. It also made them more vulnerable to demands for change.

In part, loss of political capacity was reflected in decreased ability to pursue populist policies and the politics of spoils. Governments in Latin America and Africa had long used allocations of public goods and services as a political resource. Frequently, public investments in physical and social infrastructure, as well as jobs, were distributed with a sharp eye toward the political capital they could engender, the political conflicts they could resolve, or the loyalties they could cement.[91] In a number of countries, the politically important urban working classes had become accustomed to government-subsidized food, housing, and transportation. In the 1980s, just as such populations were feeling the brunt of economic crisis and the pinch of adjustment dislocations, governments became less able to call upon state resources to respond to public protest and concerns. Herbst argues that the austerity measures and reforms of structural adjustment in Africa "may impose so many limits on politicians' ability to direct resources to clients that old networks of support may no longer be viable ... The real losers in structural adjustment may be African leaders themselves."[92]

In a number of countries, political dynamics changed as leaders became more vulnerable to claims for better and more services, wider participation in decision making, or greater autonomy to address local problems at the community level. In Latin America, grassroots political organizations achieved national prominence in Brazil, Mexico, Colombia, and Chile, challenging the behavior of political bosses and authoritarian leaders.[93] In Africa, grassroots movements and the non-governmental sector became principal movers of the "winds of democracy." Universally, such movements were part of "a changing political culture, where popular movements no longer make petitions or ask for benefits but make demands and insist on basic rights."[94] Public criticism of government and of political leaders heightened; leaders were often powerless to respond, unless they were able to provide a vision of how current sacrifices would result in future benefits. All too often, they simply reacted to conflict and increased pressure for participation and autonomy with repressive acts or brutality, further undermining both the institutional and political capacities of their government.

CONCLUSIONS

Economic and political crises in Latin America and Africa were interrelated, but not synonymous. Economic hardship increased public dissatisfaction and encouraged protest against governments in power, regardless of regime type. It also decreased the ability of leaders to use state resources to maintain their core constituencies of support. In these ways, the economic crisis made political leaders more vulnerable to demands for change by weakening their ability to control political dissatisfaction or to shore up political support through the use of state patronage, rents, and access to spoils. But the pressure for political opening which accompanied demands for economic redress was fueled also by the desire to participate more fully in the selection of national and local leaders, to be included in national decision making, and to reclaim space for autonomous community and individual action.

Although events varied from country to country, the end result of a decade of the interaction between economic and political crisis was the weakening of relationships long in place between state and economy and state and society. In the economic realm, state policies put in place in prior decades to encourage industrialization and state control of economic interactions were widely credited to be root causes of the crisis. The mechanisms adopted to pursue such goals – protection, regulation, state industries, marketing boards, widespread subsidies, and other means – encouraged the development of weak and inefficient industrial and agricultural sectors and eventually destroyed the capacity of states to garner resources from the economy.[95] After turning to deficit spending and external borrowing, governments were unable to maintain such policies when international economic conditions turned sharply downward. In this context, long-conditioned expectations about the leadership role of the state in national economic development were called seriously into question by elites and non-elites alike.

Long-accepted relationships between state and society were equally called into question. Increasingly unable to claim broad-based legitimacy or the loyalty of traditional support groups, political regimes demonstrated their inability to dominate and lead civic society as they had done in the past. Increasingly, their role was questioned by the renewed capacity of civic organizations to demand resources, participation, accountability, and local autonomy. Where existing regimes resorted to increased use of repression and brutality to respond to protest and demand making they further undermined their own capacity to interact effectively with society and further weakened their own bases of support. Increasingly, civic societies in both Latin America and Africa were no longer willing to accept centralized and unresponsive states; increasingly, the nexus between such states and quiescent citizens was broken.

But historic crises such as those experienced by Latin America and Africa in the 1980s and early 1990s must be understood both from the perspective of what they reveal about the weakness of prior development strategies and regime configurations and the opportunities created for the emergence of new strategies and political relationships. In earlier periods, the depression of the 1930s exposed the weakness of a primary export development strategy and of political regimes that were captive to coalitions of landowners and exporters in Latin America; at the same time it opened up opportunities for import-substituting strategies and more inclusive populist coalitions of urban middle- and working-class, reformist military, and bureaucratic interests. In Africa, the independence struggle exposed the weaknesses of colonial economic exploitation as well as undercutting the capacity of colonial elites and their national counterparts to exert effective political power, opening the way for state-managed strategies of development and new coalitions of urban and bureaucratic interests.

Similarly, the historic crises of the 1980s and 1990s called policies, strategies, and power relations of the past into question and opened opportunities for new initiatives to manage economic and political tasks. How those crises are played out in individual countries depends in large part on the strength and durability of existing institutions for conflict resolution and the skills and orientations of political leaders in using the expanded space available to them to define new strategies for economic development and to build new and durable coalitions of political support. Chapters 3 through 8 detail the extent and nature of economic and political crises in Mexico and Kenya, the impact of such crises on state capacity, and the response of state leaders and institutions to the challenges created by a significant historic moment.

3

Crisis and breakdown in Mexico and Kenya

Prior to the 1980s, Mexico and Kenya had strong reputations for effective state-led economic development and sustained state-dominated political stability in their respective continents. This chapter documents the extent to which expectations based on these reputations eroded and then broke down. The experiences of the two countries differ, yet the combined effect of economic and political change altered the context for state action in similar ways. In Mexico, the interaction of economic and political conditions indicates that economic crisis sharpened and accelerated an emergent political crisis. In contrast, Kenya provides a case of a country whose political crisis contributed significantly to deepening its economic problems.

Deep and sustained economic crisis has farreaching consequences, as the case of Mexico explored here demonstrates. Although most frequently measured and discussed in terms of stagnant or declining rates of growth and indices of social welfare, extended economic crises also stimulate critical reassessment of the intellectual underpinnings of national development strategies. Such crises encourage citizens, policy makers, and politicians to question prior growth strategies and policy regimes, even those that had produced positive results in the past. In consequence, long-accepted notions about how development is best achieved become subject to greater skepticism and at times are held responsible for creating current conditions.

Along with this questioning of appropriate routes to development, sustained economic crisis also has a profound impact on the economic interests supporting and benefiting from existing policies. The economic basis for their cohesion and power is undermined and government is less able than previously to respond to demands for continued policy support or rents. It should not be surprising, then, that when economies stagnate or decline over extended periods, elite coalitions that had been instrumental in sustaining prior policy regimes weaken. This dynamic presents governing elites with a dual challenge: it simultaneously robs them of long-familiar political support but opens up the possibility of constructing new coalitions around alternative policy regimes. The context for state action vis-à-vis the economy is thus altered.

Similarly, political crises involve far more than protest, uncertainty, and instability. They affect the bases of political power and authority in society and can result in the inability of regimes to maintain existing patterns of social control. Under the impact of sustained political crisis, long-entrenched institutions such as

47

dominant parties and officially sanctioned interest groups can be challenged by their own constituents and by groups historically marginal to political influence. Civic mobilization can call into question the right of such institutions to continue to interpret or represent societal interests and to define the limits of effective political voice. Or, as in the case of Kenya, political leaders actively seeking to redistribute policy benefits and introduce new mechanisms for managing political dissent can contribute to the erosion of existing relationships. Even in regimes noted for their centralization and hegemonic control of political expression, the breakdown of relatively stable relationships between state and society can be difficult to forestall. Thus, the context for state action vis-à-vis civic society is also altered.

This chapter traces the emergence and trajectory of economic and political crises in Mexico and Kenya. In Mexico, I am particularly concerned with the period between 1982 and 1988: the economic crisis had its most profound effect between 1982 and 1987; the crisis of political legitimacy and continuity was felt most fully between 1985 and 1988. In Kenya, the period of greatest interest is 1987 to 1993, when the sense of crisis heightened and undermined the country's reputation for strong economic performance and relatively stable politics. The case histories demonstrate that the parameters for economic policy and political interaction changed profoundly in both countries during these years.

The beginning of the end of the "Mexican miracle"

Mexico was in an enviable position among developing countries by the early 1970s. The violent Revolution of 1910 had destroyed the control of feudal landlords, the church, and foreign interests over the economy. The creation of the PRI in 1929 had established a mechanism for elite conflict resolution, mass support, and political control. The Revolution and the party had given birth to a strong nationalist ideology. Land reform, extensively pursued in the 1930s, and heavy investment in basic industries and infrastructure in the same decade had set the basis for economic growth after 1940.[1] As an early adopter of import substitution and as a country with a relatively large domestic market, Mexico had experienced over three decades of sustained growth as industrialization and urbanization responded to the stimulus of supportive government policies.

Between 1940 and 1950, gross domestic product grew at an average of 6.7 percent annually, with manufacturing production increasing at an average of 8.1 percent annually. GDP annual growth in the decade of the 1950s averaged 5.8 percent, with manufacturing growth at 7.3 percent; in the period between 1960 and 1970, these rates were 7.6 percent and 10.1 percent respectively.[2] Foreign investment increased, the middle class grew significantly, and indicators for health and welfare steadily improved. By the early 1970s, life expectancy in the country was over sixty years and adult literacy was 74 percent.[3]

During the 1960s, Mexico urbanized at a rate of 4.7 percent a year, with about a third of the total urban population gravitating toward Mexico City.[4] Employment in agriculture dropped from 58 percent of the labor force in 1950 to 39.4 percent by 1970. The industrial labor force grew from 16 to 23 percent of the total, rising from somewhat more than 8 million people to almost 13 million people in the same period. Employment in the service sector increased more rapidly than that in industry, however, indicating a longer-term problem of industrial employment failing to keep pace with population growth and urbanization.[5] Although income became more concentrated in the upper middle income brackets during the thirty years between 1940 and 1970, real incomes for all groups probably rose, particularly among urban sectors.[6] If Mexico remained a country of extensive poverty and severe inequalities between rich and poor, urban and rural, it was also a country in which there was widespread expectation of upward economic mobility.[7]

Politically, by 1970 the country had the most durable regime in Latin America, its continuity stretching back for over fifty years. During that time, Mexico's leaders had successfully diminished the political relevance of the military and had implanted civilian government under the hegemonic control of the PRI. The PRI itself was the result of a historic and inclusive pact among the political elites who emerged as victors of the Revolution of 1910 and the struggle to consolidate power in the 1920s. Based on corporate representation of peasant, labor, and middle-class groups, the PRI managed a system of clientelism and cooptation that encouraged group leaders to be more responsive to the needs of the regime than to their membership. Meanwhile, elite economic groups lobbied formally and informally with regime leadership outside the structure of the control-oriented party, giving them greater capacity to influence policy, although rarely to impose it. Thus, the party's structure encouraged control of dissent by subordinate classes and accommodation to elite interests. Sustained economic growth facilitated political stability by increasing the material goods available to government to distribute as rewards for conformist behavior. Such rewards also moderated class antagonisms through the extensive distribution of subsidies to capital and wages. Individual and regional interests were similarly incorporated through the distribution of development projects and access to credit, jobs, licenses, and other state-controlled resources.

Mexico's strong and interventionist state was presided over by a caesar-like president on six-year rotation and a bureaucracy and political party cemented through patron–client linkages that spanned the political and economic elite down to urban squatter settlements and remote peasant villages.[8] Formal and informal links between the government and the party meant an unusually effective system of patronage and political mobility. Moreover, within the broad parameters of a general development strategy, there were periodic opportunities for adjusting policy to new interests and exigencies when presidential administrations changed, as they did with unquestioned regularity every six years.[9] This relationship between party and government was based on a consistent division of labor in which the PRI was centrally engaged in political mobilization, control, and conflict resolution, while the government bureaucracy and its political executives focused primarily on policy development and implementation. If it was a country of extensive and increasing inequalities between those who had access to power and those who did not, between organized groups of industrialists and workers and captured groups of peasants and lumpenproletariat, it was also a country that escaped the instability and overt brutality and repressiveness of many political regimes in Latin America.

Mexico's development model, characterized by generous protection to domestic producers of manufactured goods, subsidies to wage employment, low inflation, expansion of domestic demand, and incentives to export-oriented agriculture, had, by the early 1970s, produced a large and prosperous industrial elite with close ties to government, a well-disciplined labor union movement with corporatist representation in political decision making, and a modern export-oriented agro-industrial elite. At the same time, the revolutionary origins of the political regime, the successful incorporation of peasants, workers, and middle class into the dominant party, and state leadership in supporting industrialization had created a strong and legitimate state that guided economic and political life in the country. Despite the fact that large numbers of Mexicans remained marginal to full participation in economic growth and political life, most considered the regime legitimate, nationalist, and effective.[10]

The beginning of the end of the "Mexican miracle"

This relatively successful model of state-capitalism and inclusionary politics was to be torn apart in the 1980s. Mexico's economic crisis, although long anticipated by domestic and international analysts, developed with a speed and depth that no one expected. As far back as the early 1970s, some economists had warned that the strategy of import substitution, first introduced piecemeal in the 1930s and fully adopted as a basic development strategy in the 1940s and 1950s, could not sustain the high rates of economic growth that the country had experienced for almost three decades.[11] Critics of the country's development pointed to the emergence of inefficiencies in the industrial sector, encouraged by high tariffs, quotas, and import licensing. They also indicated that subsidies for energy, transportation, and wage goods encouraged industrial inefficiency while social expenditures were constrained by low tax rates.

Moreover, by the early 1970s, it was becoming more evident that the size of the population and the structure of income distribution impeded the effective pursuit of industrial deepening through the production of durable consumer, intermediate, and capital goods.[12] In addition, price controls for producers and extensive subsidies to consumers generated so few incentives to the peasant agricultural sector that the country was increasingly unable to meet domestic demand for basic foodstuffs.[13] By 1973, in fact, the inefficiency of the peasant agricultural sector was identified by the government as the cause of a significant drain on the country's foreign exchange. Some analysts linked increasing disparities in income, coupled with high population growth rates, to the emergence of political dissent in the 1960s, such as rural guerrilla movements and student protests. Thus, over the long term, Mexico's development strategy had "generated growth, but at increasingly higher costs."[14]

In the early 1970s, the policy response to emergent economic and political problems was to increase the role of government in the economy through investment, control over foreign capital, and greater attention to escalating social needs.[15] Under the leadership of President Luís Echeverría (1970–1976) and the banner of "Shared Development," the state expanded development expenditures beyond traditional concerns with urban and industrial infrastructure and rapidly became the principal purveyor of goods and services not only in urban areas but also in remote rural areas. Subsidies were increased for industry and agriculture and for producers and consumers. In 1972, public expenditures increased by 21.2 percent in real terms and by 23.2 percent in 1973, an expansionary pattern that continued unmodified until 1977. The number of central government employees grew from 0.3 to 1.3 million between 1969 and 1976; the number of state-owned enterprises increased from 391 to 499 in the same period.[16]

Increased government expenditures and activities were not supported by increased concern for revenue expansion or for encouraging other sources of growth in the economy. As a result of these policies and the 1973 oil shock, a set of economic problems assumed crisis proportions by 1976 (see Table 3.1).[17] The overall public sector deficit increased from 2.8 percent of GDP in 1972 to 4.6 percent in 1975. Inflation, which stood at 5.2 percent in 1970, was 23.7 percent in 1974, 15.2 percent in 1975, 15.8 percent in 1976, and 29 percent the following year. The foreign debt grew from 6.4 billion dollars in 1971 to 20.5 billion in 1976. The peso became seriously overvalued and investor confidence was further undermined by President Echeverría's populist style. Capital flight increased significantly, reaching 3 billion dollars for 1976.

In response to mounting evidence that current policies could not be sustained, the government announced a devaluation in 1976 that ended the traditional fixed exchange rate regime. It also signed a stabilization agreement with the IMF. In accordance with this agreement, the incoming administration of José López Portillo (1976–1982) was pledged to reduce government spending, reform revenue collection, and cut back on money supply. An "Alliance for Production," superintended by the government, sought to rebuild political peace with the private sector and to reintroduce more moderate political rhetoric. Little progress was made in reformulating the existing set of policies, however, because, just as the seriousness of the economic situation of the mid-1970s was dawning on political consciousness, major new finds of oil were reported.

Between 1978 and 1982, Mexico was transformed into a major oil exporter. In 1978, the average per barrel price of Mexican oil was 13.3 dollars. In 1979, it was 19.6 dollars per barrel, and it rose to 31.2 dollars in 1980. In 1981, oil reached a peak of 33.2 dollars per barrel. Estimates of Mexico's reserves were adjusted significantly upward in 1979, further buoying expectations about the economy. The government embarked on a policy to "sow the oil" in the economy and to "administer the abundance," with vast investment projects in virtually all sectors and major new

Table 3.1 *Mexico: economic indicators, 1970–1992*

	1970	1971	1972	1973	1974	1975	1976	1977	1978	1979	1980	1981
GDP annual growth	7.3	4.2	8.5	8.2	6.1	5.7	4.2	3.2	8.2	9.3	8.4	8.8
Real GDP per capita growth	NA	0.8	5.0	4.8	2.8	2.6	1.3	0.5	5.5	6.4	6.0	6.2
Public sector current revenue (% of GDP)	NA	NA	9.5	9.4	9.9	11.4	11.5	12.2	13.0	13.5	15.1	14.6
Growth in (constant 1987) revenue	NA	NA	NA	6.8	12.3	20.9	5.4	9.8	11.2	17.3	21.3	3.4
Public sector current expenditures (% of GDP)	NA	NA	7.9	8.6	9.6	10.5	10.7	11.3	11.1	10.8	11.3	13.8
Growth in (constant 1987) expenditure	NA	NA	NA	18.0	19.0	15.5	6.5	8.2	3.1	9.5	14.3	29.6
Public sector overall deficit (% of GDP)	NA	NA	2.8	3.8	3.5	4.6	4.4	3.1	2.5	3.1	3.0	6.4
Public sector deficit (index of constant data, 1980 = 100)	NA	NA	55.6	81.0	80.5	110.8	109.7	80.5	69.0	96.5	100.0	228.1
Consumer prices (average annual growth rate)	5.2	5.3	5.0	12.0	23.7	15.2	15.8	29.0	17.5	18.2	26.4	27.9
Real wages (average annual growth rate)	NA	NA	NA	NA	NA	NA	NA	NA	NA	NA	NA	3.5
Minimum wage growth rate	NA	NA	NA	NA	NA	NA	NA	NA	NA	NA	NA	1.0
Current account balance (millions of US dollars)	−1,068.0	−835.5	−916.3	−1,415.1	−2,875.5	−4,042.4	−3,408.7	−1,854.0	−3,171.3	−5,459.0	−10,750.0	−16,061.0
Trade balance (millions of US dollars)	−888.0	−749.0	−894.0	−1,515.0	−2,791.0	−3,272.0	−2,295.0	−1,021.0	−1,745.0	−2,830.0	−3,385.0	−3,846.0
Share of oil in total exports (percent)	3.2	2.4	1.2	0.9	4.2	15.5	16.0	23.7	28.6	43.8	66.8	72.1
Total external debt (millions of US dollars)	5,965.6	6,416.4	7,028.0	8,999.0	11,945.5	15,608.5	20,519.5	31,189.1	35,712.2	42,773.9	57,377.7	78,215.3
Interest payments due/exports of G & S	NA	NA	NA	NA	NA	NA	NA	NA	NA	NA	27.4	NA
Capital flight (billions of US dollars)	NA	NA	NA	NA	NA	NA	3.0	0.9	0.1	0.0	−0.3	11.6

Table 3.1 (contd)

	1982	1983	1984	1985	1986	1987	1988	1989	1990	1991	1992
GDP annual growth	−0.6	−4.2	3.7	2.7	−3.9	1.8	1.2	3.4	4.5	3.6	2.8
Real GDP per capita growth	−2.9	−6.3	1.5	0.7	−5.6	0.0	−0.5	1.6	2.7	1.6	NA
Public sector current revenue (% of GDP)	15.5	18.0	16.2	16.5	16.0	17.5	17.3	18.4	14.2	NA	NA
Growth in (constant 1987) revenue	7.4	10.6	−6.7	4.7	−6.8	11.4	0.5	9.9	−19.5	NA	NA
Public sector current expenditures (% of GDP)	22.4	20.5	18.5	20.4	24.8	27.3	24.9	20.6	15.1	NA	NA
Growth in (constant 1987) expenditure	64.4	−12.9	−6.2	13.3	17.3	11.9	−7.6	−14.6	−23.5	NA	NA
Public sector overall deficit (% of GDP)	14.8	7.6	7.1	8.4	13.1	13.6	10.4	5.3	−0.8	NA	NA
Public sector deficit (index of constant data, 1980 = 100)	535.1	261.4	253.3	307.4	463.6	488.3	376.7	197.5	−29.5	NA	NA
Consumer prices (average annual growth rate)	58.9	101.8	65.5	57.7	86.2	131.8	114.2	20.0	26.6	22.7	NA
Real wages (average annual growth rate)	0.7	−22.8	−7.1	−2.7	−5.9	−1.9	−1.3	9.0	2.9	2.4	NA
Minimum wage growth rate	−0.1	−21.9	−9.0	−1.2	−10.5	−0.2	1.8	6.3	5.7	5.0	NA
Current account balance (millions of US dollars)	−6,307.0	5,403.0	4,194.0	1,130.0	−1,673.0	3,968.0	−2,443.0	−3,958.0	−7,117.0	−13,282.0	NA
Trade balance (millions of US dollars)	6,795.0	13,762.0	12,941.0	8,451.0	4,599.0	8,433.0	1,668.0	−645.0	−4,433.0	−11,063.0	NA
Share of oil in total exports (percent)	77.2	64.4	61.8	60.1	43.8	41.7	32.1	33.9	36.8	34.5	NA
Total external debt (millions of US dollars)	86,019.0	92,964.3	94,821.9	96,865.5	100,880.0	109,460.0	100,780.0	95,450.0	97,360.0	101,740.0	NA
Interest payments due/exports of G & S	40.4	34.8	34.7	34.4	35.1	27.7	27.0	25.5	16.7	17.3	NA
Capital flight (billions of US dollars)	6.5	2.7	1.6	0.7	−2.2	0.3	1.1	−2.9	NA	NA	NA

Sources: World Bank, World Tables, various years; IMF (1992a, 1992b); Lustig (1992).

initiatives to reduce poverty and deal with declining agricultural productivity. Public spending increased at dramatic rates. It grew 13.7 percent in 1978 and 24.9 percent in 1981.[18] At the same time, economic growth was unprecedented, reaching a four year average of 8.6 percent. Oil revenues paid for much of this expansion, but the foreign debt also mounted rapidly as both public and private sectors borrowed heavily to finance investments and lavish consumer spending. The foreign debt, much of it in short-term loans and incurred at much higher interest rates than in the past, reached 35.7 billion dollars in 1978 and 78.2 billion in 1981. The overall public sector deficit grew to 6.4 percent of GDP in 1981, and the exchange rate became seriously overvalued.

The government grew and expanded its role under both Echeverría and López Portillo, but did so well within the tradition of state leadership that had been instituted in the 1930s and 1940s. Thus, "The outburst of public spending was not the outcome of a single individual intoxicated by a terms of trade shock; it was also produced by a set of institutions that simultaneously placed great expectations on what the government should provide and few restraints on the nature of its intervention in the economy."[19] What distinguished both Echeverría and López Portillo administrations, however, was a concern to create a vibrant economy that was not subject to the "vagaries of private investment."[20] Traditionally, the government had sought development tied to extensive incentives for the private sector; beginning with Echeverría, relations with the private sector became less harmonious and more subject to dispute.

The collapse of the economy

The underlying structural weaknesses in the economy and the excesses of the oil boom years set the stage for the economic collapse of 1982. By that year, Mexico's foreign debt had risen to 86 billion dollars. Oil accounted for 77.2 percent of the country's total exports, up from a modest 4.2 percent in 1974, radically increasing vulnerability to fluctuations in international prices. The overall public sector deficit escalated to 14.8 percent of GDP and inflation reached 58.9 percent. Then, dramatic changes in international conditions precipitated a major crisis. Oil prices began to fall, from a high of 33.2 dollars per barrel in 1981 to 28.7 dollars in 1982 and 26.3 dollars in 1983. At the same time, the United States tightened its monetary policy. The resources from exports and foreign borrowing that had fueled the boom dried up rapidly, capital flight assumed major proportions, and Mexico's international creditors demanded repayment on their loans. GDP growth sank to −0.6 percent in 1982.

Repeated efforts to deal with these problems characterize the policy history of the 1980s. The crisis was initially understood by government officials to be primarily a short-term problem of stabilization; only in the mid-1980s did the depth of the problem and the need for altering the underlying structure of the economy become clearer to them.[21] Moreover, many of the policy measures, particularly at the outset of the government's efforts to bring the economic situation under control, were contradictory.[22] Initial actions conformed to neoclassical prescription; announcements of two major devaluations, cutbacks in government spending, and higher domestic energy prices punctuated 1982. In August, the government declared a moratorium on payments of foreign debt principal. Then in September, the outgoing López Portillo administration nationalized the banking system, bringing the number of public sector enterprises to 1,155, and imposed controls on foreign exchange. These actions, along with the government's role in increasing wages, caused a major crisis of private sector confidence in the government and exacerbated already high levels of capital flight.[23] At the end of the year, the incoming administration of Miguel de la Madrid (1982–1988) confronted historically low growth and high inflation, financial sector panic, depleted foreign reserves, severe imbalances in the external sector, rapidly maturing debt, and a new stabilization agreement with the IMF.

The stabilization package, to be in effect from 1983 until 1985, included a large devaluation, draconian measures to control the budget deficit, and initiatives to increase public sector revenues. In return, Mexico was able to reschedule the foreign debt and reduce payments of principal due over the short term. Government investment was cut back by 36 percent in 1983 and allowed to expand by only 4 percent in 1984. While these efforts offered some relief and the budget deficit dropped to half of what it was in 1982, 1983's GDP growth rate of −4.2 percent was well below target and the inflation rate of 101.8 percent was well above the targeted 55 percent. GDP growth recovered to 3.7 percent in 1984, but this encouraged the government to relax its efforts to control the deficit and balance of payments situation. The latter problem was exacerbated by a further dramatic drop in international oil prices. By mid-1985, the economic picture looked much darker than it had the previous year. Inflation continued high, public spending increased, and macroeconomic policy proved unable to arrest economic decline. GDP grew only 2.7 percent in that year.

Another stabilization plan was introduced in mid-1985, involving an agreement with the IMF to reimpose an austerity budget and begin to address structural issues in the economy.[24] In particular, trade liberalization was placed more centrally on the agenda for government policy action. Shortly following the agreement, however, massive earthquakes rocked Mexico City on September 19 and 20. The policy agreements and IMF were virtually forgotten in their wake, which caused 8,000–10,000 deaths, 4–5 billion dollars in damage, and incalculable loss through the destruction of communication networks, chaos in the physical infrastructure, and disorientation among citizens and officials alike. The country's economic managers were again disappointed in 1986 as petroleum prices dropped precipitously to 12 dollars per barrel.[25]

The dual impact of the earthquake and oil prices redefined the task of economic management from that of trying to lower inflation to trying to contain it. This goal was elusive, however, and inflation rose to 86.2 percent in 1986. More generally, there were few positive signs in the economy as GDP growth measured −3.9 percent, the public sector deficit rose to 13.1 percent of GDP, and the total foreign debt reached 100 billion dollars. By 1986, real wages had lost over half their 1978 value. The country's economy improved in 1987. Although inflation continued to rise – reaching 131.8 percent – and the public sector deficit reached 13.6 percent of GDP, growth recovered to 1.8 percent, petroleum prices rose to 16.1 dollars a barrel, the debt was successfully renegotiated with the IMF, and foreign reserves grew. The government was able to continue the liberalization of the economy with a series of deregulation measures. A run on the peso following the October stock market crash in the US, however, encouraged policy makers to refocus their attention on controlling inflation.

In light of continued high inflation, the most significant accomplishment of 1987 was the negotiation of the Pact of Economic Solidarity among government, industry, workers, and farmers.[26] The pact, engineered by the government, sought to cement agreements among the parties to reduce inflation to 2 percent per month by the end of 1988.[27] The government agreed to discipline public finances, cutting spending to 20.5 percent of GDP and increasing revenues. Workers agreed to moderate their future wage demands in return for a short-term adjustment of 38 percent and an incomes policy based on a basket of basic commodities. In return for wage restraint, business promised to increase productivity and lower profit margins. The bargain for farmers included relative price adjustments in return for increases in productivity. The government committed itself to tight monetary policy, an exchange rate policy to minimize the need for major devaluations, expansion of trade liberalization, and privatization of the large public enterprise sector. With this pact in place, and the promise to renegotiate it at regular intervals, a more concerted effort in terms of fiscal and monetary policy and liberalization could be pursued in 1988.

The collapse of the political economy

The depths of Mexico's economic crisis were probably faced in 1986 and 1987. The Pact of Economic Solidarity laid the basis for significant policy changes in 1988 and after. But the crisis encouraged changes that were far more transcendental than those relating to macroeconomic management. First, commitment to the model of import substitution was firmly broken among policy makers and large portions of the intellectual community during these years of crisis. Critiques of the inward-oriented growth strategy, which had emerged by the mid-1970s, gained widespread acceptance by the mid-1980s. Such critiques, widely produced and circulated in academic institutions, government offices, and editorial rooms, focused on the failure of import-substitution policies to generate sufficient employment for the burgeoning and impoverished majority of the population, the inefficiency of industrial and agricultural production, the cost of extensive subsidies to capital and labor, and the potential for increased economic dependence on industrialized countries, particularly the United States. There continued to be contention over alternative models of development and about the speed of change required to replace the old policy set, but there were few economists, policy makers, or economic advisors in the late 1980s who continued to define Mexico's future in terms of deepening its industrialization through import substitution.

Equally important, an ongoing debate about the appropriate role of the state in the economy shifted significantly toward a more market-oriented approach by the mid-1980s. The highly statist orientation of the Echeverría and López Portillo administrations gave way to the much more liberal stance of the de la Madrid policy makers, and the proponents of a highly interventionist state within Mexico's lively intellectual community were clearly on the defensive by mid-decade. The change in orientation can be traced in part to the political need to respond to extensive disaffection of the private sector that had developed under Echeverría, was mollified under López Portillo until 1981, and then reached unprecedented levels with the imposition of exchange controls and the nationalization of the banks at the end of 1982.[28] Some can also be traced to experience demonstrating that, even under favorable economic conditions, the government did not have the technical or administrative capacity to manage such a large role effectively.

Altered thinking about the country's development strategy and the role of the state related also to changes in the profiles of policy makers and the leverage of international agencies. As we will see in Chapter 5, a new generation of technocrats, many trained in economics in the United States, emerged in powerful positions under Miguel de la Madrid. Moreover, the international financial institutions that locked horns with these technocrats in negotiations over the debt and domestic policy were firmly set against the country's traditional development strategy and had considerable leverage to make their point of view known. Nor were Mexican policy makers alone in reconsidering appropriate development strategies and the role of the state; many other countries were experiencing economic crisis and their policy makers were also rethinking the validity of prior orientations. The result of these trends was a widespread reassessment of the intellectual and empirical foundations of import substitution and a much greater domestic and international consensus on its vulnerability as a long-term development strategy. By the mid-1980s, debate about the role of government in economic development, a constant in Mexican politics since the era of Echeverría, was enjoined with those arguing for its traditional leadership, protectionist, and social welfarist role in a much weakened position.

In addition to the final undermining of what had been considered an appropriate development strategy for the country, the power of economic interest groups and their ability to influence government policy were profoundly altered by the crisis. Mexico's industrialists, particularly owners of small and medium enterprises, had long been powerful in supporting protectionist policies, generous subsidies to the industrial sector, and limitations on foreign capital. The peak business organizations in the country had extensive informal links to policy makers, even though they were not represented in the formal structure of the PRI. In fact, this gave them added power, as much of the institutional strength of PRI leaders came from their ability to control and coopt constituent groups. Outside the PRI, protected business interests lobbied successfully for the continuation of supportive policies and subsidies and were the principal impediments to liberalized trade.[29]

Prolonged economic crisis hit this traditional protected business sector particularly hard. When the economy stagnated, declined, and failed to recover rapidly, private debts had to be repaid, inflation and rising unemployment diminished domestic demand, government subsidies were repeatedly cut back through austerity measures, and most public investment plans were put on hold. While the government had traditionally been a large consumer of the production of domestic firms, it could not sustain this role in the face of the crisis. The nationalization of the banking system not only undermined business confidence; it also significantly restricted the availability of capital to small and medium firms. The inevitable result was the loss of economic viability of many of the country's domestic firms. Bankruptcy and recession exacted their toll on the fortunes of even large entrepreneurs and capital flight turned the interests of others to economic conditions in the US and elsewhere.[30] Then, the reprivatization of the banks that was begun in 1985 and 1986 increased the power of private sector groups that were not linked to the old protectionist interests.[31]

As economic hardship affected their constituent members, the traditional business organizations lost economic power and, in consequence, the ability to speak effectively with government.[32] Some organizations moved into open opposition to the government and the PRI, calling for political protest and support for alternative parties. But many business associations could not agree on an appropriate response, and their lack of cohesion diluted the capacity to influence government.[33] Within the peak organizations, these differences of opinion about appropriate policy also led to dissent and increased impediments to collective action. Thus, private sector ability to resist liberalization was considerably less in 1987, when the government moved to enter the General Agreement on Tariffs and Trade (GATT), than in 1980, when it was instrumental in government's rejection of such a move, or in 1976, when it successfully stalemated efforts to liberalize.[34]

Similarly, the country's relatively privileged official unions lost bargaining power with government over the issue of wages and trade liberalization.[35] In part, their power was undercut by the rise of independent unionism, a trend that accelerated in the early to mid 1980s. Independent unions challenged the right and legitimacy of the National Confederation of Workers (CTM) and its venerable boss, Fidel Velázquez, to speak for labor interests in negotiations with government and with the private sector.[36] The CTM, which represented the corporate interests of labor in the PRI, was also challenged internally by dissent over issues of leadership and policy. Decades of union bossism, corruption, and manipulation of workers left many with little desire to rally around traditional structures. Union leaders' willingness to support government policies that were hurting rank and file members also sparked increased internal dissent.

The government fueled the inability of labor organizations to speak with a unified voice by making separate deals with them.[37] In addition, the government used its legal powers to restrain strike activity. Inflation focused many of the country's workers on day-to-day household survival rather than on union militancy, and a shift in employment from the formal to the informal sector further fragmented what had once been the most powerful sector of the PRI.[38] Austerity affected subsidies for public transportation, food, electricity, and gasoline and increased economic pressure on workers. The combination of these factors weakened the capacity of labor to resist policy adjustments away from protectionism and a large, paternalist state.

The economic crisis affected the political landscape in Mexico in other ways. The presidency, the preeminent political institution in Mexico, did not remain untouched by events in the 1970s and 1980s. Long revered as politically unassailable, the presidency began to fray around the edges under Luís Echeverría, whose populist policies caused some estrangement with the country's business sectors. Under José López Portillo, the fraying of presidential legitimacy became more visible with accumulating evidence of extensive corruption in high levels in government and political circles and with the patent inability of the administration to deal with the economic crisis. After successfully courting private sector support throughout the boom years with policies that provided something for everyone, his administration ended with private sector outrage over the nationalization of the banks and exchange rate controls imposed in an effort to stem capital flight.

The change of administration did not resolve the crisis of the presidency. Miguel de la Madrid was publicly attacked for his failure to deal effectively with the economic crisis and his failure to respond adequately to the human suffering and dislocation caused by the 1985 earthquake. Carlos Salinas de Gortari (1988–1994) assumed office as the weakest president in the modern history of Mexico, having been effectively challenged by two other major contenders during the election and having won a bare majority of 50.7 percent of the votes. In fact, his victory was hotly contested in the congress and in the courts, with his principal rivals contending that Salinas won only because of massive electoral fraud. Indeed, there was a generalized belief that had the elections been honest, he would not have won.[39] The president, traditionally above reproach in Mexican politics, had become a very human and fallible figure to most citizens by 1988.

The PRI was also a far different organization with far less political coherence in 1988 than it had been in earlier periods. Internally, its hold over labor was challenged by the rise of independent unionism. Mexico's formal sector workers had forged alternatives to the boss-led control, corruption, and manipulation that characterized the CTM and its relationship to the PRI leadership. Peasant movements also emerged to challenge the hegemony of the PRI.[40] While less politically powerful, these movements were significant because the peasant sector had long been the most loyal and "captured" of the PRI's constituencies. Table 3.2 illustrates the decline of urban and rural support for the PRI in the presidential elections of the 1980s. Within the leadership structure of the party, there was an unusually open debate between those who favored greater pluralism and those who defended the old clientelist and patronage system.[41] The debate centered not only on internal democratization but also on the extent to which the party was willing to allow even modest democratization of the party system.

Table 3.2 *Support for the PRI by type of congressional district (percentage of total vote)*

Districts	1979	1982	1985	1988	Average of 1979–1988
Federal district (Mexico city)	46.7	48.3	42.6	27.3	41.2
Other urban[a]	53.4	56.2	51.1	34.3	48.8
Mixed[b]	67.9	66.2	59.2	46.4	60.0
Rural[c]	83.5	80.9	77.3	61.3	75.8

[a] Urban districts are those in which 90 percent or more of the population lives in communities of 50,000 or more inhabitants. Total number: 40 in the Federal district and 56 in other urban areas.
[b] Districts in which more than 50 percent but less than 90 percent of the population lives in communities of 50,000 or more inhabitants. Total number: 44.
[c] Districts in which less than 50 percent of the population lives in communities of 50,000 or more inhabitants. Total number: 160.
Source: Cornelius and Craig (1991: 70).

Equally important was the independent mobilization of the country's relatively large middle class. What is important about this period is not that civic society was mobilized – there was a high degree of political organization in the country – but that a wide variety of interests became politicized and mobilized outside the confines of the PRI, where they were less susceptible to cooptation and control.[42] In this regard, the earthquake of 1985 was a watershed for civic society. Severely let down by the government's failure to respond to the problems created by death, destruction, disorientation, and homelessness, hundreds of communities took the initiative to organize rescue efforts, soup kitchens, shelter, and rehabilitation initiatives.[43] A surge of a sense of political empowerment developed, as groups long accustomed to dependence on government learned that they could deal with basic social and economic problems better without government than with it.

As indicated above, the PRI was also challenged by the increased popularity of other political parties.[44] One challenge came from the National Action Party (PAN). Centered in the north of the country, this party had traditionally played the role of a protest party whose principal purpose was to dissent from the PRI rather than to achieve political power. By 1988, the PAN's presidential candidate was taking himself seriously as a presidential alternative. A much greater challenge came from the newly organized National Democratic Front (FDN), which became the Democratic Revolutionary Party (PRD) in 1988. The FDN presented Cuauhtémoc Cárdenas as its candidate in the 1988 elections. Cárdenas was not only the son of Mexico's most famous and revered president, but also a PRI insider until party leaders virtually ejected him and other insiders for demanding internal democratization of the party and commitment to a platform emphasizing social justice. This incident clarified the extent to which political conflicts could no longer be resolved by elites within the confines of the party. Table 3.3 provides a historical view of the

Table 3.3 *Voting in presidential elections, 1934–1994*

	Votes for PRI candidate [a] (%)	Votes for PAN candidate (%)	Votes for all others[b] (%)	Turnout of eligible adults[c] (%)
1934	98.2	—	1.8	53.6
1940	93.9	—	6.1	57.5
1946	77.9	—	22.1	42.6
1952	74.3	7.8	17.9	57.9
1958	90.4	9.4	0.2	49.4
1964	88.8	11.1	0.1	54.1
1970	88.3	13.9	1.4	63.9
1976[c]	93.6	—	1.2	59.6
1982	71.0	15.7	9.4	66.1
1988	50.7	16.8	32.5[d]	49.4[e]
1994	50.1	26.0	23.9[f]	—

[a] From 1958 through 1982, includes votes cast for the Partido Popular Socialista (PPS), and the Partido Auténtico de la Revolución Mexicana (PARM), both of which regularly endorsed the PRI's presidential candidate. In 1988 they supported opposition candidate Cuauhtémoc Cárdenas.

[b] Excludes annulled votes; includes votes for candidates of non-registered parties.

[c] Eligible population base for 1934 through 1952 includes all males ages twenty and over (legal voting age: twenty-one years). Both men and women aged twenty and over are included in the base for 1958 and 1964 (women received the franchise in 1958). The base for 1970–1988 includes all males and females aged eighteen and over (the legal voting age was lowered to eighteen, effective 1970).

[d] Includes 31.1 percent officially tabulated for Cuauhtémoc Cárdenas.

[e] Estimated using data from the Federal Electoral Commission. However, the Commission itself has released two different figures for the number of eligible voters in 1988. Using the Commission's larger estimate of eligible population, the turnout would be 44.9 percent.

[f] Includes 16.8 percent tabulated for Cuauhtémoc Cárdenas.

Source: Cornelius and Craig (1991: 65); preliminary figures for 1994.

declining hegemony of the PRI and the extent to which the 1988 elections were indicative of a breakup of the old political coalition and the traditional mode of elite conflict resolution. Indeed, the PRI had fallen far from its former position of political dominance.

The political crisis that reached a peak in the period between the earthquake of 1985 and the elections of 1988 did much to destroy the old bases of political power and support in the country. Presidents after 1988 could not count on the unquestioned support of a firm coalition of economic and political interests nor could they assume that the PRI could ensure their election. They could no longer assume that the bases of presidential leadership were intact or that citizens continued to consider the government legitimate even when they did not agree with its policies. Conditions for political leadership and political organization had fallen apart, just as the bases for economic power and state leadership had been undermined by the crisis. The state was the victim of these changes, in that its dominant role in economics and politics was deeply eroded.

THINGS FALL APART IN KENYA: POLITICAL CENTRALIZATION, ETHNIC ALLIANCES, AND ECONOMIC DECLINE

Conditions of economic and political development in Kenya differ in important ways from those of Mexico. In 1980, Kenya's economy was more agrarian, its society much less urban, and its political institutions in existence for a much shorter period of time. Mexico traced its governing system to the Revolution of 1910, the constitution of 1917, the political bargains struck in the 1929 consolidation of power in the PRI, and the inclusion of peasants and workers into its corporatist representational system in the 1930s. Kenya looked back to the legacy of settler colonialism and British administrative structures, the struggle for independence that culminated in 1963, the consolidation of the KANU in 1964, the power of the civil service and the provincial administration, and the presidential style of Jomo Kenyatta to trace its institutional heritage.[45]

Yet, within Africa, and until the mid-1980s, Kenya enjoyed much the same position that Mexico held in Latin America. It was regarded as a relative success story economically, often held up as an example of effective state-led development that encouraged the emergence of a thriving private sector. After independence, Kenya's economy managed to sustain moderate rates of growth in a continent wracked by stagnation and the fluctuations characteristic of economies based on export of primary commodities. Its agricultural sector performed extremely well compared with the rapid destruction of agricultural production in most African countries.[46] The country developed thriving industrial and commercial sectors and proved a much more attractive destination for foreign investment than most other countries in the region.

Overall, Kenya's economy performed well, spanning the decade of the 1960s with a 5.9 percent annual GDP growth rate and the 1970s with a 5.8 percent average. During the latter decade, manufacturing growth averaged 9.5 percent annually, spurred in part by government policies stimulating import substitution and by returns to the country's dynamic agricultural export sector.[47] At independence, a successfully managed transfer of land controlled by Europeans in the rich central highlands maintained the productivity of the agricultural sector and encouraged the continuation of beneficial pricing policies, credit and marketing facilities, and public investment in agriculture and infrastructure.[48] Elites in the civil service and urban business invested heavily in land and exerted considerable pressure on government to maintain policies favorable to agriculture. This resulted in a development strategy that was far less urban biased than was the case in many other countries.

Similarly, building on a colonial institutional and policy base, the Kenyan government sought to stimulate commercial and industrial development through extensive investment in the economy and the development of a large number of parastatals in basic industries, infrastructure, and other activities. Joint ventures with state capital and extensive trade barriers also stimulated industrial development. This development was noted for the balance achieved between indigenization and foreign investment and for low inflation rates.[49] In agriculture, the emphasis was on export promotion, in industry on import substitution; in both cases, "nurture capitalism" defined the role of the state.[50] Kenya also achieved more than many of its African neighbors in the social sectors. Its population became relatively more educated than that of most other African countries, with a 69 percent adult literacy rate in 1990.[51] The country also achieved greater strides in public health and welfare, with a life expectancy of 59.7 years in 1990, compared to sub-Saharan Africa's 51.8 years.[52]

Just as Mexico was noted within Latin America for the strength and durability of its political institutions, Kenya had a similar reputation among African countries. The political system, characterized as civilian and authoritarian, provided sustained stability and relatively durable institutions compared to the frequent regime changes and political upheaval of most other countries in the region after independence. Despite an army mutiny in 1964 and an attempted coup in 1982, the regime was more noted for its continuities than for its changes. Close interlinkages among government, agricultural, commercial, and industrial elites encouraged an accommodationist style of conflict resolution among politically relevant and mobilized groups.

Kenya also developed a well-institutionalized state, with a firmly embedded civil service bureaucracy molded by British colonialism. The civil service achieved a strong professional identity and benefited from a broad array of official perquisites. Neither parliament nor KANU threatened its autonomy or prestige; in the 1960s and 1970s, it was not unusual for permanent secretaries to have more power than ministers. While the task of politics in Kenya was in some ways more difficult than it was in Mexico – the country was poorer, its colonial history more recent, and its ethnic diversity more politically divisive – within the African context, Kenya managed the tasks of political and economic conflict resolution much more effectively than did many other countries.

In more direct comparison to Mexico, Kenya's presidency emerged as the preeminent institution at the apex of the political system. This institution placed the incumbent in a powerful position to manage political relationships, to superintend policy initiatives, and, until the 1980s, to remain above the fray of daily politics as a national figure. In a 1988 article reviewing twenty-five years of independence, the country's influential *Weekly Review* argued that "The history of Kenya's politics is very much the history of the evolution of the country's presidency. More than any other institution, the presidency has shaped the destiny of other institutions, such as parliament and the judiciary," statements that could also have been written about the presidency in Mexico.[53] An important difference between the two institutions, however, was that while Mexican presidents could not be reelected, in Kenya's presidentialist-parliamentary system, they could be. This translated into the longer-term personalization of presidential power in Kenya.

KANU, for many years the only legal party, was organized through patron–client networks similar to those that traditionally provided cohesion to the PRI in Mexico. These networks linked regional bosses to national elites and to remote villages and were cemented through exchanges of state patronage for votes.[54] In contrast to the

PRI, competition for nomination to electoral candidacy within the party encouraged a greater degree of leadership accountability to voters.[55] Moreover, the party lacked the centralized direction and corporatist national structure of the PRI, and was more aptly described as a coalition of regional notables, or "big men," than as a party of centralized control.[56] In this regard, the patronage networks were far more important than the party itself. The core support of the party traditionally came from the more economically developed groups and regions in the country, a "coalition of 'the bigs,' 'the mobilized,' and 'the haves.'"[57] These were predominantly Kikuyu "bigs" and Kikuyu-dominated regions of the country. As with the PRI in Mexico, the primary tasks of KANU were electoral mobilization and patronage distribution. The tasks of policy making and implementation were carried out almost exclusively by the presidency, the cabinet, and the civil service.[58]

In Mexico it is difficult not to focus primary attention on the economic crisis of the 1980s, but the more compelling story in Kenya is the emergence of political crisis. During the course of the decade, clientelist networks shifted, the presidency became a focus of controversy, KANU became a more assertive mechanism for presidential control and ethnic identities, and tensions steadily increased. Civic organizations directly challenged the presidency and the party system and violence escalated. The political crisis greatly exacerbated an emergent economic crisis and significantly delayed the ability of the regime to respond to it. There is no question that by the early 1990s, the familiar relationships among state, society, and economy had been deeply disrupted in Kenya.

Pulling apart the bases of political power

The story of the political crisis is primarily the story of the presidency of Daniel arap Moi, but some trends can be traced to the final years in office of Jomo Kenyatta, the country's first president. During most of the 1960s and 1970s, Kenyatta enjoyed the reputation of a master at managing or suppressing political conflict in the country, which characteristically involved ethnic and regional identities and access to land and state resources. Kenyatta successfully superintended the incorporation of the Kenya African Democratic Union (KADU) – the most important other political party at independence – into KANU, in part by apportioning the vice-presidency to Daniel arap Moi, KADU's leader and a prominent politician representing an alliance of Kalenjin and other minority ethnic groups. He thus engineered the destruction of the only potential opposition party to KANU at independence. He proscribed the Kenya People's Union (KPU), another potential opposition party, in 1969.[59] Had they survived, these two parties would have challenged Kikuyu dominance and the elite and ethnic bias of agricultural and industrial policy; in suppressing them, the "radical critique of the government [was] effectively sidelined from the political system" by Kenyatta.[60] In addition, Kenyatta ensured that a centralized rather than a federal state would develop, further entrenching the power of the Kikuyu-based coalition.[61]

Throughout the 1960s and 1970s, most political conflict centered on access to state patronage, including land, credit, development projects, party nominations, and jobs. Kenyatta allowed power structures to remain unchallenged at regional levels as long as they did not threaten his leadership or the power of the central government to set policy directions. Competition for favors centered on the patron–client networks that linked ethnic and regional elites to villages and Nairobi. During this period, KANU was primarily "a loosely knit grouping of politicians," a characteristic that enhanced the position of the president.[62] Nor did Kenyatta do much to bring ideological or policy cohesion to the party, preferring instead to have presidential control over the policy agenda. Diversity of views within KANU decreased its ability to play a role in national policy formation.[63]

In turn, elections encouraged incumbent members of parliament to concentrate on delivering patronage to their constituencies, developing networks with bureaucrats and political influentials to get access to state resources, and supporting local self-help (harambee) initiatives through personal donations and access to powerful patrons in Nairobi.[64] Politicians who demonstrated their competence in these areas were generally assured of continued election and promotion to assistant ministerial and ministerial status.[65] Kenyatta set a standard for careful ethnic arithmetic in the composition of his cabinet, an institution that was expanded over time by increasing the number of ministries, effectively broadening his political base and spreading the reach of economic and political opportunities through the patronage networks. Eventually, "with more than one-third of the National Assembly receiving ministerial appointments, Kenyatta developed a powerful tool for maintaining support from prominent politicians and ensuring that they remained popular in their home areas."[66]

In significant contrast to the highly politicized public administration that was established in Mexico, Kenyatta ensured some distinction between policy making and politics. By keeping political competition and patronage focused on local and regional politics, the presidency and the civil service gained autonomy to set national agendas. The consequence of this was a bureaucracy that became as central to policy making and implementation as Mexico's was. In fact, the civil service at the national and provincial level became the principal instrument of state and presidential power. The permanent secretaries and the provincial commissioners became powerful actors in their own right, although always dependent for their autonomy on the president.[67]

The administrative officers [at the provincial level] not only collected taxes on behalf of local authorities but they also chaired land boards, loan boards, agricultural committees, licensing committees, etc. They were coordinators of all governmental activities in the provinces and districts, and because some departments had no representation at provincial and district levels, they also filled certain technical roles. But most important for the centralization of authority and the wide range of functions carried out by officers of provincial administration was their political power, which they acquired by being the personal representatives of the head of government – they became "governors."[68]

More generally, Kenyatta did little to encroach on the privileges of the already economically, socially, and politically established Kikuyu and their coalition partners, the Kamba, Luo, and several smaller ethnic groups.[69] At the same time, however, he promoted a market for both political and economic mobility that provided opportunities for ambitious individuals from all regions and ethnic groups to join the ranks of the advantaged. It was, Widner notes, a "Kikuyu-dominated meritocracy."[70] Strategic use of state patronage was also important in building bases for national cohesion and identity. Strategically employed violence and legal forms of intimidation further enhanced presidential power. Particularly when political challenges incorporated populist appeals that threatened the ethnic elites, response was unambiguous.[71]

This system worked remarkably well for almost fifteen years. A strong presidency that remained generally unchallenged because it did not challenge entrenched structures of economic and political privilege was matched by a relatively well-managed civil service that was nevertheless central to political power through its control of the resources of state patronage. By the latter half of the 1970s, however, the aging Kenyatta became more prone to surround himself with cronies, wink at corrupt activities, be intolerant of dissent within KANU, and encroach increasingly on the civil service to promote his own political ends.[72] Ethnic tensions incorporated serious economic conflicts and, with time, the Kikuyu-led elite had more and more to fear from losing political power to rival groups. This concern sparked a contentious – and ultimately unsuccessful – effort in 1976 to change the constitution so that the Kalenjin vice-president, Daniel arap Moi, would not become president in the event of Kenyatta's death in office. When the president died in 1978, he left behind this conflict between the constitutionally designated successor and those who spoke for the politically and economically powerful. The central issue of elections in 1979 was the degree to which rival groups could capture state resources to build political support in the regions; with Moi in control of the presidency in the interim period, this competition quickly took on strong ethnic overtones as he sought to shift such resources from Kenyatta's core constituency group to his own ethnic minority supporters.[73]

Despite this tension, President Moi gave few clues that extensive political change was in the offing in his early years in office. A political insider, although from the minority Kalenjin group, he knew well the rules of Kenyan ethnic, regional, and elite politics.[74] While he moved some members of his own and other minority groups into positions of power, and moved against some close associates of Kenyatta, he appeared to be pursuing a political strategy of careful distribution of state patronage, ethnic arithmetic, and regional political autonomy similar to that of Kenyatta before him. Many of his initial acts as president – amnesty for political detainees and free milk for school children, for example – were highly popular.

Nevertheless, Moi faced a difficult situation as president. He was surrounded by appointees, politicians, and civil servants who had primary loyalties to interests, regions, and ethnic identities that differed greatly from his own. A number of them had, through the change-the-constitution movement, attempted to ensure that he could not succeed to the presidency. The army, air force, police, and civil service were all dominated by members of the Kikuyu-based coalition. And, within months of his election, the country faced severe economic problems. These issues exacerbated the new president's dilemma: building a base of personal political support, ensuring the loyalty of those in influential positions, and providing state resources to regional and ethnic constituencies within the context of declining public resources to do so. In seeking to redistribute resources and power to groups and regions that had been marginalized under the colonial and Kenyatta governments, Moi's tactics were much less subtle than those of his predecessor, despite his reputation as a skillful politician and survivor. The objectives he sought placed him in direct opposition to the political and economic establishment.

Gradually, changes were noted, particularly in the appointments of non-Kikuyu to positions of power, greater use of state security measures, and allocations of patronage.

There could be no better summary of this change than the difference between the slogans employed by Kenyatta on the one hand and Moi on the other. The celebrated cry of "Harambee!" with which Kenyatta concluded his speeches had encapsulated the late president's approach to politics. At one level harambee bespoke a preference for local-level community action to achieve collective benefits or "development." At another level it embodied a strategy of bargained exchange; Kenyans could "pull together" by compromise ... and by refusal to enshrine the interests of one group above all others in the party, or, indeed, in the cabinet. Moi introduced a different slogan and a different conception of appropriate political strategy. "Nyayo!" ("Follow in the footsteps") took the place of "Harambee!" Although the slogan was intended to convey respect for Kenyatta and highlight the need to pursue the course the first president had set for the country, *nyayo* acquired a second interpretation: do what the Office of the President tells you to do. Politics as control began to take the place of politics as exchange.[75]

Criticism of government policy was increasingly suppressed and Moi began to use KANU's structure more fully as an instrument of control. The office of the president took over control of the police, security measures were tightened, and security budgets increased.[76] The power of the provincial administration was undermined by strengthening the central ministries. Parliamentary debate, particularly over amendments to the constitution, was curtailed. In 1980, regional and ethnic welfare societies, which had become vehicles for lobbying, political competition, and patronage, were suppressed.[77] Within KANU, Moi demanded greater political conformity. In May 1982, a constitutional amendment made KANU the only legal party, in fact moving Kenya from being a de facto one-party regime to a de jure one. Symbolically, Section 2A of the 19th amendment to the constitution was indicative of a more generalized and growing intolerance for dissent. Intolerance was also reflected in much greater controls on the press and public debate, actions that sparked considerable criticism of Moi as president. Economic difficulties, and the policy measures taken to deal with them, also encouraged disaffection with the new president. In August of 1982, officers of the air force attempted a coup and riots tore through Nairobi, involving groups of students and impoverished urbanites.[78] These events undercut the confidence of many Kenyans in their country's stability and political superiority to other African countries.

The coup attempt also had a profound effect on Moi. It exacerbated his own sense of insecurity. Most analysts agree that beginning in 1982, the history of the presidency can be recounted in terms of a marked trend toward the centralization of personal power in the president's office and in the president himself. The coup provided an opportunity for the president to remove a number of rival politicians from ministerial and party positions and to reorganize the command structure of the military and police.[79] It also enabled Moi to use his legal power and the security apparatus to detain political opponents and increase surveillance on those he suspected of dissent. The tendency to surround himself with ethnic and family loyalists became a more notable aspect of his style. As political opposition and challenge mounted later in the 1980s, this tendency was exacerbated.[80]

The centralization of personal power in the presidency was complemented by much more pronounced efforts to redistribute economic and political power to minority ethnic groups. Concretely, this meant a shift in agricultural policy and increased development expenditures in areas of the Rift Valley, Coast Province, parts of Western Province, and other provinces inhabited by Kalenjin and other minority groups supporting Moi. The Kikuyu-dominated Kenya Farmers Association (KFA) was replaced by the Kenya Grain Growers Cooperative Union, which provided representation to the new support coalition. The Kenya Tea Development Authority was confronted with a new parastatal, the Nyayo Tea Zones, that provided greater support to the tea industry in western Kenya.[81] There were also personnel changes in government. Kikuyus in the bureaucracy, for example, became increasingly aware that their chances for upward mobility were being constricted, just as the fortunes of Kalenjins and associated ethnic groups improved. Because Kikuyu had long enjoyed the greatest access to education, land, civil service positions, and business opportunities, they were quick to point out that many official positions were being filled by ill-educated and greedy tribesmen of the president, eager to "eat" at the public trough. Jobs, development resources, opportunities to do business with government, licenses and permits – their distribution demonstrated similar shifts.

By the mid-1980s, ethnic rivalries that had always been salient, but that had been managed relatively effectively under the old rules of Kikuyu dominance and ethnic and regional arithmetic, became infused with much higher levels of animosity. Political power and economic power no longer coincided as neatly as they had under Kenyatta. By the early 1990s, these tensions led to violence, particularly in areas inhabited by both the old favorites and the new favorites.[82] Ethnic clashes, particularly in western Kenya and areas bordering the Rift Valley, in "frontier" areas of ethnic migration, flared over rights to land and were widely believed to be officially incited.[83]

Similarly, Moi sought to destroy the political fortunes of potential rivals by attacking the patron–client links between regional and local political officials, by stimulating in-fighting, and by undermining the ability of local MPs to deliver patronage goods and thus build up support for reelection.[84] Purges limited dissent within the party.[85] The elections of 1988 were dominated by debate about the introduction, at the president's behest, of a two-stage voting system that mandated queuing in the first stage. This system was held responsible for widespread intimidation and for a turnout of only 24.6 percent of registered voters.[86] The same year witnessed significant curtailment of press freedom. The civil service commission, once a powerful and relatively independent institution with authority to appoint, promote, and discipline members of the civil service, and the judicial services commission, with similar responsibility in the judicial system, were brought under the control of the office of the president, which became the initiator and arbiter of all policies and decisions. Differential promotion practices gradually eroded civil service autonomy and made public officials reluctant to question presidential authority and policies. Similarly, voluntary organizations representing economic, professional, and religious interests were either incorporated into KANU or targeted for increased repression, including harassment and detention of their leaders. Business owners, farmers, and business associations began to experience varying degrees of difficulty in acquiring licenses, credit, and access to foreign exchange.

In 1988, the attempt to centralize and personalize power, shift the ethnic composition of dominance, and control dissent was clearly in evidence in massive rigging of elections for parliament. This practice, along with growing awareness of the extent of corruption and cronyism in government, lack of capacity to participate freely in politics, and increasing evidence of truncated political and economic opportunities for the majority Kikuyu, encouraged mounting opposition to the regime and to Moi personally.[87] Organizations representing the clergy, lawyers, and some non-government associations became increasingly mobilized around opposition to Moi. In July 1990, Nairobi and other urban areas were the scenes of violent demonstrations against the government. The murder of Foreign Affairs Minister Robert Ouko in 1990, and an officially sanctioned effort to cover it up, fueled further disaffection. Many believed that Ouko meant to expose extensive high level corruption in government.

Increasingly, political opposition unified around the effort to force the government to introduce multiparty elections. In 1991, political opposition coalesced in the founding of the Forum for the Restoration of Democracy (FORD), which brought together a number of old guard political insiders representing the KANU of Kenyatta's era with newly mobilized urban professionals, clergy, and non-governmental organization (NGO) leaders.

In addition, Kenya's relations with most of the international agencies that had dealings with the country became overtly political, as these organizations began to press the government to adopt multipartyism. Losing patience with the failure to deal seriously with economic problems or to move against escalating corruption, they coalesced around a series of demands for reform, eventually substantiating these demands with a decision at a consultative meeting in Paris in November 1991 to cut off all quick disbursing aid to the country until they were met. Reluctantly, Moi acquiesced. A constitutional amendment to repeal Section 2A was introduced and passed in December 1991; elections were called for in late 1992.

Moi's acquiescence to multiparty elections signaled neither a conversion to pluralist politics nor to greater accountability in government. Throughout the electoral campaign, the opposition parties were kept on the defensive by efforts to restrict their ability to campaign freely. Despite these efforts, and despite widely reported abuses in the election process and fraud at polling places, Moi won only 36 percent of the vote. Only the fragmentation of the opposition, with three major parties fielding candidates, allowed him to win the presidency. The geographical distribution of voting for KANU and for opposition parties was an ethnic map of the country, with KANU winning most of the peripheral and rural regions where Kalenjin and other minority groups predominated, and the opposition parties winning all of the central and urban zones in which the Kikuyu dominated (see Table 3.4).[88] In January 1993, and for the first time, Moi faced an organized opposition in parliament, whose combined representation robbed him of the possibility of passing constitutional amendments with the support of KANU.

The patterns that led to increasing political crisis in Kenya emerged tangibly in the wake of the 1982 coup attempt. The height of political tension and mobilization of dissent and repression fell between 1987 and 1993. The coalition of ethnic, regional, and economic interests that had originally dominated political life in the country was weakened, increasingly distanced from the more centralized and personalized structure of power engineered by Moi. Corruption reached new heights as ministers and other high level public officials used their positions to amass huge fortunes.[89] Official acts of brutality, lawlessness, and abuses of authority further fueled criticism and opposition. By late 1992 and early 1993, Kenyans at all levels in society doubted the ability of the country to sustain its reputation for political stability and relatively effective management of political conflict. In 1992, Joel Barkan wrote:

In the thirteen years since the death of his predecessor, Daniel arap Moi has consistently sought to fragment and capture all independent bases of authority to reduce his dependence on institutions controlled by ethnoregional interests that were never part of his political coalition. In the process, he has established a form of personal rule that seeks to exert authority directly vis-a-vis the Kenyan population, thus bypassing established institutions and power brokers ... [E]xisting institutions have been undermined, particularly the informal procedures that had previously established a predictable relationship between state and society.[90]

Economic decline and the failure of policy

The political crisis made the management of economic policy more difficult. It is significant, however, that until the early 1990s, economic policy management was not a centerpiece of political conflict in the country, and, except for agricultural producer prices, was not even an issue in the increasing rivalry between the Kikuyu-based alliance and the emergent Kalenjin coalition. Agricultural pricing policy was important because Kenya's coffee producers had traditionally been favored by government policies; producers of grain, many of whom came from Moi's support constituencies, had been less well treated. In the mid-1980s, subsidies to coffee were

Table 3.4 *Kenyan election results 1992 by province*

	Total	Nairobi[a]	Central[a]	Eastern[a]	Coast	North	Rift	Western[a]	Nyanza
Provincial % of total vote	100	7	19	15	6	1	27	10	15
Turnout as % of registered	68	56	84	62	48	41	76	63	63
Presidential (% of vote)									
Moi (KANU)	36	17	2	37	62	78	66	40	14
Matiba (FORD-A)	26	44	60	11	11	11	19	38	2
Kibaki (DP)	19	19	36	50	10	3	8	3	7
Odinga (FORD-K)	17	20	1	2	16	8	6	18	76
Parliamentary (seats won)									
KANU	100	1	0	21	17	8	36	10	7
FORD-A	31	6	14	0	0	0	4	7	0
DP	23	0	10	9	1	0	2	0	1
FORD-K	31	1	1	1	2	1	2	3	20
Others	3	0	0	1	0	1	0	0	1
Total seats	188	8	25	32	20	10	44	20	29
% incumbents won	26	12	—	34	45	60	34	25	14
% "old faces" won	54	38	36	59	65	50	59	55	55

[a] Kikuyu coalition heartland.
Source: Barkan (1993: 96).

decreased while grain production received increased support.[91] More generally, however, economic policy was made and implemented – or not implemented – beyond the confines of the political conflicts and the realignment of political power that characterized this period.

Kenya's economic growth in the 1970s and 1980s was strongly affected by periodic external shocks. A pattern of long-term deterioration in the country's terms of trade was initiated by the first oil shock of 1974–1975. Until the late 1970s, however, the effects of negative external shocks were masked by subsequent booms in commodity prices and supportive international financial conditions. As a result, deeper structural problems in the economy – such as the rate of private sector employment creation, a gradual loss of dynamism in the agricultural sector, and the rapidly expanding size of the population – were easy to ignore. The oil shock of 1974–1975 led to a 1975 adjustment program, but shortly thereafter coffee and tea prices improved and Kenya benefited from an unprecedented beverage boom. GDP grew by 2.2 percent in 1976, 9.4 percent in 1977, and 6.8 percent in 1978 (see Table 3.5). At the same time, high export prices and economic growth encouraged foreign borrowing, government spending, and inflation. When coffee and tea prices fell in 1978–1979, these trends continued. The second oil shock of 1979 had equally serious implications for the country's balance of payments and, unlike the first shock, was not followed by strong growth in the industrialized countries, expansionary international credit markets, or rising commodity prices.[92]

The late 1970s, then, brought warnings of serious economic problems. Economic growth slowed in the early 1980s, even while inflation remained high. A devaluation, pressed for by the IMF in 1979, was postponed by the Moi government until 1981; it was followed by a second and larger devaluation in the same year. GDP growth declined to 1.9 percent in 1982, 1.5 percent in 1983, and 1.7 percent in 1984. Public sector revenues declined as the economy weakened, yet government expenditures continued to expand. Controlling the fiscal deficit therefore became a centerpiece of negotiations with the IMF, the World Bank, and other international institutions. In other areas, such as producer and consumer prices and the use of subsidies, the Kenyan government's performance received relatively high marks from the international financial institutions, at least until the late 1980s.[93] In raising consumer prices, the relatively weak position of the country's unions assisted the policy position of the government.

Despite almost continuous negotiations with the international agencies, the government demonstrated little interest in controlling public spending in the first years of the 1980s. Development investments, civil service salary increases, drought relief, and expenditures related to the 1982 coup pushed government budgets upward. Nevertheless, although the attempted coup resulted in greater politicization of the bureaucracy and greater centralization of power, it also encouraged the government to take measures to stabilize the economy and control the budget deficit. And, despite the move toward greater political control and evidence of "crony capitalism," the policy-making influence of the economic ministries and their high level technocrats was important until 1986.[94] In 1982, the finance ministry increased its power to control spending, resulting in clear improvement of the budget deficit. Devaluations in 1982 had a positive impact on the effective exchange rate, and a crawling peg system was introduced. Devaluations had been firmly resisted by business groups that were heavily dependent on imports; once the government moved to a crawling peg system, however, protest became muted.[95]

These measures improved relations between the government and the IMF, and the government continued to pursue some efforts to stabilize the economy through 1985. It also initiated efforts to liberalize trade. Inflation was reduced to 12 percent by 1984, and the overall deficit was cut to 4.8 percent of GDP by that year. A civil service census removed some 85,000 shadow names from the payroll roster in 1984.[96] GDP growth recovered in 1985 and continued to improve in 1986. The structural problems of the economy, however, lay outside these reform efforts. Admittedly, import liberalization, decontrol of the important maize market, and increased consumer prices were placed on the government's reform agenda, but implementation of these measures did not always follow from the announcement of policy. Moreover, the severe drought of 1984 raised concerns about food security and the impact of deteriorating infrastructure and increased population on agricultural production. By late 1985, structural problems related to population, agriculture, employment, and the role of the state became more insistent and more prominent on the agendas of the international financial institutions that dealt with Kenya.

In 1986, Sessional Paper No. 1, "Economic Management for Renewed Growth," was taken by the international institutions as a recognition of the need for substantial economic policy reform by the government.[97] It indicated a new recognition for the leadership of the private sector in development and a need to move from import substitution to promotion of exports and freer trading relationships if the economy were to become more dynamic. It recommended a range of policy reforms that needed to be made to achieve this goal, and particularly signaled the importance of sound policy management in the agricultural and industrial sectors. As in 1975, however, a boom in coffee exports weakened the pressures to adopt reforms and encouraged higher spending and inflation. Lower commodity prices in 1987 were replaced by higher prices and greater agricultural production in 1988 and then by another reversal in 1989.

By the late 1980s, mounting political crisis and the economic situation intersected to discourage significant progress in undertaking reform initiatives. The inability to manage inflation, for example, undermined public confidence in the government, while increasing budget deficits were spurred by expanding public sector employment, mismanagement of parastatals, and widespread corruption. In a situation of weakened political support, Moi was not willing to dismiss public sector employees or curtail the activities of his high level supporters in government. Instead, he responded with efforts to quash dissent, buy further support through patronage, tolerate increasingly large-scale corruption in high levels of government, and rig electoral outcomes. Economic management in the late 1980s was characterized by increasing conflict with the international institutions and increasing evidence of extensive rent seeking and corruption on the part of government officials. A pattern

Table 3.5 *Kenya: economic indicators, 1970–1991*

	1970	1971	1972	1973	1974	1975	1976	1977	1978	1979	1980
GDP annual growth	-4.7	22.5	18.3	5.8	3.6	1.3	2.2	9.4	6.8	7.5	5.4
Real GDP per capita growth	NA	18.3	14.2	2.1	-0.1	-2.3	-1.5	5.3	2.8	3.4	1.3
Public sector current revenue (% of GDP)	NA	NA	18.0	16.1	17.4	18.9	18.3	17.2	22.8	21.7	22.6
Growth in revenue	NA	NA	NA	-5.5	12.2	9.9	-0.9	2.4	42.2	2.0	10.1
Public sector current expenditures (% of GDP)	NA	NA	15.6	14.9	14.5	16.7	16.7	14.9	18.6	20.2	19.4
Growth in expenditure	NA	NA	NA	0.9	1.0	16.8	1.8	-2.5	33.9	16.3	1.3
Public sector overall deficit (% of GDP)	NA	NA	3.8	5.1	2.8	4.8	5.9	3.6	4.0	6.5	4.5
Public sector deficit (index, 1980 = 100)	NA	NA	56.0	80.9	45.2	79.6	99.4	66.0	78.4	137.4	100.0
Consumer prices (average annual growth rate)	NA	10.9	18.5	16.7	20.8	12.8	21.5	28.0	10.2	13.7	15.7
Real wages (average annual growth rate)	NA	NA	NA	NA	NA	NA	NA	NA	NA	NA	NA
Minimum wage growth rate	NA	NA	NA	NA	NA	NA	NA	NA	NA	NA	NA
Current account balance (millions of US dollars)	-49.0	-111.7	-68.1	-126.0	-307.9	-218.4	-124.2	27.5	-660.5	-498.4	-886.0
Trade balance (millions of US dollars)	-86.3	-184.9	-116.8	-74.9	-316.9	-213.7	-63.8	18.1	-675.9	-562.8	-1,083.4
Total external debt (millions of US dollars)	NA	426.0	497.1	722.7	986.7	1,107.3	1,281.8	1,712.2	2,240.0	2,779.7	3,449.0
Interest payments due/exports of G & S	NA	NA	NA	NA	NA	NA	NA	NA	NA	NA	11.7

Table 3.5 (contd)

	1981	1982	1983	1984	1985	1986	1987	1988	1989	1990	1991
GDP annual growth	4.1	1.9	1.5	1.7	4.3	7.1	5.9	6.0	4.6	4.3	1.7
Real GDP per capita growth	0.0	−2.1	−2.5	−2.2	0.5	3.3	2.1	2.5	1.1	0.8	−1.8
Public sector current revenue (% of GDP)	22.5	21.7	20.9	20.4	20.2	20.5	22.2	22.6	24.0	22.1	NA
Growth in revenue	3.5	−1.7	−2.5	−0.4	3.2	8.9	14.4	7.9	11.2	−3.8	NA
Public sector current expenditures (% of GDP)	20.7	23.3	21.3	21.7	21.6	21.4	22.9	22.6	24.9	21.6	NA
Growth in expenditure	11.2	14.7	−7.2	3.2	4.1	5.8	13.4	4.9	15.3	−9.5	NA
Public sector overall deficit (% of GDP)	6.5	7.8	4.8	4.8	6.2	4.4	6.3	4.1	6.5	5.5	NA
Public sector deficit (index, 1980 = 100)	150.3	184.3	116.0	117.4	158.3	119.8	183.9	126.9	208.2	184.1	NA
Consumer prices (average annual growth rate)	15.0	13.4	13.3	12.0	12.9	16.6	11.6	15.3	14.3	15.0	14.3
Real wages (average annual growth rate)	NA	NA	NA	NA	NA	NA	NA	NA	NA	NA	NA
Minimum wage growth rate	−25.3	−5.6	−21.3	−11.6	−7.2	7.5	NA	NA	NA	NA	NA
Current account balance (millions of US dollars)	−558.4	−302.1	−44.9	−123.4	−110.3	−36.6	−494.0	−459.8	−579.4	−502.1	−230.9
Trade balance (millions of US dollars)	−752.7	−532.2	−271.3	−313.7	−326.6	−284.4	−713.9	−784.7	−1,037.3	−998.2	NA
Total external debt (millions of US dollars)	3,307.7	3,450.8	3,715.3	3,570.9	4,181.2	4,670.1	5,730.0	5,768.8	5,783.1	7,005.6	7,014.0
Interest payments due/exports of G & S	NA	15.4	15.1	14.5	15.7	14.1	16.8	15.0	14.1	14.8	14.5

Sources: World Bank, World Tables, various years; IMF (1992a, 1992b).

of rhetorical commitment to reform and failure to take action dominated the policy arena through the early 1990s. Some reforms were more easily adopted and pursued, such as a modernization of the tax system, because political and economic priorities of the government coincided. More frequently, however, such as in the cases of import liberalization, maize market decontrol, and health sector user fees, a pattern of on and off implementation prevailed, undermining private sector confidence in economic recovery and further souring relations with the international organizations. GDP growth rates moved steadily downward from 1988 and inflation moved steadily upwards.

The implosion of politics

In historical perspective, the 1980s and 1990s were a critical period for Kenya. The coalition that supported the government and the country's development strategy throughout the first two decades of independence was systematically fragmented and marginalized by Moi's use of appointments, repression, constitutional changes, electoral manipulation, and patronage. Declining productivity in agriculture, policies that had a negative impact on the export sector, and decreasing incentives to investment weakened the economic power of the alliance that united the coffee- and tea-growing regions of the central highlands, the public bureaucracy, and the industrial and commercial sectors. In Kenya, then, a dominant coalition was broken apart less by a crisis caused by prior economic policies and external shocks than by deliberate political actions to shift the basis of political power in the country and to reconstitute the support base of KANU.

These actions fueled increasingly high levels of open political dissent and declining economic performance. The international financial institutions, disenchanted with the ramifications of economic and political disarray, increased the conditionalities on assistance and increasingly refused to assist Kenya in its foreign exchange shortfalls. They gave their public support to the movement for multiparty elections. Both sets of actions further undermined investor and international confidence in government and the economy. In a similar way, political instability in the mid- to late 1980s discouraged tourism, by that time the country's largest foreign exchange earner.

By the early 1990s, political and economic crises combined to encourage efforts to mobilize a coalition of KANU dissidents, new professional groups from the country's urban middle class, and urban constituencies more generally. Their objective? For some, it was to remove Moi from office and to regain their previous position of power and privilege. For others, it was to remove Moi from office and to open up the political process to greater accountability. Many were also motivated by a combination of these three goals. What they agreed upon was that Moi and his cronies had to go. For most of them, the introduction of multiparty elections was the clearest way to achieve their objective.

CONCLUSIONS: ECONOMICS AND POLITICS IN DISARRAY

Things fell apart in Mexico and Kenya in the 1980s. In Mexico, a development strategy that had effectively promoted economic growth until the early 1970s and that was kept in place through the early 1980s by massive inflows of oil revenue was widely rejected by the mid-1980s as inappropriate for rescuing the country from the deep crisis that it faced after 1982. Not only were policy makers and analysts convinced that import substitution and state-led growth were no longer a reasonable path toward Mexico's development, the economic crisis also undermined the economic interests that helped keep that set of policies in place. The industries that had long been protected from both domestic and international competition by government policies were deeply affected by the crisis and, as they lost economic power, they also lost their ability to pressure government effectively. Real wages fell dramatically and formal unemployment increased, weakening official unions that had long played an important role in Mexican politics. The economic crisis thus had both ideological and political implications: policy makers lost faith in the policy regime of the past and the coalition of interests that kept that model in place was fundamentally altered.

Politically, there was also breakdown. By 1988, long-term observers of Mexican development were asking if the political regime, so artfully constructed in the period between the Revolution of 1910 and the early 1950s, was in the process of collapse. Many considered that the autonomous mobilization of civic society and its increasingly insistent demands for greater choice in elections and enlarged participation in decision making was leading inevitably to a more open and pluralist democracy. Others argued that increasing contestation and open divisions in society could easily lead to a right wing reaction that would include the politicization of the military and a possible coup or coup attempt.[98] At the very least, they argued, the government might be pushed to open repression of dissent and political mobilization.

In considering the extent of political upheaval and open criticism of government there was little question that the old bases of political control and hegemony had broken down. Some were surprised by the rapidity with which the underpinnings of political control seemed to evaporate; others argued that the society had been undergoing fundamental change since the early 1970s. Most analysts agreed, however, that as economic crisis mounted, an extensive range of latent grievances became rapidly politicized outside the confines of traditional political structures. Despite the fact that the economy was somewhat improved in 1988, the combined impact of six years of economic hardship, a massive earthquake, falling oil revenues, and widespread and autonomous political mobilization reduced public confidence in government to a historically low level.

If Mexico in 1988 is compared to Kenya in 1993, significant differences emerge in terms of the dynamics of breakdown. In Kenya, the political crisis was initially more profound than the economic crisis and had its origins in the actions of the president to strengthen his power in ways that weakened support for the regime. President Moi's efforts to centralize and personalize power and to shift the ethnic and regional basis of KANU and the civil service backfired in the sense that these actions stimulated political mobilization outside of KANU and extensive elite defections from it. Political centralization undermined the ability of the regime to respond to diverse constituencies and to reach timely decisions about the management of the economy and government. Most fatally, perhaps, it stimulated the rapid expansion of the politics of cronyism, rent seeking, and corruption that further undermined faith in the system.

In the economy, the sense of crisis was slow to emerge and less central to the escalation of the political crisis than it was in Mexico. While economists, some policy makers, and the international agencies repeatedly argued that there were deep structural problems in the Kenyan economy, and while Sessional Paper No. 1 provided a critique of import substitution and a prescription for renewed growth, Kenya experienced less of the ideological transformation that occurred in Mexico. By 1993, there was increasing recognition that something was wrong with the economy, as growth rates followed a long-term declining trend and unemployment and capital flight continued to rise. The causes of that "something," however, were most frequently located in extensive corruption and the failure of investment programs to produce concrete results, largely as a result of the same corruption, rather than in the nature of the country's prior development strategy. To an extent even greater than Mexico in 1988, however, the capacity of the Kenyan state to manage the economy was deeply questioned.

Thus, by 1988 in Mexico and 1993 in Kenya, the old parameters of politics and economics no longer held. In each case, regimes that had reputations for their ability to ensure basic political stability and coherent economic development policies were no longer as much in control of either politics or economics as they had been. The story of breakdown through economic and political crisis is usefully told through the cases of Mexico and Kenya because they are states that had managed to develop the strength and durability to set ongoing conditions for state–economy and state–society interactions.

But a more challenging question has to do with how these two states responded to the problems created by economic and political crisis. When old relationships fall apart, they create possibilities for developing new ones. In the cases we are concerned with, this means the potential to recast the rules of the game for economics and politics, refine the policy-making process, restructure the public service, and recapture the ability to manage political conflict. The potential to reinvent state–economy and state–society relations is, of course, difficult to fulfill when the regime has been weakened both politically and economically. Yet some countries have been able to respond to these challenges. What makes it possible for them to do so? What factors impede such efforts? These questions lie behind the remaining chapters in this book.

4

Imposing state authority

States are unique among social institutions in that they seek to ensure that their rules predominate over the rules of other institutions such as the family, the community, the tribe, or the market.[1] In fact, the capacity to exert authoritative control has long been a defining feature of states.[2] Characteristically, modern states must make and enforce sets of rules related to property rights, contracts, civil and criminal justice, and the selection of those who make and implement the rules. Part of their purpose is to "reduce uncertainty by establishing a stable (but not necessarily efficient) structure to human interaction."[3] The most authoritative states are those in which the right to make and enforce rules is based on widespread acceptance of their legitimacy to do so.

But the history of economic and political development in Latin America and Africa is a useful reminder that institutions of state dominance are not always authoritative. The 1980s and early 1990s were replete with conflict and uncertainty over whose rules would predominate and be accepted as legitimate. Informal markets, ethnic conflict, armed subversion, sectarian claims on personal loyalties, corruption, and other evidence of institutional instability recalled the notion of the soft state, initially used by Gunnar Myrdal to refer to states that lacked capacity to enforce obligations on citizens – states unable to govern.[4] As many states failed in authoritativeness, rival sets of institutions often set the terms for economic and political interactions.

Of course, rules that structure the interaction of state, economy, and society are always being contested and often being restructured through the normal processes of representation of interests, law making, and regulation.[5] A decade and more of crisis in Latin America and Africa, however, encouraged conflict not just about the rules but about the basic legitimacy of the state to set the terms for rule making and enforcement. Thus, while existing rules were undermined by crisis and pressures mounted to redefine them, political leaders and institutions were engaged in a more fundamental conflict about the capacity of the state to assert legitimate authority. The institutional capacity of the state – the ability to prevail over other social institutions in setting the terms for economic and political interactions and doing so through processes whose basic legitimacy is largely uncontested – was at stake.

This dynamic was clear in Mexico and Kenya, where state institutions regulating economic and political relationships lost authority and legitimacy during the 1980s and 1990s. Of course, neither Mexico nor Kenya can be compared to countries such as Peru, Liberia, Ethiopia, or Somalia, in which the state virtually collapsed under the impact of economic and political conflict. Nevertheless, both states lost preexisting institutional capacity. At the most general level, the ability and right of government to define the terms for economic development and political expression were severely challenged. Capital flight, parallel markets, and corruption undercut the capacity to generate resources for development and to prescribe the rules for large numbers of economic agents. For the first time in the modern history of both countries, dominant political parties were almost unseated, in turn weakening their ability to encapsulate political conflict and diminishing the power of the presidency and the bureaucracy to shape policy directions.

In earlier periods, political elites in Mexico and Kenya played important roles in shaping the rules that linked the state to the market and to civic society. They worked to institutionalize the capacity to allocate and regulate private property, particularly in the case of land, and to regulate access to markets for capital and labor. Moreover, in both countries, governing elites and their core constituencies articulated and adopted national development strategies that gave the state the right to intervene extensively in the market to spur economic development. Similarly, they assumed leadership in setting the terms for reviewing government performance, enumerating the obligations of citizens, and providing the national government with a wide range of powers over sub-national levels of government. Both formally and informally, the presidency and the dominant political parties set most of the conditions for political participation and political mobility. Nationalist ideologies in both countries ensured that the authority to regulate the economy and manage political conflict would be viewed as legitimate by broad sectors of their populations, even when it was widely acknowledged that the rules, or their application, were inequitable. Mexico and Kenya are useful cases for assessing how the institutional capacity of the state changes over time. Due to skillful political engineering in prior periods, both countries could boast relatively stable rules of the game that provided predictability for economic and political interaction into the early 1980s.

The dynamics of how this capacity was weakened during the 1980s varied in the two countries. Divergent processes of change are partially explained by the strategies and objectives sought by political leaders and the mechanisms available to them and to state institutions. In Mexico, economic crisis exacerbated a mounting political crisis that political elites and institutions were hard pressed, at least initially, to resist. The authority and legitimacy of the regime suffered as a result. Over time, however, leaders, through their influence over the presidency, bureaucracy, and party, seized the initiative to rewrite the rules to suit changed economic realities and new definitions of national development and to reassert presidential power. In Kenya, political incumbents sought to alter the basis of power for the regime, and in altering the roles traditionally assumed by the bureaucracy and the party, undercut the efficacy of existing rules. Political crisis exacerbated mounting economic problems and encouraged further loss of state authority and legitimacy. The 1980s and early 1990s in Kenya were characterized by greatly expanded conflict over whose rules would be asserted – those of the opposition centered in civic society and the international financial institutions, or those of regime leaders.

CHANGING THE RULES OF THE GAME IN MEXICO

In the fall of 1988, the authority, legitimacy, and coercive capacity of the Mexican state was at its lowest point in decades. Not only was there widespread dissatisfaction with the performance of the economy, the structure of government intervention and regulation was widely questioned; evidence mounted that it was not working and was encouraging extensive corruption. Similar disillusion was voiced about the government's commitment to the ideals of the Mexican Revolution; more people became convinced that existing laws and regulations benefited only a few. In 1988, many Mexicans believed that the president-elect won the election only through widespread fraud at the polls. The PRI's capacity to marshal votes had fallen to historically low levels, as indicated in Figure 4.1 and Table 3.3. Public opinion polls also reflected serious reservations about the basic legitimacy of the regime in power; a 1989 poll indicated that half of the respondents believed that a revolution within the next five years was likely.[6] Government claims that inflation was being controlled and economic recovery was on the way were met with skepticism; public attention focused on the costs and inequities of the crisis, not on the promise of reform and recovery. A rapidly expanding informal economy attested to the ineffectiveness of the rules governing the formal economy.

The de la Madrid administration had grappled with these problems. Some progress in adjusting economic policies to an exigent situation had been made, but the institutional context for economic interactions remained ambiguous. In the mid-1980s, for example, some trade liberalization and initial efforts toward privatizing public sector enterprises had been introduced. These efforts were tentative, however, and were stymied by the intensity of day-to-day management of the macroeconomic crisis and repeated external shocks that occurred during the decade. In the political arena, the administration was noted more for its failure to manage the political challenges of widespread mobilization and its inability to bring reform, coherence, or responsiveness to the PRI than for any initiatives to strengthen the institutional context for state–society interactions.

Thus, among the principal challenges to the administration of Carlos Salinas de Gortari were basic questions about the institutional capacity of the Mexican state. Although the mantle of presidential power was badly tarnished as a result of the administrations of Luís Echeverría, Jóse López Portillo, and Miguel de la Madrid, the six-year cycle of political administrations in Mexico continued to provide opportunities for leadership. Salinas inherited what remained of the institutionalized charisma that accompanied the office of the president, control of extensive powers of appointment, almost all of the government's informational and analytic capacity,

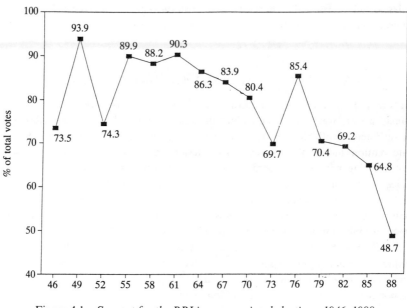

Figure 4.1   *Support for the PRI in congressional elections, 1946–1988*
Source: Cornelius and Craig (1991: 66).

power to restructure the executive, and a strong tradition of executive initiative in policy matters. Indeed, from his inauspicious assumption of power, marred by an unprecedented walkout of opposition congressmen from his inaugural speech, Salinas made exceptional use of the formal and informal powers of his position to reinforce and extend a major reversal of the country's development strategy and to rewrite the terms on which the state would relate to the economy. To a lesser extent, he worked to redefine the relationship of the PRI to the government and of citizens to the state.

After 1988, the rules of the game changed in a variety of ways: liberalized trade broke the dependency relationship between industry and government; deregulation placed a greater burden for productivity and management on the private sector; privatization created new centers of power; one constitutional revision fundamentally altered property rights in the countryside and another changed existing church–state relationships; financial sector reform created powerful new institutions for banking, brokerage, and insurance; and a fractionalization of the corporatist structure of the PRI made it possible to centralize even more power in the presidency. Among these many initiatives, deregulation, redefinition of property rights, and the reassertion of presidential power are indicative of ways in which the formal and informal rules of the game were altered to reinvigorate the flagging institutional capacity of the Mexican state. In each case, the initiative to revise existing rules was spearheaded by the government.

Altering formal rules: deregulation

One of the early activities of the Salinas administration was to create an Office to Coordinate Economic Deregulation in the ministry of commerce and industrial development (SECOFI). The office, which was to grow appreciably in power after 1989, was symbolic of the administration's interest in revised rules for economic interaction. Its goals were ambitious. "Ultimately, what we are trying to do is limit the discretion of the government," stated one official deeply involved in this process of change.[7]

This was a daunting task. By the 1980s, government policy had created a vast web of restrictions, licensing mechanisms, and restraints that necessitated a large bureaucratic apparatus and encouraged extensive rent seeking by private agents and public officials. In 1982, 100 percent of Mexico's imports required licenses; until 1989, all internal freight transport required government-approved contracts; until 1989 only the government could exploit an extensive list of basic petrochemicals; until 1990, only government-approved cooperatives could fish for certain species of fish; and the list continued, including extensive control of prices and wages. On a day-to-day basis, commercial establishments needed numerous permits in order to operate legally, and barriers to entry of new firms were great.[8] In everything from advanced telecommunications to traditional agriculture, from aquaculture to prices, extensive regulation was the norm. Although the administration of Miguel de la Madrid had engineered and sustained the social pact of 1987, dealt repeatedly and harshly with the public sector deficit, and introduced initial efforts at trade liberalization and deregulation, the role of the government in the economy continued to be very large.

In practice, the rules that structured the relationship between the state and the economy were frequently circumvented through side payments to public officials, contributions to the PRI, or special friendships and arrangements between business elites and high level government officials. Often they were simply ignored, as the growth of the informal sector attested. The consequence of widespread defection to alternative rules was obvious to one Mexican public official who argued that, "When the law closes off options to people, they find a way around the law in order to make things work. This is inventive, but eventually it undermines the legitimacy of the system when so much occurs outside it."[9] Moreover, the government maintained the right to implement a host of regulations, a fact that significantly increased its bargaining power with individuals and firms from the private sector, but undermined business confidence in fair treatment by the regulators. Increasingly, as the web of regulations and interactions became more complex, so did relationships with government. Many private sector firms maintained offices in Mexico City staffed with lawyers, political influentials, and go-betweens whose primary responsibilities entailed managing relations with the government.

As the economic crisis continued in the 1980s, this model of state–economy relations lost credibility. The mission of the new office for deregulation was to "overcome the absurdities of the regulatory system. Much of it is patently illogical –

and clearly so to anyone concerned ... It is often hard to find a justification for the regulations that exist."[10] Behind the commitment to deregulation was the idea that more rational policies would be both more effective and more authoritative. "Our primary purpose here is to make markets work better – anything that we consider needs to be done to make this happen can be considered. We want to encourage competition and competitiveness."[11]

Procedurally, the office was to report to the president and his economic cabinet through the minister of SECOFI. The office would select a sector thought to be in need of deregulation, carry out studies of the regulatory environment within which the sector operated, consult with the regulators and the regulated industries, and draw up recommendations.[12] Office staff sat down to negotiate with the affected ministries and industries only after receiving SECOFI, presidential, and economic cabinet approval to move ahead with the plan. Extensive negotiations were then often required, but the deregulation office came well armed with research and technical studies to back up its positions, as well as with presidential support. The deregulation of freight transport is a good example of how these factors worked together to spur the deregulation project.[13]

Prior to its deregulation, freight transport in Mexico was controlled by a formal cartel of fifteen families, which monopolized all trucking routes. Routes were awarded to cartel "associates" by committees formed of members and officials from the ministry of communications and transportation (SCT). Permits were issued by SCT officials at regional centers for each one-way haul of freight. Under this system, there were many powerful winners: the cartel controlled shipping and was able to extract rents from trucking concessionaires; these associates had assured access to routes with no competition; ministry officials had ample opportunities to reward friends and extract rents from truckers who wanted their freight contracts approved; middlemen flourished by doing deals between government and truckers; the PRI acquired access to trucks from grateful owners for periodic political mobilizations. Outside the cartel arrangement, a pirate trucking industry also prospered. Shippers, who paid higher prices for freight services, had no voice in this cozy set of arrangements.

Negotiations with SCT to change this system required six months; a deregulation agreement was signed by President Salinas in July 1989. Opposition came primarily, although not surprisingly, from SCT. Despite presidential backing, ministry officials at first treated the deregulators with scorn. Citing legal precedent, the threat of social violence, the probable emergence of regional inequities with deregulation, and the mandate of SCT, officials refused to negotiate at first. They were clearly protecting their organizational and political turf. The deregulators, however, continued to press for discussions. They produced technical studies and presented evidence of the costs of the current system, the benefits of the proposed system, and cases based on the experience of other countries. They also produced videos of corrupt practices that implicated cartel members and SCT officials. High level officials disdained these meetings; the deregulators could only gain access to operational levels in the ministry.

In the context of frequent meetings and concerted effort on the part of the SECOFI negotiators, more collegial working relations eventually began to develop between them and lower level ministry officials who were delegated to deal with the undesirable interlopers. Within the ministry, a group of officials interested in unseating its leadership also demonstrated willingness to reach an agreement. Gradually, the deregulation initiative gained momentum. As the SCT negotiators and insurgents proceeded with the talks, and as it became clearer that the Salinas administration was committed to deregulation, the old guard at the head of the ministry was increasingly left out of the discussions, losing considerable power to oppose the advancement of talks. In addition, politically astute officials soon began to realize that to miss being on the Salinas administration's bandwagon of economic reform was to risk losing very real political advantages, including their positions of leadership in the ministry. Moreover, the ministry as a whole had little technical capacity to resist the studies and arguments of the deregulators, who based their position firmly in cost-benefit analysis and evidence from studies of deregulation in other countries. To make their job easier and to give more leeway to negotiators on both sides, the deregulators focused on altering the regulatory framework that derived from a law passed in 1939, rather than on altering the law itself. "The strategy finally adopted was to *redefine* the spirit of the law without abrogating it: trucking routes were therefore redefined as 'all federal highways' and tariffs were redefined as 'ceiling prices ... '."[14]

Opposition from the regulated industry was less intense than might have been expected because of differences that emerged within the trucking cartel. Under the traditional arrangement, and under a highly protected international trade regime, the profitability of most freight routes was roughly similar. With the move toward liberalized international trade and greatly increased import prices in 1988, import and export activity across the US–Mexican border increased greatly, making northern routes in the country much more profitable than most other routes. Increasingly, associates of the cartel eyed these lucrative northern routes and chafed at the constraints that prohibited moving into them. The community of interests in maintaining the regulated system was thus less clear than it had been. The government also promised increased investment in the road network and in vehicle replacement, further undermining industry opposition to change. The dynamics of the negotiation process and the divergence of interests within the trucking industry gave the reformers the upper hand.

Deregulation throughout the economy was supported by similar sets of events and strategies. By mid-1992, almost fifty economic sectors had been deregulated, including freight transport, fisheries, public health, aquaculture, banking, insurance, petrochemicals, mining, and telecommunications.[15] Several factors help account for extensive and rapid change. First, presidential support was extremely important in managing the opposition of regulatory ministries, whose officials had an interest in the jobs and discretionary power that regulation entailed. According to one official actively involved in interministerial negotiations,

When the cabinet decides to move ahead with any actions, I am provided with a presidentially signed decree giving me authority to act. With this in my back pocket, I go to negotiate with the ministries. I do this in the spirit of negotiation, to try to get them to come up with an understanding of the situation and options, but I always have the trump card of the president's letter in my back pocket if it is needed. We discuss possible avenues of action, but never whether action will be taken or not. That is already decided.[16]

Second, the language of negotiation was set by the deregulators. They spoke the technical language of economic rationality, not the traditional language of politics in which both regulators and regulated were proficient. With support at ministerial, cabinet, and presidential levels from officials who also spoke this technical language, the deregulators had a clear advantage in bargaining relationships. The deregulators also chose to work through regulatory and administrative action rather than legislative action in order to introduce change. This speeded up the process considerably and gave the executive greater discretion to take action. Third, deregulation was a policy area that was easier to implement than some others; it required government to cease doing something, not take on responsibilities that required institutional innovation and behavioral change among bureaucrats. It was difficult to negotiate deregulation, but once it had been agreed to, it immediately wrested power from the regulators. As a result, their opposition became irrelevant to whether the initiative would be sustained or not.

Finally, economic crisis and policy change altered the power and perspectives of entrenched interests. In some cases these groups no longer had the political importance to resist effectively and in other cases the traditional coalition was weakened by differential opportunities to become winners under the proposed reforms. Moreover, an improved economy in the early 1990s meant that the potential to benefit from deregulation was greater than under conditions of economic stagnation. Very shortly after changes were introduced, winners emerged in the deregulated sectors to defend the initiative and to press for even more action. It could reasonably be predicted, then, that deregulation would set the structure for relationships between government and the economy for some time to come. In a similarly ambitious initiative, the Salinas administration sought fundamental changes in the rules about property rights in the countryside.

Altering formal rules: property rights

The Constitution of 1917 guaranteed Mexico's large peasant population access to grants of communally held land, called ejidos.[17] These grants were made to organized groups of peasants who fulfilled requisite criteria and accomplished a complicated set of legal and administrative procedures. The ejido, modeled on Mexico's traditional landholding system, was chartered by the state; ejidatarios, the recipients of ejido land grants, were protected from loss of their land by constitutional prohibitions on its sale or rental.[18] The ejido was governed by an elected council and a commissioner, whose job it was to adjudicate ejidal affairs and represent the community to government. The land reform, based on Article 27 of the constitution, was only sporadically implemented until the mid-1930s, when massive land distribution and the organization of a large peasant movement were spearheaded by President Lázaro Cárdenas. During his presidency from 1935 to 1940, 17.9 million hectares of land, 9.1 percent of the country's surface, were distributed as ejidos to petitioning groups of peasants.[19] By the 1980s, about half of the country's agricultural land was incorporated into some 28,000 ejidos.

With time, ejido peasants became dependent on the state not only for land but also for credit and access to inputs, markets, and social services.[20] In 1938, they were incorporated into the PRI as one of its three corporate pillars, the National Confederation of Peasants (CNC). From that time, the peasant sector became the most loyal and least autonomous and articulate base of political support for the PRI and the regime.[21] Support for the government was consistent, rarely questioned, and easily manipulated, given that the government retained the right to determine legal access to land and wielded control over much needed credit, inputs, development investments, and jobs. With time, also, ejidal commissioners became closely tied into the patron–client networks that were the basis of the PRI's hegemony. As local level political bosses, they worked in close association with municipal officials and state governors, who were frequently the strongmen managing the PRI patronage machinery within a region.

While commercially oriented export agriculture, dominated by large capitalist farmers, expanded greatly after the 1940s and benefited from government investments in infrastructure, research, extension, and credit, the ejido sector, occupying the least productive land throughout the country, was increasingly tied to government and dependent on government largesse for access to credit, agricultural inputs, and markets.[22] Because the land could not be sold or rented, ejidatarios lacked collateral to participate in commercial credit markets. Access to government credit became dependent on political orthodoxy and loyalty and came with numerous restrictions on its use. The government invested little in small infrastructure projects through the 1960s and, because of tenure relationships, ejidatarios had little incentive to provide their own infrastructure. Agricultural research and extension focused on the large farm sector. Controlled prices for basic foodstuffs, and the extensive presence of the state marketing board, CONASUPO, rounded out the lack of incentives to the ejidos for investing in greater productivity. Not surprisingly, the ejido sector consistently reported low and declining productivity. By the mid-1960s, Mexico was importing increasing amounts of basic foodstuffs and, despite massive investments in the countryside under the presidencies of Luís Echeverría and José López Portillo, the sector remained underproductive and backward.

Despite their persistently poor performance, ejidos were little short of a sacred cow in Mexican politics and development ideology. Because they formed such an important political support base for the regime, because the rural and regional bosses had been so successful in managing political dissent and organization, and because much of the land was not commercially exploitable, it was political heresy to question them, even though analysts increasingly questioned their economic viability. The ejido was an important ingredient of Mexican nationalism and sense of historic uniqueness, embedded in the rhetoric and symbolism of the Revolution, the PRI, and the government. It is little wonder, then, that the Salinas administration's ability to revise Article 27 and the accompanying Agrarian Code to alter tenure relationships took most people by surprise. What made such a change possible?[23]

Discussions about changes in the structure of tenure in the countryside began quietly in 1989. Analysis of the problems of productivity surfaced first in SECOFI's office of deregulation. Soon, the president indicated interest in the project and asked for more analysis and discussion of the issues and their solution. The action then moved to the ministry of agriculture and water resources, where a small working group established by the president in January 1990 began assembling data and thinking about what might be done. The group was composed of young lawyers and economists and its leadership was assumed by a young official with a PhD in economics from MIT, who had impressed the president in prior positions in the ministries of planning and finance. He became vice-minister in charge of planning in agriculture. Despite the appointment of a new agriculture minister who would shortly become an advocate of their initiative, however, the team was in hostile territory. The ministry of agriculture was fundamentally opposed to any changes in the agrarian law, and even the minister initially voiced skepticism. They could expect no help from the ministry of agrarian reform, either; this ministry derived its power from the ability to grant access to land.

Before thinking of managing this opposition, however, the group had to consider the problem. Their data was unambiguous – the ejido was not an economically productive institution and most ejidos and ejidatarios were poverty-stricken and powerless economically and politically. The issue was what to do about it. A member of the working group summed up the dilemma facing them.

There have been two basic views on what to do in the countryside and this encouraged the ambiguity of what needed to be done. On the one side you had those who focused on the asphyxiating role of the state in the rural economy and its authoritarian political relationships with groups in the countryside. For these people, the solution involved getting the state out, period. On the other side, you had those who argued for the state maintaining its supportive role ... This boiled down to those who wanted the magic of the marketplace and those who said, "Don't abandon us."[24]

The group's initial analyses focused on issues of prices and credit. Gradually, however, they came to believe that institutional constraints related to tenure and organization were much more important. Meeting in secret, they eventually focused on three areas: (1) the land market and the immobility of land under existing law; (2) security of land tenure; and (3) legal restrictions on the use of land. They became convinced that legal reform of property rights was essential.

The pace of work picked up after team members visited Eastern Europe and the Soviet Union to study issues of land reform and made a presentation to the president on their return. Those involved in the discussions were often frustrated by the magnitude of the issues involved. "There was a sense that it was all just for discussion, that the issue was so big that no action would ever really be taken on it ... In all of this work, [the vice-minister] took the radical approach – do away with regulation in the countryside. He shocked other members of the group."[25] In the end, the team was converted to this view of the problem, even from a political perspective. "In the end, we realized that we would incur the same political costs and high political risks if we went for modest and marginal reforms as if we went for a complete package of reform ... We decided it would be just as well to go for the big change."[26]

By spring of 1991, the group was meeting with the president and with the leadership of other ministries; the initiative was discussed in cabinet meetings. Importantly, although leaders of some peasant organizations were consulted, the CNC was not involved in the discussions until the very end of the process, just before the initiative was sent to congress. "This was the president's choice. He was worried about leaks. The president was very clear. There was to be no noise about this until it was announced. And we thought the CNC needed to protect itself with its membership by being able to claim that it had not participated."[27] Some peasant groups did protest once the plans became more public. They were particularly concerned about their exclusion from the decision-making process. In response, the president met with peasant leaders and issued a document that clarified the new law. This discussion, however, came too late to shape the policy; its purpose was more political than substantive.

The reformers anticipated extensive opposition from the ministry of agrarian reform – which, although lacking resources, political importance in Mexico City, and personnel, derived considerable power from its mandate to interpret the extensive agrarian law – from the CNC and other peasant organizations, from the ministry of agriculture, from the political left, and from those in the intellectual community who had long celebrated the country's agrarian heritage. Although confident that their analyses were correct, the Salinas group was far from confident that the reforms could be undertaken. They also knew that a constitutional revision was impossible until the PRI regained a two-thirds majority in congress, lost for the first time in 1988.

For this and other reasons, the congressional elections of August 1991 were a significant victory for Salinas. The constitutional revision could now be introduced, as it was in November, and dutifully affirmed by the PRI-dominated congress. With the amendment in hand, the vice-ministry group moved ahead to a more daunting task, revision of the lengthy agrarian code – "an incredible nightmare of regulations and stipulations."[28] By early 1992, a revision was presented to congress and, although there was discussion and some opposition, the president's team won approval. These changes were remarkable for how quickly they happened and for the virtual absence of public dissent about them. It was, after all, a set of reforms that would strip some two million peasant families of their protection from land and labor markets. However much this protection made them exploitable by rural bosses and locked them in poverty, it did provide them with assured rights to their land. Moreover, the constitutional change stripped the ejido commissioners, local bosses, and governors of great power over the ejidatarios.

Indeed, throughout the reform process, observers and participants were struck by the lack of effective opposition to the reform initiative after it had become public. One reason for this was the difficulty of defending the only known alternative to the proposed plan – the old system. The existing system had, in fact, become so discredited and notorious for the degree of exploitation and corruption it encouraged that few were willing to defend it. Although ejidatarios faced direct exposure to the "tyranny of the market" and the strong possibility that they would eventually lose their lands because of their level of poverty, they did not go to the barricades for the preservation of a system that clearly exploited them. Mexico's leftist intellectuals, who had long believed in the possibility of a peasantry with a special relationship to the market mediated by a nationalist state, had no clear alternative to offer that would deal with the problems of poverty, underproductivity, and disenfranchisement of the ejidos.

As with the deregulation initiative, those arguing for demise of the corporate basis of land tenure and for expanding markets for land, labor, and capital in rural Mexico captured the initiative because of the technical information and analyses they commanded. In an administration dominated by economists, the language of economics resonated well and gave the working group important credibility with the president and his cabinet.[29] Their argument was also unambiguous. "What you need for a market economy in the countryside is clear – property rights, clear rules of the game, and macroeconomic stability."[30] Alternative arguments tended to be based on more philosophical, historical, or nationalist bases and, in the end, could not provide convincing plans for how the productivity of the ejido sector could be increased without extensive infusions of government investment, an alternative ruled out by the government's commitment to keep spending closely controlled. Additionally, the secrecy of the planning process gave the upper hand to those who had the data and the analyses. "In the end," suggested one participant in the process, "[the vice-minister] just overpowered the other side with arguments and technical analysis."[31] The ejidatarios, the CNC, the PRI, the ejido commissioners, local bosses, and governors were simply not consulted about the change. Moreover, given the complexity of the agrarian law, the revision to it, and the technical language used to discuss it, it is likely that few really understood what the revision meant at the level of the ejido. It was not until two years after the initiative was passed by congress that the reformists became fully aware of the extent of opposition to the change. On January 1, 1994, a rural uprising in the southern state of Chiapas, led by the Zapatista National Liberation Army (EZLN), alerted the government to the consequences of their closed decision-making process. The peasants demanded, among many other changes, repeal of the revision of Article 27.

Whether strong opposition existed or not, implementation of the new legislation would be problematic. Unlike deregulation, implementing new rights to property would require an extensive administrative infrastructure. Under the new laws and regulations, each ejido could decide whether or not its members would receive individual property rights. In order to grant individual title to land, the government needed to settle a vast number of outstanding ejido land claims.[32] It also needed to clarify the individual status of ejidatarios and to assess the value of agricultural land if a market in land was to be introduced. An extensive system of land courts was set up as part of the reforms, but their operation was not clearly understood, even by the reformers. Ejidatarios needed to be informed of their new rights and how to implement change.

Given these difficulties, the impact of the new rules of the game for property rights in the countryside would not be immediately felt. Increases in agricultural productivity among the new class of smallholders were anticipated, but not expected to appear for several years. The reformers – and their critics – also anticipated extensive rural to urban migration as the poorest farmers would be forced to sell any commercially viable land they had and look for wage employment in the cities. An extensive rural income support program, Procampo, would similarly have some economic impact on producers of basic staples. Introduced in 1993, the program was intended to provide these peasants with an economic cushion to adjust to lower prices for their crops once the North American Free Trade Agreement (NAFTA) was fully implemented. Whether it would promote migration, investment in diversified production and non-farm income-generating activities, or simply sustain rural poverty and political dependence could not be predicted, however.

Politically, the redefinition of property rights in the countryside also had the potential for unpredictable outcomes. The CNC lost its main source of power, ejidal commissioners and local and regional strongmen lost their direct relationship to the PRI's patronage machine, and peasant farmers ceased to be virtual wards of the state. The rebellion led by the EZLN in Chiapas sparked sympathetic support throughout much of Mexico and spurred increased efforts to organize the rural poor to make demands on government. The rules had been changed, but how the new rules would operate or what economic and political consequences they would have over the longer term remained unclear. A similar statement could be made about the consequences of the centralization of presidential power that was a notable aspect of the Salinas administration.

Altering informal rules: reasserting presidential power

As he took office in late 1988, Carlos Salinas inherited a position that had lost much of its traditional legitimacy and authority. The system was still strongly presidentialist, but incumbents were treated with much greater skepticism and could not count on the degree of public, party, and bureaucratic support that was available to presidents prior to the 1980s. Salinas found himself with a bare majority of 260 out of 500 seats in congress. Only 27.3 percent of the population of Mexico City had voted for him in 1988. He faced active and vocal opposition parties and movements, his election was widely thought to be fraudulent, and many of the barons of the PRI resented his technocratic background and style.[33] In fact, his greatest liability as an incumbent was the institutional weakness of a presidency whose political machine could no longer ensure electoral victory.

By 1993, however, the presidency was stronger than ever. Through a series of initiatives and supported by encouraging economic recovery, Salinas centralized and personalized power and separated the power of the PRI more fully from the power of government and the presidency. Reasserted presidentialism was instrumental in the introduction of a new set of relationships between the state and the economy. It also encouraged the beginning of a restructured relationship of citizens to the state. By working to atomize and marginalize the PRI, the Salinas administration encouraged more direct interaction between the political executive and individuals and groups in society. In this, it was setting the basis for the emergence of a political system far less corporatist in nature than it had been since the 1930s.

At the outset of the new administration, the presidency was certainly undercut by the historic disarray of Mexican politics that had emerged in the 1980s. At the same time, however, that disarray provided some opportunities for restructuring political relationships. As argued in the previous chapter, those who had benefited from the old system – protected industries, union bosses, the leaders of the PRI – had already lost considerable influence in government because their economic power and social cohesion had suffered under the impact of economic crisis. The new administration, although met with extensive cynicism and disaffection, was not without resources to take advantage of the more ambiguous political context. Mexico's presidents have extensive powers of appointment that can be used to build an administration that is responsive to the views of those at the top.[34] Presidentially appointed ministers and heads of agencies have a virtual free hand to assemble teams of officials who serve at their discretion and that of the president. This system of appointments, which reaches down to middle levels in many ministries and agencies, provides opportunities to repay and incur political debts; it can also provide an effective vehicle for assembling like-minded officials who are highly motivated to respond to their superiors – ultimately the president – to whom they owe their positions and their opportunities for upward mobility. Presidents also have the power to remove national, state, and local elected officials from office and to determine the PRI's leadership cadre. Unions are chartered by the state and their leaders can be challenged through the use of federal laws.

These resources of presidential power were put to immediate use by the new administration. In particular, Salinas used appointments – and dismissals – as a vehicle for sending signals about the importance of being on the presidential bandwagon. Other presidents have taken similar action, but Salinas was particularly clear about defining the terms for being part of his team. He indicated that those on the bandwagon – the winners – would be those who identified themselves unequivocally with "modernization." Modernizers were to be in the forefront of supporting economic liberalization and moving the country toward an important place in a new, more competitive international economy. They would be those with the skills and perspectives needed to support a market economy and a "rational" state. They would be those who welcomed a different future and looked askance on the past. They would be those who confronted the losers – the "dinosaurs" wedded to the old and discredited system. Salinas indicated that dinosaurs were to be found in the private sector, among business people who expected protectionism, and among those in the poor and working population who were content with the paternalist state. They were found among the PRI and union bosses who were comfortable with the system of patronage and spoils, as well as among bureaucrats and elected public officials who sought to extract rents from their positions and who resisted transparency and accountability in decision making.

During the first year of his administration, Salinas worked to establish that it was politically and economically astute to be on the side of the modernizers. He used his power of appointments to identify those who held firmly to his vision of a new, modernized Mexico, and he surrounded himself with a set of advisors that included those already identified as modernizers in the PRI, the government, and the private sector. Those who had ambitions to be appointed to public office, to be influential in policy discussions, to receive presidential support for electoral campaigns, or to hold on to jobs they already had, were impressed by the unusual cohesion of those appointed to the most important top level positions and the extent to which common political and ideological criteria were applied. On a more public level, and within weeks of taking formal control of the presidency, Salinas ordered the arrest of "La Quina," the notorious, corrupt, and heretofore untouchable boss of the petroleum workers' union. This was followed by a showdown with the powerful head of the national teachers' union. These actions significantly increased Salinas' image as a powerful and effective leader. Both union leaders had reputations for corruption and extensive abuses of power, and they had also been vocal and powerful opponents of the policy reforms that would weaken their hold over the national petroleum company and the national education system.[35]

Similarly, Salinas placed close allies at the top of the PRI and made it clear that their task was to modernize the political bases of the regime's support. While rhetorically the president pledged himself to the internal democratization of the party and a more open political society, the commitment to party reform was centrally a commitment to enhance presidential power at the expense of the PRI. In the aftermath of the August 1991 elections, presidential power was exercised against the governors of two important states, Guanajuato and San Luís Potosí, whose elections were widely viewed as fraudulent. The PRI incumbents were removed from office and new elections scheduled. While these actions were meant to signal both nationally and internationally the president's commitment to fair elections, even if that meant a PRI loss, many political insiders saw another purpose: moving against the PRI governors placed the party apparatus on notice that the president was more powerful than the party and that he could make or unmake PRI politicians.

The task of modernizing the party was directed at weakening still further its constituent pillar organizations of workers, peasants, and middle-class interests by introducing individual memberships and one-person-one-vote policies for internal decision making. Efforts were also made to distance state governors from control over the state party organizations. According to one party official, modernization meant increasing centralized control over local party activities.

In the past, the governors selected the heads of the state executive committee of the party – the local presence of the PRI. Now, when a governor is recalcitrant about going along with our aims, we have taken this power away from him, in some cases sending a central person to take over at the state level in the party. This is the only way to break the power of the governor and the local powers such as bosses and dinosaurs, where they still exist.[36]

Modernization also meant encouraging local constituency organizations to connect directly with the reformist leadership at the top of the party in Mexico City rather than through the old patronage networks that led, level by level, to the top of the party hierarchy.

The Salinas administration sought further changes in the way the patronage machinery worked. On the one hand, the automatic right of PRI operatives to distribute government largesse was extensively curtailed. On the other hand, the availability of resources for local development expenditures, which had been severely cut through austerity programs, was increased by creating a fund from the sale of state-owned enterprises to service the debt and then using budget funds freed up by this move to fund the National Solidarity Program.[37] The program – created in late 1988, organized within the office of the presidency, and located in the presidential compound – made funds available to local communities for small infrastructure and social service projects with the dual purpose of addressing the social costs of adjustment and encouraging local communities to address their own development problems.[38] Until 1992, the program's quick disbursing funds were distributed directly to local community organizations by the president's office, bypassing the old PRI-dominated networks of patronage and including the party only when local party officials actively identified themselves with the modernizers.[39] Indeed, these funds helped the modernizers within the PRI fortify their positions, gave the government a source of largesse to distribute to constituencies that had been wooed by the opposition, and provided a way of rebuilding the vote for the PRI at the local level without at the same time providing resources to the local bosses of the party. Mexicans at the local level were quick to identify the source of funds as presidential and to connect their good fortune with Salinas and the government rather than with their relationship to the PRI bosses. The August 1991 elections, in which the PRI garnered 61.5 percent of the vote, was credited as a vote of support for Salinas, not for the PRI.[40]

The effort to enhance presidential power received help from other sources as well. First, the economy showed signs of improvement. GDP growth averaged 3.4 percent in 1989, 4.5 percent in 1990, and 3.6 percent the following year. Perhaps more important, consumer prices, which increased 114 percent in 1988, grew only 20 percent in 1989 and 26.6 percent in 1990. By 1991, the rate had fallen to 22.7 percent and many were ready to believe that the country's economy was on the road to recovery. In addition, as discussed in Chapter 7, the political parties that had mounted a historic challenge to the PRI in 1988 appeared unable to consolidate their positions organizationally or to develop coherent alternatives to the Salinas reform agenda.

The effort to centralize and enhance presidential power in Mexico exposed the Salinas administration to considerable risk. By simplifying the options for bureaucratic and political actors – being with the modernizers or with the dinosaurs – the president risked the ability to put together a winning coalition of insiders in the political game. His policy reforms met with extensive opposition in government and could have been stymied through official sabotage or inaction. The Salinas team could only meet this challenge by demonstrating that the president's bandwagon was the appropriate vehicle for bureaucratic and political survival. But this could only be accomplished by ensuring the continued ability to win elections. Despite the discredit that had fallen upon the PRI, the party apparatus was essential to the ability to win elections and pack the congress with enough delegates to pass constitutional amendments. Moreover, traditionally it had been the PRI that linked the president to the state governors, regional bosses, official union leadership, urban popular sectors, and ejido commissioners. Undermining the structure of the PRI unsettled the traditional basis for resolving conflict at regional and local levels. As with the changes in Mexico's agrarian regions, the consequences of these actions could not be fully predicted.

In Mexico, economic and political disarray provided a new presidential administration with opportunities to reestablish the authority of the state over the broad sets of rules that govern the relationship between the state and the market and the state and civic society. In the economy, new rules lessened the degree of state intervention while simultaneously legitimizing the state's role in defining the rules. In political relationships, enhancing the authority of state institutions meant subverting the power of organizations that had long ensured the regime's stability. The initiative to establish more authoritative rules for economic and political interactions was taken by political elites who shared perspectives on what those rules ought to be and who used the resources available to them to pursue their reformist agenda. In doing so, they were attempting to reassert the institutional capacity of the Mexican state after this capacity had been undermined by both economic and political crises. The dynamics of altered institutional capacity in Kenya were very different, yet political elites are just as central to understanding what occurred.

CHANGING THE RULES OF THE GAME IN KENYA

The multiparty elections of December 1992 in Kenya signaled the extent to which the institutional capacity of the Kenyan state had declined in the previous decade. The elections were forced on a reluctant administration by an alliance of civic organizations and international actors. The campaign was marked by abuses of official power to intimidate and deny opposition candidates opportunities to hold meetings or travel to certain areas. The results of the election, which denied KANU a two-thirds majority and almost denied Daniel arap Moi the presidency, were widely questioned by election monitors and observers. In their aftermath, allegations of fraud and evidence of official and KANU tampering with election boxes were widely discussed. A number of opposition members declared their intention of boycotting parliament.

In other areas as well, although the government continued to make rules to structure the relationships among state, economy, and civic society, the authoritativeness of those rules was seriously questioned, as was their legitimacy. The extensive growth of the informal market, massive corruption in public and private interactions, and alterations in the functioning of public enterprises undermined formal rules that had been accepted as the principal means to regulate the economy. Rules that protected individuals from the power of the state were also violated with greater frequency. As the 1980s and early 1990s unfolded, growing numbers of Kenyans became convinced that the rules imposed by the state were improper or misused.

In fact, the authority and legitimacy of the Kenyan state were highly contested issues during this period. The efforts of the president to build a new coalition of support within KANU, to centralize and personalize power, colonize the public service with political loyalists, and create new bases of economic power met with countervailing efforts of civic organizations and international agencies to insist on the introduction of rules that would ensure predictability and accountability in politics and the economy. This was a period of intense conflict over whose rules would become authoritative – those supported by regime incumbents and their coalition partners or those championed by alliances between domestic and international opponents of President Moi.

Among the numerous arenas of contention over whose rules would prevail were the constitution, presidential power, economic liberalization, and privatization. In each case, regime incumbents used political resources to influence the outcome of conflict, while civic organizations had recourse to the courts, the press, and the streets. In turn, international agencies used conditionality to insist that the rules they favored for structuring economic and political relations be adopted. Despite the extensiveness of the power of the presidency to determine the outcome of these conflicts, it did not always emerge the victor. In the one case in which civic organizations and the international donors allied to insist on their definition of appropriate rules for governance, they were able to bring about the change they sought.

Altering formal rules: the constitution
and the party system

Kenya's constitution is no stranger to change. After independence, this long and complex document that sought to define a wide range of political relationships in the country was repeatedly amended to correspond to the political goals of governing elites and to enhance the power of the state vis-à-vis society.[41] Originally, the document provided for strong regional governments, a bicameral legislature, protection for minority groups, and extensive protection for citizens against abuses of power by government. Some of these original provisions – such as regionalism and bicameralism – were never effectively implemented. Many more were altered through formal processes of amendment. Thirty years after independence, a revised constitution granted extensive powers to the national government, provided the executive with great capacity to control other institutions and levels of government, and prescribed a unicameral legislature.

So extensive were these changes that they became a focal point for opposition to the government. The *Advocate*, the journal of the Law Society of Kenya, for example, published an article noting that the constitution had been amended on average once a year.

Speak of a dismantled Constitution and you will be speaking about the Kenya Constitution. Since 1963, the Kenya Constitution has been "tampered" (read amended) with so much that it can no longer be classified as rigid. Most of the amendments that this document has been subjected to have not been for the better. Indeed, most were intended to legitimise undemocratic and authoritarian administration.[42]

President Moi superintended important changes to the constitution that consistently increased the capacity of the presidency to dominate political life. But he was not the first president to use constitutional change to achieve his political goals. His predecessor, Jomo Kenyatta, was active in restructuring the constitution to enhance central and presidential power long before Moi used the same means to achieve similar ends. Under his administration, seventeen amendments dismantled regionalism, gave the president power to appoint and dismiss civil servants, restricted the ability to form opposition parties and to stand for election, extended presidential powers over issues of public security and justice, restructured parliament and rules related to voting, enabled the president to appoint "special" members of parliament and the electoral commission, altered eligibility for voting, and determined languages to be used for public business.[43] Changes in the rules also altered the speed with which amendments to the constitution could be passed, to the point that by 1979, an amendment could be introduced and approved in as little as eight days.

President Moi initiated a series of amendments that continued the process of political centralization. Among others, changes to the constitution introduced by his government abolished appeals about electoral outcomes, gave central authorities the right to regulate appointments to local governments, expanded police powers, and eliminated security of tenure for the attorney general, the auditor general, members of the public service commission, and high and appeals court judges. These formal rules, embodied in the constitution, ratified the powers of an authoritarian ruler who used them to enhance the welfare of those loyal to him and to discourage dissent. Through these changes, Kenya's president became, not a parliamentary leader, but "an African king" according to one observer.[44] And the constitution became, according to another, "a weapon in power politics to be manipulated to subdue or eliminate opposition."[45]

As with Kenyatta before him, several of Moi's amendments were added to the constitution to respond to very immediate political threats.[46] This was the case with amendment 19, which contained the stipulation that Kenya was to become a de jure one-party state. Section 2A of this amendment effectively inhibited several prominent politicians from forming the Kenya Socialist Party to present an electoral challenge to KANU. The 1982 amendment outlawed all opposition; henceforth, only KANU members could hold public office.[47] While considerable opposition to the amendment was known to exist, parliamentary approval was swift with all but two MPs giving it their approval, an outcome encouraged by suppression of public and parliamentary debate on the issue.[48]

Section 2A became a focal point of opposition to the rule-making power of the regime.[49] Among those most active in opposing the official one-party state and later in pressing for multiparty elections were organizations of urban professionals, particularly lawyers and clergy, and the country's burgeoning non-governmental organizations (NGOs).[50] The involvement of the Law Society of Kenya (LSK), the National Council of Churches of Kenya (NCCK), and the NGO sector helped bring international attention and public opinion to bear on the government. For those who focused on the repeal of Section 2A, the central issues involved the extent to which it could be used as a vehicle for personal rule, and the extent to which citizens could hold their elected representatives accountable for their actions while in office. In addition, the international financial agencies weighed in with conditions to increase pressure to repeal Section 2A. The combination of civic protest, international attention, and donor conditionality proved to be effective in convincing the government that one-party rule could not stand. On December 3, 1991, Section 2A was repealed through the 27th amendment to the constitution.

Multiparty elections were held in December of 1992. After these elections, the capacity to contest constitutional issues was limited for both KANU and the opposition parties as none of them had the necessary two-thirds majority to pass amendments. Nevertheless, the parliament offered itself as a forum for discussing such issues. In June 1993, for example, opposition members raised the issue of limiting presidential powers over such matters as the appointment of administrative officers, directors of state corporations, and the attorney general. Although recognizing that they did not have the power to alter these constitutional provisions, they nevertheless argued that it was appropriate for them to raise the issue for public debate.[51] In this case, the conflict over whose rules would prevail attracted extensive public attention, domestically and internationally. There was much less debate about a series of rules that determined the relationship of the national government and of the executive branch to the country's regions.

Altering formal rules: district focus and centralization of presidential power

Under Kenyatta, the movement toward greater centralization of power in the national government was clear and consistent. Nevertheless, regional autonomy remained important to the political style of the coalition held together by KANU. As indicated in Chapter 3, regional strongmen continued to wield significant power as long as basic loyalties to Kenyatta and KANU remained intact. In many cases, regions were managed as near fiefdoms of the politicians who were so important to the Kenyatta government. For administration, Kenyatta relied heavily on the provincial commissioners to manage regional affairs in the interests of the national state. These administrative officers were the instruments through which national ministries implemented development projects and administered law and order.[52]

At the same time, as far back as 1966, the government had experimented with various forms of decentralization.[53] These initiatives were generally introduced as important for achieving development goals such as increased efficiency in agricultural production and the need to plan resource allocation in accordance with information on local conditions and needs. Nevertheless, while decentralization was supported rhetorically for its purported positive impact on efficiency and participation, the schemes were never implemented with significant political support from the center.[54] They therefore tended to languish after they had been announced and provincial and district administrations had been reorganized.

District Focus for Rural Development, introduced in 1983, was different. It was implemented with considerable impetus from President Daniel arap Moi. The idea for District Focus originated with a plan whose intent was to strengthen the districts as decision-making units; this was expected to encourage greater efficiency in the use of public resources to promote development.[55] The plan originated with a presidential initiative. Moi, stimulated in part by the need to respond to flagging economic indicators, appointed a working party to explore the more effective use of public expenditures. Their report was delivered to the president shortly before the 1982 coup. In the post-coup environment of greater political insecurity, its recommendations offered a means for addressing political and economic dissatisfaction and regional inequities in the distribution of public resources.[56] Counterintuitively, it also offered an opportunity for centralizing presidential power.

As officially outlined, District Focus had two objectives. The first was to make the district the central location for bringing together local needs and national priorities and resources. Committees at the sub-locations and locations that composed each of the country's forty districts were directed to consider what local level needs were and to forward them on an annual basis to district level development committees (DDCs). According to the plan, these committees would also receive annual information from the central government about national development priorities and the availability of budgetary resources for various types of investments. With technical assistance from their planning units, the DDCs were then expected to integrate the two streams of information and prepare development plans for the district which would be forwarded to Nairobi to become part of the annual budget preparation process. The second objective of District Focus was to set in motion a process to equalize development expenditures across districts, to assist the less developed ones with greater resources.

The groundwork for District Focus had already been laid through a series of unsuccessful efforts at decentralization. As a result of earlier initiatives, the district had acquired an administrative infrastructure that gave it greater capacity to manage some development activities at the local level. When District Focus was introduced as a means of development planning and expenditure control, an institutional infrastructure of DDCs and district development officers (DDOs) already existed to deconcentrate planning capacity. The DDCs, composed of civil servants and elected officials, were chaired by the district officer, a presidentially appointed civil servant. These committees could bring together upwards of sixty people from government and communities to consider how central budget resources would be used at the district level to promote rural development.[57] The District Focus scheme required that development projects implemented at the district level by ministries, non-governmental organizations, or harambee groups be integrated into a district development plan under the administration of local DDCs. The purpose of this approach was "strengthening planning capacity at the district level, improving horizontal integration among ministry field agents, and expanding authority to district officers for managing financial and procurement aspects of local project implementation."[58]

Beyond the ostensible purpose and structure of the strategy, however, District Focus had a number of political implications that were particularly attractive to the president.[59] It provided a means for redirecting development expenditures from the provincial to the district level. Development expenditures authorized by the treasury would now be under the control of a presidential appointee – the district commissioner – who reported directly to the permanent secretary in the office of the president. The composition of the DDCs was also weighted toward central officials, such as the district level representatives of various national ministries. The amount of local input into development decision making could be closely controlled. One analyst of District Focus summarized how a decentralization initiative could increase central power.

The local committees that are supposed to send needs to the DDCs are exclusive, not really the "voice of the people." They are usually composed of the chief or subchief – appointed by government – and locational and sublocational officers and local headmasters. In many places, these local committees don't even exist. The same is true at the district level. Most decision making and work are done by the planners and central government officials assigned to the district. These officials usually don't come from the area and are often there only 9 to 12 months. They have no loyalty to the district. They are just an extension of central government ... District Focus translates into increased penetration of central government into district and local life.[60]

District Focus strengthened presidential discretion at the expense of the power of the clientelist networks established by Kenyatta that linked central politicians to "big men" at provincial and district levels and that allowed them to develop their own political constituencies at more local levels. This system had provided these political bosses with considerable independence. Clientelist networks continued to exist, but they were more directly linked to the office of the presidency than under Kenyatta. District Focus also undercut the power of the provincial commissioners, who had been favored under the Kenyatta system with a central role in administration and political control. Similarly, senior politicians who traditionally played important roles in the distribution of government largesse could also be circumvented or made more dependent on the president's control over district level resources. Even harambee activities had to be officially sanctioned through this new system.

Second, District Focus reduced the discretion of national ministries over their budget allocations. Because of the new way in which the budget process was to work and because of the principle of equity among regions, the capacity of the ministries to concentrate resources in their own priority areas or to move expenditures from one district to another was reduced.[61] For the ministry of agriculture, for example, greater openness in the allocation process "placed a great deal of pressure on [ministry] headquarters officials to be more egalitarian in their district allocations. There were no standards set as to what regional spending patterns were appropriate, but officials knew that if they were not to be accused of 'tribalism' they would have to be able to justify deviations from equality."[62] District Focus brought local offices of line ministries more closely under the scrutiny of the district officers and provided a vehicle for channeling patronage and influential politicians to officials from the districts.

Third, District Focus meant that politicians had to focus their efforts to deliver development resources and patronage on smaller constituency units. In fact, competition for resources increased among districts, limiting the extent to which politicians had an incentive to form alliances with politicians from other districts. Individually, then, MPs became less likely to acquire extensive constituencies of support that would increase their autonomy from Moi. Collectively, they were less likely to find reasons to collude against him. In this way, Moi "reduced the room for maneuver of the local politicians."[63]

Despite the rhetoric of local participation and empowerment, District Focus constituted a formal means for centralizing presidential power, atomizing interest-aggregating structures to the district level, and altering the allocation of public resources in ways that supported the changing nature of state–society relations in the country.[64]

The District Focus Strategy is out to ensure that local authorities behave according to the requirements of the central Government. Therefore, local authority decisionmaking on all financial matters as well as in development ones have now been subjected to approval by the DDC. This subjugation applies equally to popular institutions like the coopera-tives and self-help committees. Their activities are now closely monitored by the DDC and subjected to its vetting. Of course this policy is not new. What is new, however, is that the DDC through its new planning unit is now well equipped to ensure the subordination.[65]

District Focus affected the political dynamic between the center and the periphery in Kenya. It promoted the power of the president to assemble and control his own base of political support and it weakened the potential of ministers and other politicians with national audiences to determine the allocation of public resources. Under the strategy, MPs had to work harder at the district level to produce the goods for their constituencies and, as a result, they became less likely to remain in office for extended periods and more likely to be dependent on Moi's patronage if they did so. The strategy clearly affected the informal rules for political mobility and accountability in Kenya and encouraged the fragmentation of the power of other politicians and the centralization of Moi's official authority and personal power.

Altering formal rules: liberalization and privatization

International financial institutions wanted to see the role of the state in Kenya's economic development diminished significantly; the country's top level decision makers had little interest in seeing this occur. The result was a decade-long dance in which the international institutions pushed for economic liberalization and the government responded cautiously, liberalizing markets that did not significantly affect the economic or political interests of state elites. Under increased pressure to change long-standing economic policies further, the dance continued as the govern-ment would first agree to and then rescind agreement to pursue such measures, only to be forced to reintroduce them at a later point in time.[66] For the international agencies, liberalization was essential for renewed economic growth. For the govern-ment, it was a direct threat to mechanisms for wielding political power. The outcome of divergent perspectives was an impasse about market deregulation and privatiza-tion of major state-owned enterprises.

Throughout the 1970s and 1980s, the Kenyan economy featured important controls such as quantitative restrictions on imports and extensive protection of domestically produced goods. Some fifty-two categories of goods fell under the General Price Control Order, and the Specific Price Control Order listed eighty-seven individual items. A wide range of regulations and state monopolies required the private sector to deal regularly with state organizations. State marketing boards, such as those for coffee, tea, pyrethrum, and grains, were among the most powerful institutions in the country. They had a virtual monopoly on the purchase and sale of these commodities. Parastatals such as Kenya Power and Lighting, Kenya Posts and Telecommunications, Kenya Pipeline Company, and others were among the largest industries in the country.[67] In 1990, parastatals contributed 11 percent of GDP and accounted for 15 percent of formal sector employment.[68] Industrial protection had been a significant factor in encouraging the development of urban areas in the country and the financial sector was dominated by state-owned banks and investment corporations.

In 1979, evidence began to accumulate that the system of protection, licensing, and public ownership was increasing inefficiency in the economy. In the aftermath of the beverage boom of the 1970s and in the face of an increasingly recessionary international economy in the early 1980s, growth in the Kenyan economy slowed and domestic criticism mounted about the performance of the parastatal sector and overall management of the economy. An official commission, set up in 1982 to study the government's economic problems, focused considerable criticism on the costs of financial indiscipline, corruption, and budget deficits; the commission singled out the problems of the parastatals, blaming poor management and government extension into activities that should be left to the private sector.[69]

Despite earlier reform recommendations and increased public awareness, liberalization got on the government's action agenda only when international financial institutions and top level government officials shared concern over mounting economic crises. Shared concern, for example, meant that the IMF standby agreement negotiated in 1982 was implemented more conscientiously than previous agreements and was relatively successful in stabilizing the economy.[70] In the same year, the World Bank began negotiating a new structural adjustment loan with the government. Among other things, this agreement called for extensive deregulation in agricultural marketing, import liberalization, and privatization.[71]

In agriculture, emphasis was placed on deregulating maize marketing, tightly controlled by the National Cereals and Produce Board (NCPB). Import liberalization was to be sought through a shift to generalized tariffs rather than the quantitative restrictions in operation, providing more uniform policies for industrial protection, and introducing incentives for exports.[72] Delays in implementing the maize market reform that had been agreed to in the 1982 package were important in delaying the agreement to subsequent sector adjustment loans with the bank.[73] The contents of the 1982 agreement with the World Bank were basic ingredients of a series of subsequent agreements negotiated during the 1980s and early 1990s.

None of these initiatives was likely to be easily implemented. Agriculture was the most important sector of the economy and the government had played an extensive role in its development, closely regulating investment and controlling trade for important crops. To reduce this role would be to give up significant influence. Government agencies involved in the marketing of food argued that the country's food security would be jeopardized unless they maintained control.[74] Manufacturers were fiercely opposed to import liberalization, fearing for their own future in the face of competition from imports. Export promotion, while viewed as important, was not expected to show immediate benefits and the private sector sought the most generous support possible through an export compensation scheme.[75]

Despite such opposition, a number of initiatives toward economic liberalization were pursued after 1982, and significant progress was made after 1986. In terms of import liberalization, quantitative restrictions on imports were removed in 1988 and tariffs were reduced significantly and simplified. The decade also witnessed a lowering of effective rates of protection. Only six categories of goods remained on the General Price Control Order and the number of specific items controlled was reduced to forty-four. In agriculture, insecticides, meat, farm machinery, animal feeds, fertilizers, agricultural chemicals, and barbed wire were decontrolled between 1986 and 1990.[76] In 1993, the government abolished the import licensing system that dated to the era of independence.[77] Parastatal reform, increasingly on the reform agenda, also showed gains in the late 1980s. The government established the Parastatal Reform Programmes Committee to oversee the restructuring and sale of parastatals and to devise procedures for divestiture. By the early 1990s, according to the government, eleven enterprises were slated for sale or liquidation, twelve parastatals were being restructured, and the government was divesting itself of shares in five industries.[78]

A closer look at market deregulation and privatization, however, suggests a strategic approach to both reforms that protected the government's central political interests. The rules could be changed, it appeared, but only to the extent that new rules did not trespass on political resources that were central to the power of the presidency. This dynamic was clear in the decade-long effort to liberalize maize marketing and diminish the monopoly power of the NCPB. In the parastatal sector, privatization efforts were at the center of conflict between the international agencies and the political leadership of Kenya.

Maize had the reputation of being "Kenya's most politicised agricultural commodity."[79] The NCPB had a monopoly on the purchase and sale of maize and its transport across district lines.[80] It maintained a network of depots throughout the country where farmers were required to sell their grain at preannounced prices and consumers could buy staples at official prices. In addition, NCPB was to maintain strategic grain reserves to ensure food security in times of harvest shortages. The board also controlled the access of millers to supplies of grain. The case of the economic inefficiency of the board had been made many times before, but a number of initiatives to deregulate the market had all met with failure. As early as 1966, when an official commission reported on the maize market, reformers had presented evidence about the inefficiency of the public monopoly, the distortions caused by price controls, and the cost of subsidies to the budget.[81] Most critics argued that the government should restrict its role to market stabilization and reserve stock management.[82] In line with such arguments, the World Bank provided data in 1982 indicating the large differences between producer and consumer prices and argued that consumer prices were adversely affected by a system that generated large rents for the board. Although the government – in the guise of the finance ministry – agreed to the adjustment package, extensive opposition to it existed within government. In particular, the marketing board was adamant that food security would be jeopardized through decontrol and that Asian traders would move in to control the marketing of maize and create political tensions.[83]

Implementation was extremely slow. A year and a half after agreeing to the package, the government announced the imminent decontrol of maize, but did not follow up on this pledge. Instead, it announced that the Kenya Grain Growers Cooperative Union, which was created by the government to replace the Kikuyu-dominated Kenya Farmers Association, could also engage in marketing of grains. The drought of 1984 provided the government with a reason to backtrack on this announcement, however, in the interests of food security. Early in 1986, growers were allowed to sell directly to millers, but the NCPB monopoly was reimposed within six months. Maize liberalization was reintroduced in 1988. The new reform package included trade and price liberalization, initiatives to develop the private market, and operational restructuring of the NCPB. This reform was agreed to because of significant pressures from international agencies. Their concern with maize stemmed largely from the fact that the NCPB was responsible for over a quarter of the total public sector deficit.[84] Between 1988 and 1992, there was a gradual expansion of the number of bags of maize that farmers were allowed to sell on the open market, but in the fall of 1992, strict limits were reimposed. A black market in maize quickly emerged, and the World Bank canceled credits that had been conditioned on agricultural sector reforms. In the spring of 1993, partial liberalization of maize markets was announced again.[85]

In defending maize market control, the government insisted on the importance of food security and the need to be able to ensure stocks of basic grains. The NCPB was reluctant to lose its privileged position in regulating the market and expanding its presence in remote areas; the farmers were reluctant to give up the above-market prices they were receiving from the NCPB. Moreover, the government benefited from its ability to supply maize through the NCPB when food shortages emerged. The political interests of the government were further advanced by the reintroduction of pan-territorial pricing, which enabled NCPB, particularly through its geographically expanded network of depots, to buy maize at high prices from farmers in remote locations, in areas that strongly supported Moi. Operating losses of the NCPB mounted steadily and maize imports increased after 1989.[86] Under such conditions, changing the rules of the game for the economy was a slow and halting process at best.

Privatization faced a similar fate. While the country's parastatal sector had built a reputation for considerable efficiency compared with other African countries, the performance of the entire sector declined after 1979, reflecting more constrained economic realities in the country, curtailed government investment, and the impact of broader financial and pricing policies of the government.[87] The political and social objectives of the parastatal sector also increased in the 1980s. Greater pressure was put on them to address questions of regional distribution and to hire additional workers; both initiatives reduced their profitability and managerial interest in generating profits. In fact, just as in many other countries, the parastatal sector was politically central to state leaders, as clearly explained by one Kenyan official.

The biggest reason that the government will not privatize is that the parastatals are absolutely central to power here in Kenya ... Senior positions in the parastatals – down to the third and fourth layer of management – are doled out as political gifts. The president hires and fires these people ... The parastatals allow the president to benefit regions that are important to him, and they provide opportunities for making political gifts. And there is another reason. If you visit any of these companies, you will see that they are all very overstaffed. They provide employment for large numbers of political loyalists. So giving away the parastatal sector is the same as giving away power. The government is clearly not going to do this.[88]

In light of this political reality, but in the face of international pressure, privatization proceeded reluctantly. In implementing privatization initiatives mandated by agreements with the international agencies, the Parastatal Reform Programmes Committee, assisted by its technical arm, the government investments division in the ministry of finance, first established a distinction between strategic and non-strategic parastatals. Strategic parastatals were not to be privatized, only restructured if necessary, because of concerns about national security. The list of strategic parastatals included virtually all of the ones that had significant economic and political presence – the National Cereals and Produce Board, Kenya Railways, Kenya Broadcasting Corporation, Kenya Ports Authority, Kenya Airways, Kenya Posts and Telecommunications, the Agricultural Finance Corporation, several sugar companies, and similar enterprises. The non-strategic parastatals scheduled for liquidation or sale provide a clear contrast in terms of their importance. They included the Tiger Shoe Company, East African Fine Spinners, Yuken Textile Industry, Synthetic Fibres of Kenya, Pan Vegetable Processing, Kenya Film Corporation, and a number of other small and medium enterprises.

In addition, the government proceeded to sell shares in companies in which it held 50 percent or less of the shares or sold a small amount of shares in its majority-owned parastatals. These actions meant little in a strategic sense because in the former case the government did not appoint directors and in the latter case, it continued to have the right to appoint directors. Jobs, control over essential services, opportunities to reward political loyalty with lucrative rents, and control over regional allocations were among the principal reasons for resisting international pressure to privatize. With privatization, a serious possibility also arose that the economically powerful Kikuyu or the Asian community would be the only ones with enough capital to purchase the firms. In addition, "state control and free provision of so many services has become an essential part of the social pact. Breaking that pact, in the form of cost-sharing or job-reducing privatizations, threatens regime continuity."[89] In fact, "left on its own, the government would not even have brought up the issue of privatization."[90]

The response of the government was to move slowly and to stall as long as possible on the initiative to privatize the state-owned enterprises. By 1993, the Parastatal Reform Committee was chaired by a politician well-known for his links to the president. For those involved in the parastatal reform activity, the message was clear.

When they put someone [like that] in, it sends a message to the rest of us that the reform will not be pursued. I think you will not see much action at all in terms of privatization for the next couple of years ... You will only see activities that have no real economic or political impact. Everybody knows that the message is "go slow."[91]

Kenya provides an example of how the persistence or change of rules relating the state to the market is profoundly affected by the goals of leaders and by the coalitions of interests that support them. The Kenyan government fought an ongoing battle with the international agencies over what these rules should be; the country's political leadership resisted changes that threatened its capacity to dominate the economy or reward its political base. Existing institutions were potent vehicles for rent seeking, often on a massive scale, and for discriminating among regions and private sector entrepreneurs on the basis of political loyalty, favoritism, or ethnicity. Reformists, largely concentrated in the international institutions, pressed hard for new rules, but in the end, they were only able to achieve results in areas that were unimportant to the strategic goals of the political leadership.

In Kenya, the rules that structured political relationships within government were rewritten through revisions to the constitution and the operation of District Focus. Rules that structured political relationships between the state and civic society were also rewritten. In this case, however, their authoritativeness was a subject of great contention and ultimately, the government was forced to rescind the one-party amendment to the constitution. Rules to restructure the relationship between the state and the economy were also an arena of contention. The government sought to maintain and even expand many of the existing rules, while international agencies and others sought to enforce redefinition. In both political and economic arenas, regime leaders sought to insist that state power be maintained in the economy and in political life and used to enhance the personal control of the president and reorient state resources to new groups of beneficiaries. Perversely, however, this assistance resulted in a state that was significantly less authoritative and legitimate at the outset of the 1990s than it had been at the outset of the 1980s.

CONCLUSION

"Institutions," writes Douglass North, "are the rules of the game in a society; more formally, they are the humanly devised constraints that shape human interaction. In consequence, they structure incentives in exchange, whether political, social, or economic."[92] These rules emerge over time through complex interactions of state, economy, and society. Ultimately, states authorize and seek to enforce rules considered binding on both the economy and society. Nevertheless, at times, the "constraints that shape human interaction" are seriously weakened and at other times, they can be abruptly changed. This is what occurred in Mexico and Kenya. Before the 1980s, constitutions, laws regulating the distribution of agricultural land

and the performance of national investment banks, the public bureaucracy, the presidency, and the parties all placed the state in a dominant position in developing and regulating the economy and in managing political conflict and controlling dissent. Until the 1980s, the authority of the state to make and enforce the rules was widely accepted as legitimate and, where it was not, these two states generally had the capacity to impose their authority. Such institutional capacity was seriously undermined during the 1980s.

The response to weakened institutional capacity in these two countries differed significantly. In Mexico, after a series of efforts to redefine the rules for economic interaction in the mid-1980s, a new presidential administration was able to introduce a major shift in the rules that determined how the state would relate to the economy. New rules relating to state–society interactions were also engineered, but their intent and impact were much less clear than in economic relations. In Kenya, the right of the state to continue to dominate rule making was the focus of political conflict during this same period; initiatives to expand state and presidential dominance and to restructure the support base of the regime resulted in further contention. The political disarray caused by this conflict spilled over into the economic arena, where the rules of the game relating the state to the economy came increasingly under siege. In both countries, despite divergent outcomes, political leaders and institutions were at the center of initiatives and conflict over the institutional capacity of the state and central to an explanation about how rules were altered. The two cases also clarify the extent to which the effort to develop new rules of the game must also incorporate a significant effort to develop widespread societal and international consensus that these rules are appropriate and legitimate.

5

Managing the economy

Technical capacity relates centrally to the influence of science and reason in policy making, the role of ideas in the search for solutions to public problems, and the institutionalization of analytic problem solving within the public sector. Technical capacity varies among states and within states over time, and technical analysis is rarely the sole basis on which public decisions are made. Nevertheless, the ability to use scientific knowledge as an input into decision making, and into the management of public affairs, is a distinguishing characteristic of modern states. As the problems faced by modern governments have grown increasingly more complex, and as the informational and analytic bases on which to make decisions has increased, technical capacity is increasingly required to identify the origin and nature of public problems and assess possible solutions to them.

A wide range of activities carried out by the state can provide evidence of its technical capacity. A national statistics agency that is able to collect, process, analyze, and disseminate information about economic and social conditions is one example. Promoting policy-relevant research on important public health issues is another, as is the ability to build bridges and roads that meet reasonable construction and safety standards. Similarly, introducing and managing complex information systems, ensuring air traffic safety, monitoring inflation, regulating financial markets, carrying out research on new agricultural and livestock technologies, and providing for safe drugs and water supplies are all functions that imply the need for technical expertise in a variety of fields. Where states have not been able to produce this expertise or fill immediate demand for it, foreign experts have often been contracted to carry out technical responsibilities.[1]

While the range of technical activities that are essential to modern states is extensive and spans all sectors and levels of government, I have defined this dimension of capacity more narrowly, focusing on the ability to set and manage macroeconomic policy. Several factors explain this choice. First, in the wide-ranging debate on the appropriate role of the state in development, explored in the first chapter, there is agreement that the management of the macroeconomy is a responsibility of the state. How this management is best organized within the state may be subject to debate and variation, but there is no dispute over whether states ought to carry out this function. In other areas – whether the state should be responsible for basic research in public health; whether the state should construct roads; whether the state should provide veterinary services to poor farmers – there is much less agreement. Second, managing the macroeconomy is not only an agreed-upon function of the state, it is a primary one. The development debates that characterized the 1970s and the 1980s were marked by increasing agreement that other development activities would not prosper unless the state were first capable of providing a secure macroeconomic environment.[2]

Third, in the extensive economic crises that characterized the 1980s and 1990s, almost all governments were under pressure to improve their ability to control inflation, generate economic growth, and ensure stable trade relations. In large numbers of countries, attention focused on the economic teams that advised presidents and prime ministers about appropriate responses to the crises and on those involved in negotiating agreements with international financial institutions. As indicated in Chapter 2, technocrats sometimes became nationally recognized figures and accumulated considerable political influence. High level positions, including those of president and prime minister, were sometimes occupied by individuals with extensive technical training, particularly in economics. The ability to manage macroeconomic affairs was thus a highly visible factor in discussions of state–economy and state–society relations throughout these difficult times.

In addition, focusing on macroeconomic management ability provides an opportunity to assess the role of ideas in the development and implementation of public policy and the relationship between ideas and the capacity to influence policy.[3] During the 1980s and early 1990s, the discussion and adoption of market-oriented and outward-looking development strategies were part of domestic and international dialogues and alliances that heightened the visibility of those who wielded influence through the promotion of ideas, particularly about economics. Communication about ideas for promoting development was facilitated because the discipline of economics provided a specialized language and standards of proof; language and standards also worked to exclude those who were not familiar with them and who did not hold accepted professional credentials. In such ways, the technical capacity to engage in debates about macroeconomic policy influenced power relationships among decision makers, affected access to policy discussion by interest groups, and shaped negotiations between national and international interests.

Finally, the degree to which technical information is assessed in macroeconomic decision making, and the extent to which technically trained professionals are consulted about policy, is largely controlled by top level decision makers. Political elites appoint, promote, support, and protect technical advisors and create technical analysis units – or fail to do so – largely as a result of their own perceptions, ideas, interests, and decision-making styles. In choosing to enhance technical input into decision making, political leaders can create opportunities to alter power relationships. Some leaders have empowered technocrats and technical advisory units as a way of wresting power from interest groups, legislatures, and line ministries.[4] Some have encouraged coalitions of political support built on technocratic alliances among emergent professional classes. And some have pursued major policy reorientations by using technical information, analysis, and language as political tools.[5]

Thus, analysis of how technical capacity emerges and influences decision making – or fails to do so – can shed considerable light on the impact of political leadership in policy and political change.

Operationally, the technical capacity of states to manage the macroeconomy can be assessed by considering four factors. First, is there a stock of technically trained individuals employed by the state whose function is to provide information, analysis, and policy options to facilitate macroeconomic decision making?[6] Second, do technically trained individuals hold important positions at middle and upper levels in government? Third, are there technical analytic units that serve decision-making bodies such as cabinets, ministers, and legislatures? And fourth, does the technical information and analysis generated by individuals and units play an influential role in decision making?

In Chapter 1, I hypothesized that, due to the imperative to focus on macroeconomic conditions set in motion by deep economic crisis, technical input into decision making would show a tendency to increase. Demands from the international financial institutions negotiating debt restructuring and policy reform would be met by heightened reliance on technocrats in government, increasing their access to and influence in high level decision making. Public discussion of problems of development would increasingly demonstrate the dominance of economic language and concepts and technocrats would become more visible and influential figures in national politics. Those who were unable to converse fluently in the language of economics would find it difficult to participate in policy discussions. In Chapter 2, I found considerable evidence to support this hypothesis, particularly in Latin America. In Africa, there were notable trends in the direction of increased technical capacity in many countries, but the evidence was less consistent than was the case of Latin America. This chapter provides an opportunity to look more deeply into changes in technocratic influence in Mexico and Kenya.

This chapter indicates a consistent pattern in Mexico conforming to the hypothesis set out in Chapter 1. Beginning in the 1970s, but accelerating rapidly after 1982, evidence of the increased influence of technical information, technically trained individuals, and technical analytic units in national economic decision making is incontrovertible. In fact, by the 1990s, Mexico had achieved an international reputation as a country in which technocratic elites and technocratic decision-making styles dominated the pinnacles of power within government. Indeed, in influencing macroeconomic decision making, private sector groups, party organizations, legislative bodies, and formerly powerful ministries were strongly outpaced by the unusual strength and unity of this technocratic elite. Political leaders actively promoted and protected the technocrats, set new standards for the discussion of public policy, and altered the norms for access to policy making.

In Kenya, on the other hand, there is evidence that those who had been trained in technical fields and who had held important policy-making positions calling upon their expertise were distanced from influence during the latter half of the 1980s. By the end of the decade, they were consulted only when immediate issues resulting from economic crisis required direct attention. As a result, the Kenyan state lost technical capacity during the decade, despite strong insistence from international financial agencies seeking to pressure the government into economic and political reform. Ideas became less, not more, important in influencing decision making during the decade. Although some technically trained officials continued to occupy high level positions, their expertise was not as important as their political credentials for their inclusion in decision-making arenas. They were prominent in discussions over debt and development assistance with international agencies, but their influence over policy was strongly opposed within government and their positions on particular issues frequently rejected or reversed. Foreign technical advisors continued to play important roles in national policy decisions, largely because they were viewed as being politically neutral.

How can this differential outcome in the two cases be explained? Clearly, Kenya had a less robust base of technically trained economists to draw on than Mexico. Nevertheless, until the mid-1980s, well-qualified people had made important contributions to the effective management of that country's economy. Well-respected technocrats occupied high level positions in central economic ministries and headed the central bank. The private sector, including a variety of think tanks, the universities, and international agencies were able to find skilled Kenyans to manage financial activities, provide advice, teach courses, and do research and analysis. The answer to the question can be only partially answered by reference to the available stock of trained individuals.

Salaries, benefits, and internal incentive systems that affect whether governments can attract and retain skilled personnel also play some role in the answer. Being a public sector technocrat in Kenya was not a financially or professionally attractive option for many skilled people by the 1990s. Given the relative scarcity of their skills, they were easily lured away to other positions, particularly to those with the international agencies, where they were rewarded with much better salaries and given important responsibilities. Nevertheless, many of Kenya's skilled professionals traditionally received income from private pursuits and were drawn to public sector activities when they believed their talents were important to solving national problems. Moreover, those who attain high level positions in government – in Kenya or elsewhere – are rarely motivated primarily by the desire to maximize their incomes; they are much more likely to be attracted to such positions because they offer opportunities to grapple with important issues, have power over significant decisions or institutions, develop contacts that can be politically or economically useful in the future, or make personal contributions to the solution of some public issue.[7] Salaries and benefits, while important, do not explain fully Kenya's loss of technical capacity.

This chapter, while not denying the influence of numbers and emoluments, provides an alternative explanation of why Mexico and Kenya differed in their ability to increase the state's technical capacity. It views technocratic influence as derivative of political power. While some countries have developed much more extensive corps of technically trained economists than others, few are completely without such talent. More important than their availability is the extent to which their skills are called upon as part of decision-making processes. The distinction between Mexico and Kenya, therefore, is largely one of differences in political leadership. Very simply, Mexico's leaders empowered technocrats while Kenya's marginalized them.

THE REIGN OF THE TECHNOCRATS IN MEXICO

President Carlos Salinas and his team of high level advisors were, according to *The Economist*, "probably the most economically literate group that has ever governed any country anywhere."[8] This team was widely credited with having created a new Mexican "miracle" through the design and implementation of an economic development strategy that differed fundamentally from its predecessor.[9] Within a few years after 1988, Mexico abandoned extensive state intervention in the economy and its highly protectionist policies for industrial development. It created modern financial institutions and confronted long-protected domestic entrepreneurs with a more internationally competitive environment. It reversed earlier stances on regional integration and negotiated a major free-trade agreement with Canada and the US. It legislated much expanded opportunities for foreign investment, privatized large and important state-owned enterprises, ended extensive price controls, and deregulated significant sectors of the economy. Unifying these actions was a vision of an internationally competitive Mexico playing a significant role in a new global economy. It was the vision of the modernizers who assumed high level positions within the Salinas administration. Almost to a person, they were technocrats who also had important political skills.

The cabinet announced by Carlos Salinas in late 1988 was clear testimony to the ascendance of a generation of foreign-educated policy makers who combined technical training with managerial experience in the politically charged world of Mexico's bureaucracy.[10] The minister of finance held a PhD in economics from MIT, the minister of budgeting and planning a similar degree from Yale; the minister of industry and commerce was also a Yale PhD economist; the president held a PhD in political economy and government from Harvard. The mayor of Mexico City, also a cabinet official, had an MA in public affairs from Princeton; the head of the central bank a PhD from Yale in economics; and the president's chief of staff had PhD level training in economics at Stanford. Salinas' appointee to head the PRI studied for a PhD in economics from the University of Pennsylvania. Several other high level officials had doctoral degrees or studied for such degrees at the University of Chicago, Stanford, UCLA, Harvard, Princeton, and MIT. Others held PhD degrees from the national university, UNAM.

These officials, and those they appointed to work in high level positions in their ministries, were not new to policy-making roles. Under the administration of Miguel de la Madrid, almost all of them had held high level positions in important economic ministries. Of the Salinas cabinet, one third had previous experience in the finance ministry and one half had prior experience in the ministry of budgeting and planning.[11] Several of them traced their initiation into government to the López Portillo administration.[12] All of them were well known to Carlos Salinas. While the technocratization of the Mexican public sector had been occurring since the 1970s, they held unusual influence under Salinas because of the president's role in recruiting and supporting them.

In Mexico's political system, it is relatively easy to recruit new cadres of elites into government service. Beginning with the president's appointment of his cabinet and other important positions, their subsequent appointment of "their people," and the further appointment of these individuals' subordinates, and so on, the initiation of a new administration is marked by extensive change within government. Because presidential candidates of the PRI are traditionally selected from among the cabinet of the outgoing president, and because these cabinet officials have worked as part of ministerial teams and personally loyal informal political coalitions known as camarillas, it is not surprising that many of the new appointees at the outset of an administration will be individuals from within government who have worked closely with the new president or have impressed him as being particularly astute. Thus, although there is great change in positions from one administration to another, many of those in new positions are people who have served considerable time in government.[13]

This system makes it possible for new administrations to recruit and promote new generations of public officials and encourage active adherence to presidential initiatives in ways that are more difficult where institutionalized civil service structures exist. Mexico has a public service that suffers from many of the inadequacies of government employment found in other systems – lack of responsiveness, productivity, and accountability – particularly in routine and lower level service providing jobs, but it is also a system that encourages extensive commitment to presidential leadership and activism at higher levels. A very great deal, in fact, depends on presidential leadership in terms of who is selected to fill high level positions and what directions are set for policy. It is a highly politicized public service, but it is not necessarily doomed to inefficiency and sloth, as popular views of politicized public administrations would have it. There is considerable potential for upward mobility in the system, particularly to those who have demonstrated hard work, effective problem-solving skills, political discretion, and loyalty to their superiors.[14]

Increasing the number of technically trained individuals in government and giving them positions that require use of these skills was part of a longer-term process of change in Mexico. Traditionally, public officials were appointed who had primarily political credentials; they had served within the PRI in a variety of capacities or they had served as elected officials at some point in their careers.[15] Even those with technical training generally apportioned some part of their careers to acquiring political credentials in organizing or running for office if they wished to move ahead in government. By the 1980s, however, the credentials required of aspiring public sector employees had changed considerably. As those with technical training emerged into more important positions, greater emphasis was placed on the technical qualifications of subordinates and correspondingly less emphasis was placed on their political credentials.

The criteria did not change overnight, of course, but a trend had become clear by the early 1980s: technical expertise, particularly in economics, was more important than extensive party service or elective office for moving upward in government. To the extent that party service was still relevant, that experience was more likely to involve strategic and policy planning at national headquarters rather than political organizing or electoral involvement.[16] According to one official,

The change began with López Portillo and de la Madrid, or even Echeverría. But it wasn't clear until this administration that you didn't need to work through the party, to be a militant, to get to a high position. I started in the last administration and I worked for the party, because it still wasn't clear. I even changed from medicine to law at the university because I was following the traditional path to a political career. You don't have to do this anymore. A political curriculum vitae can be invented for you when you become minister or vice-minister or general director. Technocrats are now in most of the important political decision-making positions.[17]

An important signal that criteria for upward mobility in government were changing was that presidential candidates were being selected increasingly from economic rather than political ministries. Presidents Díaz Ordaz (1964–1970), Echeverría (1970–1976), and two preceding presidents had held prior positions as interior ministers, while López Portillo had been minister of finance and de la Madrid and Salinas both served as ministers of budgeting and planning. Gustavo Díaz Ordaz was the last Mexican president to have held elective office prior to assuming ministerial and presidential roles.

In addition, the number of cabinet officials with training in economics was increasing. The percentage of cabinet officials holding degrees in economics or a closely related field was 17 percent under Díaz Ordaz, 22 percent under Echeverría, 44 percent under López Portillo, 42 percent under de la Madrid, and 59 percent under Salinas.[18] This was part of a broader trend that affected most high level positions. In a 1983 sample of 1,278 high level government officials, 97 percent had university degrees and 40.6 percent of those who held their first government position after 1970 had masters degrees or higher and 51.8 percent had studied economics or administration. This compares with 27.8 percent with masters degrees and 35.4 percent with economics or administration training among those who held their first jobs before 1970.[19]

The ascendance of those with technical training and bureaucratic career trajectories sent clear signals to politically ambitious young people. Beginning in the 1970s, larger numbers sought education abroad, particularly in the US, in economics and related fields and larger numbers sought economics degrees at home. Prestigious private universities offering rigorous training in economics and the social sciences, such as the Colegio de México and the Instituto Tecnológico Autónomo de México (ITAM), became more popular than the traditional choice, the national university (UNAM), for highly motivated aspirants to public positions. In these ways, the change of credentials increased the supply of technically trained people with interest in public sector careers.

Despite the emphasis on technical credentials, those appointed to positions that required them to use their technical skills were also expected to be politically astute and to utilize political skills – discretion, accommodation, submission to presidential leadership, loyalty, effective use of alliances and networks, and political correctness in terms of administration goals – if they were to be successful in their careers.[20] For those at upper levels in government in particular, political skills continued to be essential. Indeed, none of the public officials who came to dominate policy making under Salinas would have made it to the top of the highly politicized public sector without becoming astute practitioners of presidential and bureaucratic politics. "People think the government is made up of a bunch of technocrats from MIT. It is, but you don't get to be president, or a general director, or a minister, or a vice-minister without learning certain skills. And these people have learned them. How to listen above all."[21]

In this regard, a variety of terms – technopols, techno-politicians, and politico-technicians – were adopted to capture the importance of the combination of technical training with political astuteness that characterized those in cabinet and sub-cabinet positions under Salinas and his two predecessors.[22]

This begins to explain how a generation of highly trained technocrats was able to emerge at the top of the government hierarchy. Efforts under the Echeverría administration to draw young and better trained individuals into government initiated their ascendance. The motivation for doing so was largely political; it was part of an effort to manage the tide of dissent that swept the country's universities in the late 1960s and led to a major confrontation in 1968 that left several hundred young people dead. The inclusion of larger numbers of technically trained individuals at that time also corresponded to the expansion of the state into a much broader range of activities, particularly in the social sectors. Civil engineers, sociologists, agricultural economists, and economists joined the ranks of government and became actively involved in rural and urban development activities and a large number of other activities that corresponded to Echeverría's view of activist government.[23] Many young university graduates shared a nationalist ideology that encouraged them to identify with Mexico as a leader of the third world and with a government that was prominently engaged in efforts to alleviate poverty, bring greater equity to economic and political development, and define Mexico's future in distinction to the industrialized nations of the north.

Some of these individuals achieved important positions under the succeeding administration of López Portillo. And indeed, this was a period of such economic abundance that their vision of an activist state providing a wide range of benefits and services to all sectors of the population was believed to be an attainable reality. Also recruited into government at this time, however, was another group of young officials who believed in a reduced role for the state and a more open economy. A lively and public debate between these two groups ensued, joined by allies in the intellectual community, universities, and think tanks. The debate became known as the "dispute for the nation" in terms of which vision – one nationalist and interventionist and one internationalist and market oriented – would shape the future of the country.[24] The debate continued through the early years of the economic crisis, as the nationalists argued for economic recovery through greater government investment and intervention in the economy and the liberals argued for the need to restrain public spending and begin the process of liberalization of the economy.[25]

Under de la Madrid, these groups came of political age as many moved into prominent positions as vice-ministers, general directors, and advisors in the core economic ministries. In the years after 1982, economic crisis focused virtually all government attention on its management and heightened the importance and visibility of those in the ministries of finance and budgeting and planning ministries. Ongoing negotiations with the IMF and international creditors further increased the visibility of these public officials. For some time, however, their influence was muted because of the debate among them about how best to manage the economic crisis and the extent to which a nationalist or liberal vision of the future would predominate. Moreover, the nature of the crisis was not fully understood in the first several years of the decade, resulting in inconsistent policies and alternative diagnoses of the route to recovery. Thus, while the liberal technocrats were becoming increasingly central to economic policy making under de la Madrid, they had not yet come to dominate the policy-making arena fully. Nevertheless, the experience of attempting to manage the crisis was important to them, according to one official involved in economic policy making.

In the de la Madrid administration, where were the leaders of today? By and large they were in advisory positions where they could understand and see what was going on but couldn't do much about it. But they developed a clear idea of what went wrong and why. They studied about why 1984 – a relatively good year – became a disaster in 1985. And they studied the experiences of Chile, Peru, and Brazil.[26]

The ideas that held this group together were of a market-oriented economy, a vibrant private sector that could compete in international markets, and a state that was strong and wise enough to intervene appropriately in the economy to promote market-based growth. These ideas, forged through graduate training that emphasized neoclassical economics and comparative analysis of Mexico and other developing countries, did not reject the state as an agent of development, but redefined it as competent rather than controlling.[27] In an address in 1992, Salinas differentiated his administration's "social liberalism" from "neoliberalism" as well as from the views of those he termed "new reactionaries."

Neoliberalism minimizes the size and responsibilities of the state, marginalizing it from national life ... The new reactionaries want to return to the expansive and proprietary state, with a growing bureaucracy ... and growing inefficiency ... Social liberalism assumes that unregulated markets create monopolies, making social injustice worse and resulting in diminished growth ... Social liberalism proposes a promotional state that supports [private] initiative but with the capacity to regulate economic activities firmly.[28]

After assuming office in 1988, Salinas moved rapidly to make clear that this more international and market-oriented vision would dominate policy making and politics. While his team could trace the roots of technocratic influence to earlier administrations, his was unique in terms of the unity of their vision, which both cemented them as a team and enhanced their influence in policy making. In addition, their diagnosis of Mexico's development problems and the origins of the 1982 crisis and their prognosis of what needed to be done for the country was supported by growing disillusion with the policies of the past and increasing awareness of the critiques of import substitution and state-managed development that had circulated since the mid-1970s. In this context, new ideas had added cachet if they promised a way out of the current crisis.[29]

Most important, the ascendance of the new vision owed much to presidential leadership and the structure of power that allowed the president to empower the technocrats who shared it. First, he made full use of his powers of appointment to fill high level positions with those whose credentials as technocrats were impeccable and whose ideological and political instincts he trusted. His team in turn appointed officials whom they trusted and who shared a common orientation. The view of what needed to be done quickly became publicly unanimous among high level officials. Similarly, the president used his powers of appointment to move like-minded people with technical skills to the head of the PRI. In the coalition-building strategy discussed in the previous chapter, the distinction between the modernizers and the dinosaurs crystallized the distinction between the liberals and the nationalists, as well as between the technocrats and the politicians.

Second, Salinas made use of executive powers to restructure government in ways that gave added influence to the technocrats. He created a formal economic cabinet, composed of the minister of finance, the minister of planning and budgeting, the minister of industry and commerce, his chief of staff, the head of the central bank, and the minister of labor.[30] For more than two years, this sub-set of the full cabinet met as much as three times times a week; then, as the economic situation improved, it met less frequently. In 1992, centralization of control over macroeconomic policy was furthered by the incorporation of the ministry of planning and budgeting, a superministry identified with the spending side of government policy, into the ministry of finance, a superministry identified with fiscal control.[31] The president also superintended the creation of a number of special technical units within ministries and within the president's office that had access, through the ministers and the economic advisor, to the president and the economic cabinet. Among these were the office of deregulation in SECOFI and the vice-ministry of agriculture discussed in the previous chapter. Such units were also shielded from direct public pressure by ministers and other members of the president's team. According to one young technocrat, this helped them achieve their goals. "It is good that we have a very low – almost non-existent – profile. If we had a lot of 'participation' in our work, it would be much more difficult to do."[32] The appointment of officials and creation of new units strengthened the role of the president and the office of the president in policy making, extracting power from ministries, the legislative arena (which never had much power to begin with), and party officials who were known to resist the ascendance of the technocrats. This gave added opportunity to the president to shape policy decision making.

Formal presidential powers to appoint personnel and structure organizations were important to increasing technocratic influence. So, too, were unwritten rules about how issues would be discussed within government. According to one high level official, economic cabinet meetings were an arena for testing technical credentials and problem-solving skills.

When I take an issue to the economic cabinet, I begin a presentation with a statement of the issue and the problem. Then I present information on what other countries are doing or have done about this set of issues and problems. Then I lay out the options that are appropriate for Mexico to take and discuss the political and technical costs and benefits of each. Then I present my recommendations. The cabinet discusses the recommendations and the president takes part in these discussions, chairing the meetings ... He is a very detail-focused manager of these meetings. He doesn't like ambiguous responses. If you say, "We are designing a mechanism to do ...," he will immediately say, "What mechanism? How will it work?" He also wants people to get to the point in meetings. He has no patience with those who speculate. He sends out a clear message: don't waste my time.[33]

Those who did not conform to these rules, who talked too long or who strayed too far from the evidence and the proposed solutions, were not invited back to the high level discussions where policy was set. According to the same official, the standards for policy discussion were high.

I go to the cabinet meetings and present the same graphs and arguments that I used [as a professor in a US university]. I present these to the ministers and they assimilate them and at times even take me to task for my analysis. You don't bring bs to these cabinet meetings, believe me. You will get blown away if you do.[34]

This technocratic style also had implications for the politics of lobbying. One official, whose responsibilities included negotiating with the private sector, noted a change in how the private and public sectors interacted.

The private sector was always more technically qualified than the government, but government officials set the tone in terms of how the private sector people could get what they wanted. They learned that government officials were not interested in hearing technical arguments, they wanted to get gifts or be taken to lunch or get some kind of special consideration. So [the private sector] behaved that way. Now we have become technical, and they are dealing with us on these terms. They have learned that there are new ways of working with the government and now we often have more information than they do. They respond to us in terms of the tone and forms set for their behavior. Of course, this is most true in the economic ministries, and much less true in the very traditional ministries like agriculture and communications.[35]

The technocratic image of the administration and its language of rational problem solving appealed to the increasing numbers of professionals and technicians in the urban middle-class sector, as well as to many who had become highly disillusioned with the old-style politics, with corruption in government, and with the political rhetoric that was characteristic of administrations of the past. Along with export and financial sector elites, these groups formed the basis of the coalition of interests that Salinas appealed to with rhetoric and policy and who were invited to become part of the modernizers who would shape the country's future.

The triumph of the technocrats under the Salinas administration can thus be credited to several factors. First, over a period of two decades, Mexico developed a large stock of technically trained individuals and an elite of well-trained, politically ambitious, and astute technocrats. When the economic crisis brought macroeconomic issues clearly to the fore of public policy and international attention, presidents had an indigenous elite to turn to for advice. Second, the structure of the Mexican government and the process of upward mobility within the system made it possible for these individuals to assume high and middle level office in government with relative ease. Presidential power and the prerogatives of office gave incumbents considerable capacity to design decision-making processes that could empower technical expertise. With presidential backing, an extensive range of technical units within government provided information, analysis, and recommendations to decision-making bodies. Presidential power insulated these units and presidential style encouraged their access to the decision makers. The backgrounds of the decision makers ensured that they spoke the same language as their advisory groups and understood the alternatives they were being offered. Moreover, the public vision propounded by Salinas and his team ensured that the analysis and advice of technical groups would be consistent with the goals of the administration. And the vision was central in creating a new coalition of interests that could expect to benefit if the vision became reality. The experience of the Salinas presidency is thus a valuable case of the marriage of political power and technocratic influence.

THE REIGN OF THE POLITICIANS IN KENYA

In Kenya, a marriage of political and technocratic power ended in divorce, one that underscored the derivative nature of the influence of technocrats. The government's ability to manage the macroeconomy had been considerable in the first two decades of independence; it declined noticeably after the mid-1980s. Kenyan technocrats were eased out of office after 1987 and the election of 1992 left the government with few individuals in parliament who had the training or experience to be appointed to high level positions to manage the central economic ministries.[36] Some technically skilled individuals remained in public office, but they were often placed in positions that did not make appropriate use of their skills, marginalized from decision-making areas, or they were "bought" to ensure their loyalty to the politicians. Thus, at the time when a large number of states were increasing the presence and influence of technical information, analysis, and roles in decision making, Kenya was moving in a different direction.

Of course, even in the best of times, Kenya's stock of technically trained professionals was low by the standards applied to Latin American and Asian countries. In an analysis of the careers of four public managers who assumed influential roles in the government after independence, David Leonard notes that

The educational pyramid these men climbed was extremely steep, littered with examinations and small rates of promotion to the next level. Those who went all the way through it ... were the leaders of a genuine meritocracy. Those ... who did not go quite so far through the regular Kenyan system were nonetheless still members of a relatively small educated company ... They had won against a colonial educational system in which the odds were heavily stacked against them.[37]

Thirty years after independence, the pyramid was still relatively narrow. In the early 1990s, technocrats in Kenya were a small elite, and were likely to be less highly trained than their Latin American or Asian counterparts due in part to much more constrained access to high quality university and graduate training.

Nevertheless, several factors combined to encourage a concentration of skilled people in government by the early 1980s. First, positions in government gave high level officials considerable power over day-to-day affairs and over policy directions. The British civil service system inherited by Kenya established a professional elite with broad powers to establish and maintain order, extract revenue, oversee economic and political life, and participate in policy decisions. Under Kenyatta, the power of administrators clearly outstripped that of party and elected officials.[38] Moreover, in the first decade after independence, the challenge of nation building and the desire to play a role in it enhanced the attraction of a public sector career for bright and ambitious Kenyans. In addition, through the mid-1980s, average wage earnings in the public sector were comparable to private sector earnings in areas such as mining, manufacturing, construction, and some services.[39] The prestige and salaries accorded to middle and high level officials were cemented through guarantees of job security and perquisites of office such as official housing, medical insurance, and living allowances.

The civil service, as it developed in Kenya, provided a stable, hierarchical system within which to develop a career, offered opportunities for additional training, and protected public officials from arbitrary dismissal. Rapid expansion in the civil service in the 1970s also meant increased opportunities for upward mobility, particularly because the expansion of the state was coupled with an expansion in the number of ministries and parastatal organizations. The development of those with technical skills in economics was also encouraged during that decade. In 1974, a specialist cadre of economists and statisticians was created in the civil service that provided specific terms of service for middle and senior level economists to encourage their professional commitment to public service.[40] By the 1990s, some 350–400 economists were part of this scheme of service, which was superintended by the ministry of planning and national development. A series of initiatives to train technical specialists also encouraged the development of these skills. The government participated in graduate level programs at York University in Canada and at Cornell University in order to increase the number of well-trained individuals in government.[41] It also sought to use foreign advisors for on-the-job training of Kenyans in important ministries.[42] A 1988 survey of 255 economists in the planning ministry indicated that some 70 percent of them had BA degrees and 30 percent had masters degrees or more.[43]

In combination, these factors helped attract well-qualified individuals to government service and encouraged a sense of professional identity among those at middle and upper levels. The political style of Jomo Kenyatta further encouraged those with technical skills to take control of economic management; macroeconomic policy, in fact, was carried out largely in isolation from day-to-day political debates. As indicated in previous chapters, normal politics involved the interaction of regional and ethnic leaders largely concerned about elections and development resource allocations. Daily politics focused on the patron–client networks through which loyalties were exchanged for local development expenditures, jobs, and a degree of regional autonomy. This system left the president, the cabinet, and the civil service relatively free to set national economic policies, although often within the conditions set by international financial agencies.

In setting these policies, Kenyatta's policy makers shared a broad consensus on how the national interest was to be defined – promotion of the coffee and tea export sector, support for the development of African commerce and industry, encouragement of foreign investment, and nation building through investment in physical and social infrastructure.[44] They shared this vision in large part because they shared educational, ethnic, and economic interests that corresponded to the pursuit of these broad objectives.[45] Indeed, extensive economic activities in the private sector characterized the administrative elite that emerged and played central policy roles under Kenyatta. Their interests coincided with those of the political elite. Together, politicians and civil servants imbued public policy with a class-based "stabilizing vision" of the country's development.[46] In consequence of these shared concerns, the exchange rate was closely monitored, inflation was held to relatively low levels, and rural–urban terms of trade remained largely favorable to export agriculture, at least until the external shocks of the 1970s.

Considerable longevity in top civil service positions permitted a small group of senior officials effectively to dominate economic policy making. Among this group were three individuals of particular importance – Philip Ndegua, Harris Mule, and Simeon Nyachae. As permanent secretaries in the ministries of finance and planning and as governor of the central bank, they were the influential technocrats who stood at the heart of macroeconomic policy making for long periods of time.[47] They generally adopted principles of neoclassical economics through their training and close association with the large numbers of foreign advisors who served in Kenya's goverment.[48] Beginning in the mid-1970s, closer interaction with the technocrats of the international financial agencies also influenced their orientation toward economic policy.

In the context of heightened economic crisis, the technocrats argued for devaluation and fiscal austerity. Under less exigent conditions, they worked together to keep the exchange rate stable, inflation under control, and producer prices up. They were instrumental in a system that regularly produced multiyear development plans beginning in 1966 and in maintaining concern for macroeconomic policy. They were also committed to a long-term view of Kenya's development, the importance of agriculture to the future of the country, and the need for professional and technical input into national policy decision making. Long tenure in positions of authority and the small size of the educational elite in Kenya brought these technocrats into frequent contact with each other and cemented their general orientation toward macroeconomic policy. Nevertheless, even under Kenyatta, with whom they shared interests and trust, their influence as individuals and as a group depended on their ability to reach the president's ear.[49]

Although generally influential in policy making until well into Moi's presidency, the high level technocrats in the economic ministries also experienced periods of increased power and visibility that corresponded to the need to negotiate stabilization and structural adjustment agreements with the IMF and the World Bank. In the aftermath of the first oil shock of 1974–1975, technocrats in the ministries of finance and planning and the central bank met repeatedly with counterparts in the IMF to hammer out a macroeconomic program. When the beverage boom of 1976–1978 decreased pressure on the economy, their visibility and influence over policy declined. It was reasserted in 1979–1980 and again from 1982 to 1986 in response to the difficulties faced in the economy and the need to negotiate with the international agencies.[50]

During the period between 1982 and 1986, however, observers began to note the distinction between the important role of technocrats in the formulation of policy and their loss of control over its implementation.[51] Moi had much less personal confidence in the technocrats than Kenyatta. They did not share the ethnic, regional, and economic identity of his constituency. At the same time, he had no indigenous corps of alternatives to replace them with and was constrained in his ability to dismiss people from the civil service, although he had considerable influence over their assignments, promotions, and access to the office of the president. The economic activities actually pursued by the state, as opposed to the formal policies announced, came to be determined by the president, the heads of line ministries, the directors of parastatal organizations, and the cronies who increasingly surrounded President Moi. The capacity of these individuals to spend money and make allocation decisions was in turn determined by the extent to which they were protected by the president and had access to him.

From the mid-1980s to the early 1990s, the government generally articulated conventional macroeconomic policies and development goals, as evidenced by the commitments made in Sessional Paper No. 1 of 1986, but increasingly left policy implementation to the whims of political favoritism, cronyism, and corruption. The technocrats' loss of influence corresponded to increasing fiscal indiscipline that reached crisis proportions in the early 1990s, even while many continued to laud the policy framework established by the government. Eventually, the weakness of the implementation process became so grave that corruption, malfeasance, and misman-agement affected rates of inflation, trade, and investment.[52] Government spending increased significantly as did the budget deficit and international trade imbalances.

The 1986 policy paper was, in fact, the technocrats' swan song in terms of the traditional distance maintained between macroeconomic policy and political decision making. After that, it was increasingly clear that they "did not enjoy Moi's confidence and therefore were unable to get supportive decisions from him in the same way they had with Kenyatta."[53] By 1993, when another and much deeper economic crisis emerged, most of the original generation of technocrats had left the public service. They had fallen victim to the staffing decisions and decision-making style of President Moi. This shift out of positions of influence did not occur rapidly. In part, the formal and institutional structure of the civil service made it difficult for the president to appoint and dismiss high level officials at will. Instead,

President Moi played a game of attrition. He established a mandatory retirement age of fifty-five, which enabled him to dispense with the services of many of Kenyatta's appointees. He would wait for the rest to make some error or for their organizations to show signs of failure. The offending executives could then be dismissed with legitimacy in the public's eyes.[54]

Gradually, through the use of presidential appointments, the economic ministries and the central bank were colonized by those who were part of Moi's inner circle of associates. As described by one high level official,

Power in this system is defined by the degree of access one has. This means access to the president and then access to people who have access to the president and then access to people who have access to people who have access and so on. And then you factor in the kind of access – how often and for what kinds of decisions. To get policy change, you have to be Machiavellian. You have to find people who have access and convince them ... There is no point in a technocrat gaining access to the president; better to work through those who have it for political reasons.[55]

When those with technical training remained in government, their influence over policy waned or was less based on their expertise than on their willingness to accommodate to the politics of cronyism.[56] This affected the ability to propose policy solutions, according to one official. "It used to be that a permanent secretary or minister or other group would go before decision makers with a proposal. That doesn't happen now because everyone is so afraid of being held responsible for a politically unwise decision."[57]

In this context, and with the gradual marginalization of the Kenyan technocrats, it is not surprising that when expertise was needed, foreign advisors assumed a larger role in setting formal government policy.[58] Because they were distanced from the bases of ethnic, regional, and economic conflict, they could be called upon to write policy papers and prepare the documents to be discussed at meetings with the international agencies. By the early 1990s, the divorce between policy and power was almost complete.

The policies are pretty good and some are excellent. They are a good prescription for the problems of the country. The problem is that they are not implemented and it is not clear if there is any intention to implement ... And the policies are essentially made by a small group of foreign advisors and a couple of high level Kenyan officials. Some senior officials don't even come to the meetings where [macroeconomic] decisions are made.[59]

There were no institutional innovations, such as the creation of an economic cabinet, that could counteract the decreasing importance of Kenyan technocrats. At a more general level, policy-making influence depended much less on institutional power or assignment of responsibilities than it did on the identity of those appointed to high level positions and their reputations for access to the president.

High level officials with technical training became increasingly scarce by the late 1980s because of the impact of presidential appointments and decision-making style. Middle level professionals with technical skills also became more scarce for a range of reasons. Many of those who had been employed in the public service left because cumbersome and slow appointment and promotion practices discouraged upward mobility and meaningful work assignments.[60] In some cases, promotions were stymied for officers who represented the Kikuyu-based coalition that developed under Kenyatta. Equally important, however, declining salaries and decreasing benefits played a role in the exodus of the technically skilled from government. Some officials were offered much more lucrative (and intellectually engaging) positions in international organizations or in some cases, in the private sector. Real average wages declined for the public sector.[61] Moreover, most of the well-trained officials who remained in government had few demands placed upon them to use their training or experience. One official noted that "There are some parts of government that are working, above all in the revenue side – revenue collection, customs, VAT. Elsewhere, I have many friends who tell me they are effectively on leave. They come to their offices but there is nothing to do and there is no real reason to be there."[62]

Such factors combined to make public service less attractive to well-trained Kenyans than it had been in the first two decades after independence. By the late 1980s and early 1990s, many of the most promising university graduates joined university faculties or entered the private sector, disdaining careers in the public sector.[63] The decline of technical expertise was also registered in organizational terms. Units created to provide technical advice to decision makers lost credibility and stature through the use of presidential appointments, as we saw in the case of the new chairperson of the government's privatization effort. By the 1990s, criticism of high levels of incompetence in Kenya's public sector was commonplace.

Kenya's loss of technical capacity was closely intertwined with the assertion of presidential power under Moi. The technocrats in high level positions were marginalized from influence because they formed part of the political and policy elite that had benefited from educational, economic, and social structures under the colonial government and under Kenyatta. In the effort to restructure political power, the technocrats were moved aside. So, too, the professional managers of the country's large parastatal sector were gradually replaced with those who were central to Moi's power. The parastatals were perhaps the most lucrative political plums to be distributed among Moi loyalists, and the performance criteria for managers became largely inconsequential by the early 1990s. The election of 1992 threw into relief the problems faced by a government that had marginalized many well-prepared people from government. The elections produced a large number of KANU MPs, fully loyal to Moi, who had little or no experience in government and often limited educations. In forming his cabinet from among these MPs, Moi had to make full use of his right to nominate twelve non-elected members to government service. He also reduced the number of ministries from thirty-three to twenty-three. Even then, only 54 percent of the cabinet held university degrees, compared with 73 percent in 1979, 78 percent in 1983, and 65 percent in 1988.[64] Where information and analysis were needed, or insisted upon by the international agencies, Moi often turned to the apolitical foreign advisors.

In Mexico and Kenya, the state's technical capacity waxed and waned in response to presidential interest and objectives. Both cases demonstrate that those who have technical expertise have influence when they have presidential attention and support. Thus, the derivative nature of technocratic influence was as evident in Kenya as it was in Mexico. In Mexico under administrations from the mid-1970s to the 1990s, and in Kenya from the mid-1960s to the mid-1980s, it was possible for those who had technical training to be both technocrats and important players in national decision making. In Kenya, especially after 1987, technocrats lost presidential support, access to the centers of decision making, and capacity to shape national economic policy largely because those who held political power no longer consulted them. Given the vulnerability of the technocrats, regaining their previous positions of influence was largely out of their control.

There are multiple determinants of presidential interests and objectives, ranging from economic, political, and social alliances to ideological and professional commitments, educational backgrounds, and short-term political calculations. In explaining differences in the presidential empowerment of technocrats in the two countries, such factors are important. In addition, the nature of the crises faced by the two countries also provide some insight into divergent choices. In Mexico, the crisis of the economy was much deeper and initially more pressing than the political crisis. In Kenya, on the other hand, the political crisis was preeminent, at least until 1993. It may well be that when crisis is defined primarily by economic conditions, technocrats are more likely to be empowered on the basis of their technical skills. In contrast, it may be that crisis defined primarily in political terms spawns the marginalization of technical skills and the politicization of the roles of technocrats.

6

Administering the public good

In the early 1980s, as governments and international financial institutions struggled to manage deep economic problems, the immediate tasks of establishing macroeconomic stability and initiating the process of structural adjustment received almost exclusive attention. Soon, however, policy makers, practitioners, and development specialists began to question why many reforms did not produce expected results more quickly.[1] As they asked this question, the issue of the administrative capacity of the state acquired greater salience.

Some policy reforms required long chains of administrative action if they were to be implemented – improved tax collection, customs reform, health sector restructuring, and decentralization of decision making, for example. Some required public officials to be active managers and problem solvers – deregulation, tariff reform, and privatization, for example. And the success of other reforms required procedures and institutional structures to facilitate market activities and to encourage risk taking by the private sector – the development of financial sector institutions and economic regulation, for example.

Initial adjustment efforts in Latin America and Africa confirmed that if government institutions were to monitor public spending, stimulate trade, expand the revenue base, manage an effective foreign exchange regime, and encourage private sector investment, they had to be organized effectively to carry out routine functions and they had to be able to count on administrators able to perform assigned tasks willingly, competently, and efficiently. The same realization applied even more to efforts to decentralize government to local and regional levels and encourage reforms in agriculture, health, and education. These changes required not only effective organizations and able administrators, but also significant resource allocations and the ability to develop innovative solutions to persistent problems.

Ironically, however, the medicine applied to correct economic imbalances often contributed to weakening the ability of the government to carry out and sustain needed reforms. Deep cuts in public sector budgets affected salaries of public officials, investment in social and physical infrastructure, and programs for social and economic development. Data presented in Chapter 2 suggested the extent to which the 1980s and early 1990s were a "lost decade" in terms of the ability of Latin American and African governments to carry out normal functions of government and to provide for the public good.

The same decade also encouraged critical rethinking about appropriate functions of the state. Beyond widespread agreement on the importance of public sector management of the macroeconomy, lively debates surrounded the question of the responsibility of government for other activities. Economists debated what the state ought to do in terms of definitions of public goods, market failures, and the comparative advantages of states and markets, while others considered what functions were central to the social contract between state and society. In practice, of course, theoretical debates about what the state ought to be responsible for were adjusted to conform to the historical traditions of specific countries, the economic and political strength and composition of the private sector in each country, and the political convenience of destatization in individual countries.

Indeed, theory and practice converged in recognizing the importance of the state for ensuring that basic social and economic services were provided to populations and the market. How government would carry out these responsibilities would vary by country, with some selecting centralized state administration, others preferring decentralization to regional and local government, and others experimenting with contracting out essential functions to the private sector or local communities. Despite these differences, there was more general agreement that states must assume responsibility for protecting and promoting the public health of its citizens, developing the human resources necessary for development, and providing basic infrastructure to support economic interaction.

In this chapter, I consider changes in the ability of the Mexican and Kenyan states to deliver and administer basic social services and provide physical infrastructure necessary for the economy. I focus on health, education, and roads as sectors that are important in their own right and that are indicative of wider issues in public management capacity. The chapter suggests that innovations and restructuring are important ingredients of improving administrative capacity, but ultimately, the problems of effective delivery of social services and physical infrastructure reflect the training, motivation, and organization of public officials in large bureaucracies, whether at national or local levels. In Mexico and Kenya, these tasks were much less amenable to improvement than were other dimensions of state capacity; the ability to implement policies, programs, and projects continued to be constrained, despite a number of initiatives to strengthen the public sector. These cases suggest that developing administrative capacity is likely to remain a daunting challenge for states in Latin America and Africa well into the twenty-first century.

ADMINISTERING THE PUBLIC GOOD IN MEXICO

Few people in Mexico escaped the devastating impact of the economic crisis of 1982 and subsequent efforts to establish stability and restructure the economy.[2] Changes in public sector spending were one way in which the impact of the crisis reached the community and household level. Austerity measures introduced in late 1982 cut current government spending by 12.9 percent in 1983 and by an additional 7.7

percent in 1984. After increasing in 1985 and 1986, expenditures declined by 18.4 percent in 1987.[3] At the same time, the proportion of debt service in current expenditures increased significantly during this period. Figure 6.1 indicates that while per capita current expenditures fell after 1982, they remained well above those of the 1970s. However, the share of programmable spending in total spending declined significantly during the decade, at an average rate of 5.2 percent each year between 1982 and 1990, decreasing by 8.9 and 15.7 percent in 1982 and 1983 alone.[4]

Social sector spending declined rapidly. Between 1983 and 1988, social expenditures, 85 percent of which was composed of spending on health and education, declined by one third, and by 40 percent on a per capita basis.[5] This trend in declining expenditures began to be reversed in 1989, corresponding to an improvement in the overall performance of the economy and new policy commitments of the Salinas administration. In many ministries, the initial impact of budget constraint fell heavily on investment allocations, as it was easier to postpone or cancel investment than it was to cut heavily into operating budgets. Indeed, public sector investment declined significantly, as indicated in Table 6.1. For ministries in which a high percentage of annual expenditures under normal conditions was tied to salaries and benefits, the impact of austerity on operating expenditures was more immediate, falling heavily on public sector employees. Overall, per capita public sector wages dropped by 46.1 percent between 1983 and 1988.[6]

Liberalization and privatization helped to diminish the number of officials on the public payroll and also saved the government expenditures on rent, energy, and other office expenses. These and other efforts probably improved efficiency in the public sector by decreasing the number of redundant workers, increasing performance demands, and eliminating obsolete practices. But the economic crisis also meant an increase in the social and physical infrastructure debt by putting off necessary investments and repairs and decreasing the ability of public officials to carry out their assigned functions. The economic crisis and the measures adopted to deal with it translated into greater numbers of teachers without chalk, doctors without medicines, tax administrators without computers and telephone lines, and roads in disrepair. The administrative capacity of the Mexican state to deliver health, education, and physical infrastructure declined during the 1980s. At the same time, however, innovative reforms were introduced to attempt to do more with less.

Delivering public health

In the mid-1980s, the public health sector in Mexico was composed of a complex of institutions that developed policy and delivered services. The overall system was highly centralized in Mexico City but at the same time fragmented among a variety of public institutions. The ministry of health was responsible for policy making, coordination, provision of services, and research. In addition, several large insurance schemes were centrally important parts of the public health care delivery system. The Mexican Institute of Social Security (IMSS) covered all non-government formal

Table 6.1 *Mexico public sector real*
investment, 1979–1989 (percent of GDP)

1979	7.50
1980	7.96
1981	9.18
1982	7.77
1983	5.33
1984	5.04
1985	4.65
1986	4.63
1987	4.29
1988	3.77
1989	3.26

Source: Lustig (1992: 100–101).

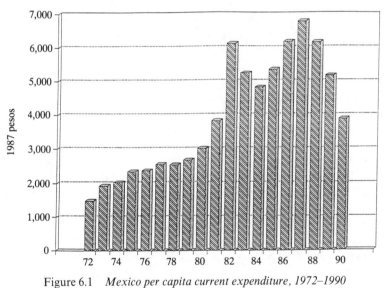

Figure 6.1   *Mexico per capita current expenditure, 1972–1990*
Source: World Bank, *World Tables* (1993).

sector workers and agricultural laborers during agricultural seasons; the Health and
Social Security Institute for State Employees (ISSSTE) provided health care for state
workers. Overall, the public health care system provided approximately 80 percent
of total health care coverage in 1987.

These public institutions, poorly funded during the best of times, were significantly
affected by the decline in revenues available for public health during the 1980s.
Health expenditures as a percentage of GDP fell from a high of 0.65 percent in 1977

to 0.41 percent in 1980, 0.32 in 1983, and recovered only to 0.39 percent by 1989. As a percentage of the total public sector budget, health accounted for 5.6 percent in 1979, and dropped to 1.53 percent in 1989.[7] Per capita expenditures for health dropped precipitously in 1980 to their lowest level since 1974; they dropped even farther between 1981 and 1983 and remained lower than expenditures from the 1970s throughout the decade of the 1980s (see Figure 6.2). Much of the impact of austerity was felt in terms of the salaries of medical professionals, which declined by one third between 1982 and 1989 (see Figure 6.3).

Infrastructure, particularly urban health facilities and especially hospitals, was cut back in terms of investment in new constructions, rehabilitation, and maintenance. The need for investment in this infrastructure was particularly severe after the 1985 earthquake that damaged or destroyed 13 hospitals, 4,387 hospital beds, 50 out-patient units, and 526 medical offices in Mexico City. More than 900 medical personnel and patients were killed.[8] Investment in medical technology also fell significantly behind during the decade. Data from 1982 to 1985 show a consistent decrease in the percentage of children vaccinated against common diseases, suggesting that the delivery of basic services were affected as well.[9] A constitutional amendment in 1983 made health protection a right of citizenship, increasing an already difficult situation by guaranteeing health care to a large number of people that the government could not in fact attend to because of extreme resource constraints.

Interestingly, however, while the sector overall declined in terms of budgets and personnel, the number of medical professionals in the system increased, suggesting that cutbacks in personnel were largely at the expense of administrative and maintenance personnel. Between 1980 and 1990, the number of medical personnel in the system increased 57.4 percent. The number of doctors increased by 44.5 percent, nurses by 24.4 percent, and paramedics by 64.9 percent.[10] The population/medical personnel ratio improved slightly during the 1980s (see Figure 6.4).

Not all parts of the system suffered equally under the impact of austerity. The two large social security schemes that provided health services to formal sector, agricultural, and state workers, IMSS and ISSSTE, showed declines in per capita availability of medical units, hospital beds, and doctors between 1983 and 1988, in part because of the expansion of the population covered under these schemes.[11] While the budget of the social security programs declined by 13.1 percent between 1982 and 1987, the insured population grew from 44.6 percent of the population to 52.1 percent.[12] As real wages fell, increasing numbers of the employed had recourse to these social insurance systems rather than pay for private care. The IMSS system was still struggling to cope with its expansion to cover much of the rural population in 1979. However, employer contributions increased during this period, partially replacing cuts in government expenditures.

Surprisingly, decreased resources in the health sector did not translate directly into increased health risks for large numbers of people, at least in the short run. National statistics indicate that infant mortality continued a four-decade trend of improvement.[13] Mortality rates for older children did not show a consistent tendency

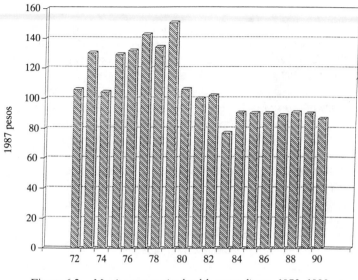

Figure 6.2　*Mexico per capita health expenditure, 1972–1990*
Source: calculated from data in IMF (1992a).

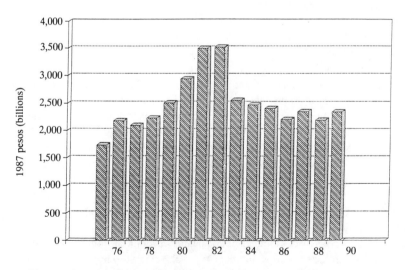

Figure 6.3　*Mexico government spending on medical salaries, 1975–1989*
Source: Instituto Nacional de Estadística Geografía e Informática

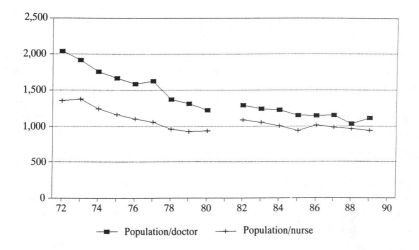

Figure 6.4 *Mexico population/medical personnel, 1972–1990*
Source: Salinas de Gortari (1990: Anexo).

to improve or worsen.[14] Life expectancy for the entire population increased by two years between 1980 and 1989, with women showing a stronger increase than men.[15] Nevertheless, there is evidence to suggest that declining real wages changed the health profile of the country. While infant mortality rates did not change, the causes of death shifted, with deaths related to malnutrition, anemia, and dysentery increasing as other causes decreased.[16] The proportion of children with low birth weight increased from 12 to 15 percent of all births.[17] The diet of most Mexicans was also affected as the consumption of meat and milk declined significantly from 1982 to 1986.[18]

Although it is not clear why there was not a more direct link between expenditures and impact, several possibilities exist. Efficiency in the delivery of health care services may have improved, or, as one official suggested, "Lots of bureaucracy can disappear without having any effect whatsoever – you get increased efficiency of those who are left."[19] This sentiment was echoed by another ministry official. "Overall, there wasn't much loss to the ministry. There were too many people to begin with and many were very unproductive. With fewer jobs and the loss of the power of the union leaders, people began to take their jobs more seriously."[20] Alternatively, the basic health profile of the population may have been strong enough to support a drop in expenditures without a corresponding rise in mortality. Another possibility is that the delivery of health care services may have become more focused on diseases and public health problems that had a large impact on indicators of mortality and morbidity. There was, in fact, an internal reallocation of budgetary support to primary health care, largely at the expense of middle-sized urban hospitals.[21]

In the context of economic crisis, some reform initiatives undertaken during the decade were focused on efforts to do more with less. The first step in this direction was taken in 1982 with a legal change that gave the ministry of health greater capacity to coordinate overall national health policy. Its mandate was expanded to cover the two major social security systems and the national family welfare system. A health coordinating group was set up to define a national health policy. This group was central in proposing a restructuring of the national health bureaucracy and delivery system. It promoted decentralization of the large and complex system and the devolution of some financial and managerial authority (and responsibility) from the ministry of health to the state level.[22] Decentralization of health care management and service provision, initiated in 1984, was slated for fourteen states, accounting for 45 percent of the total population. Full decentralization in twelve states was completed in 1986 and 63 percent of the health ministry budget was passed on to the state level.[23] The social insurance programs were also restructured by deconcentrating their activities from the national to the state level, but with centralized control remaining in Mexico City.[24] At the policy level, emphasis was placed on preventive medicine and on rural populations, those least likely to be covered by any existing social security scheme.

Paradoxically, an initiative to restructure the health care system by decentralizing to the state level probably made such services less accessible to poor populations because of the failure to deal with differentials of wealth among states.[25] Wealthier states simply had greater ability to provide health services for their populations than did poorer states and poorer states had greater need for primary and preventive health care for their large low-income populations. Within the decentralization initiative, delivery of effective health care was also dependent on the capacity of state level personnel to manage the system and the political priorities of governors.[26]

In addition, the social security institutes resisted greater control by the ministry of health and competed directly with the ministry for shares of the declining health care pie. State and municipal governments resisted taking on added responsibilities for health care, particularly within the context of shrinking budgetary allocations for health.[27] Thus, "although decentralization was meant to alleviate the ill effects of the crisis, the depleted federal budget could not cover the costs of readying state-level administrative infrastructures to handle the additional responsibilities."[28] Under the Salinas administration, the de la Madrid restructuring initiative died a quiet death, with seventeen states unaffected by any decentralization. The health care bureaucracy remained large, centralized, and inefficient.

Another initiative sought to circumvent this national health bureaucracy as much as possible. The Solidarity program encouraged community involvement in the provision of health care and public health infrastructure. Programs were initiated through IMSS and the ministry of health that emphasized quick response to community needs and flexibility in funding and approval mechanisms. According to program documents published in 1993, Solidarity activities resulted in the construction of 770 medical units, 1,480 health centers, and 140 hospitals. In the public health sector defined more generally, Solidarity activities involved the installation of potable water and sewage systems to benefit nearly 3 million people and the expansion of basic commodity and milk distribution centers.[29] The target groups for benefiting from Solidarity activities in health were children, women of childbearing age, and other vulnerable groups; the program focused on malnutrition as the principal cause of disease and death for priority groups. Solidarity's activities relied on local initiatives to provide labor and materials for construction, thus allowing government to focus its inputs on personnel and supplies. In 1992, 6.8 percent of Solidarity's budget was allocated to health (see Table 6.2).

Although the Solidarity program was potentially threatening to the ministry of health, because it circumvented traditional control and delivery systems and sought to alter access to health services, it was seen as a welcome innovation for some. One official, for example, stated,

I consider Solidarity to be a very interesting and very important effort to speed up the provision of government services. There is so much rigidity, so much bureaucracy, and so much slowness in established systems that this new effort is necessary and extremely important. It is breaking ministerial boundaries, jumping across jurisdictions, and it is working, primarily because it has the president's backing.[30]

The crisis helped open possibilities for more direct service provision and community involvement in health care delivery. Nevertheless, allocations were spread widely across the country with little concern for follow-up. In particular, the development of health infrastructure begged the longer-term issue of staffing, provisioning, and maintenance.

In both cases of reform initiatives, innovation in public health in Mexico attempted to deal with the constraints imposed by overcentralization and lack of managerial and organizational capacity. In this regard, the problem was less one of financial resources than one of effective management and administration of a large, complex, and centralized system. Decentralization focused on the existing system and attempted to define policies and structures for making it work better. In the end, it failed to achieve these goals, and the old system remained intact, underfunded and poorly administered. The Solidarity initiative was an effort to bypass the existing system by providing alternative ways of increasing health care infrastructure and services in the country. Although apparently successful in providing resources to many communities, it did not adequately address the central issues of poor ministerial performance. The problems of delivering effective health care to large numbers of Mexicans, many of them poor and ill-educated, remained major challenges to the government, even in the context of economic recovery.

Organizing public education

The public education system that developed in Mexico from early in the twentieth century was similar to the health care system in that it was vast and highly centralized. By 1980, the ministry of education serviced almost 21 million students,

Table 6.2 *Solidarity allocations: percentage of total budget, 1989–1992*

	1989	1990	1991[a]	1992[b]
Health	6.5	5.8	5.7	6.8
Education (construction and rehabilitation of facilities)	13.0	13.8	13.8	7.6
Roads	17.4	11.2	15.2	14.4
Social service scholarships	3.0	3.1	2.7	2.5
Potable water/drainage	9.8	10.8	9.5	12.0
Urban services	9.1	10.4	9.7	7.0
Electrification	5.5	5.4	4.7	4.8
Productivity enhancement (rural credit and technical assistance)	—	12.0	9.3	10.3
Other	35.7	27.5	29.4	34.6

[a] Preliminary.
[b] Programmed.
Source: calculated from data in Solidaridad (1992).

including 14.7 million primary school students, 3.0 million secondary school students, and 2.3 million students enrolled in higher education.[31] In that year, education expenditures accounted for 26.6 percent of current government expenditures.[32] By 1989, there were 25 million students enrolled in the national system, accounting for 11.8 percent of current government expenditures. Throughout this period, Mexican education policy was determined, as it had traditionally been, from Mexico City. Norms for curriculum, schedules, parent–teacher interaction, and student governance were set in central ministry headquarters for the vast majority of schools; textbooks were vetted at the national level and distributed throughout the country for a uniform curriculum.[33] According to one educational official, "Down to the most remote village, if a new blackboard is needed, it has to be authorized by Mexico City."[34] It was a system that was widely recognized to be both rigid and ineffective.

Per capita education expenditures rose rapidly in the 1970s to a peak in 1982. With the bursting of the petroleum bubble, expenditures decreased rapidly in 1983 and continued to be low throughout the rest of the decade (see Figure 6.5). Figure 6.6 indicates that intrasector allocations between primary, secondary, and higher education remained relatively constant throughout the crisis years of the 1980s. Within the sector on a per student basis, Figure 6.7 suggests that allocations to secondary and tertiary education were slightly more volatile on an annual basis than were allocations to primary education from 1983 to 1989. This may represent some effort on the part of the government to make modest reallocations to basic education at the expense of secondary and higher education. At best, however, such reallocations were modest.

Salaries of teachers and administrators were the principal way in which the education budget was reduced; salaries and other forms of remuneration accounted for about 90 percent of the budget. Improved student/teacher ratios suggest the

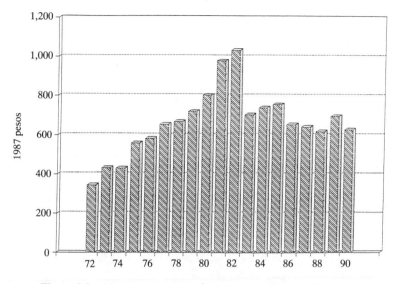

Figure 6.5   *Mexico per capita education expenditure, 1972–1990*
Source: calculated from data in IMF (1992a).

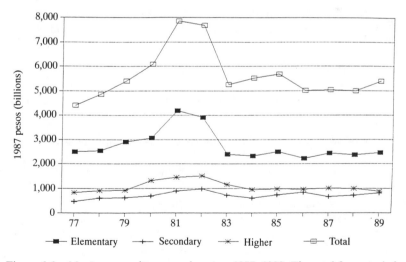

Figure 6.6   *Mexico expenditure on education, 1977–1989. The total figure includes*
adult education, indigenous education, didactic materials development, and
administration.
Source: Salinas de Gortari (1990: Anexo).

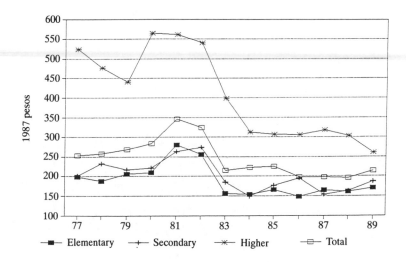

Figure 6.7   *Mexico per student expenditure on education, 1977–1989. The total figure includes adult education, indigenous education, didactic materials development and administration.*

Source: Salinas de Gortari (1990: Anexo).

degree to which cutbacks affected salaries. In 1980, there were 28.5 students per teacher in the educational system, compared with 22.8 students per teacher in 1990.[35] As expenditures dropped and numbers of personnel increased, the cost of austerity fell most heavily on salaries, administration, materials, and other recurrent expenditures.

This had a real impact on the quality of education because many teachers went out and got second jobs because their salaries did not pay enough to cover their needs. At the same time ... demand for education actually grew strongly as many people who had their children in private schools shifted them to public schools because of the crisis.[36]

Reform of public education became a priority of the government after 1988 more out of concern for its manageability than for its impact on the public budget, however. Mexican administrations had long despaired of reforming the system to bring better quality education to students. The greatest constraint, they believed, was the national union of teachers that, with close to a million members, was reputed to be the largest and strongest union in Latin America.[37] The teachers' union had been mobilized and active during the entire course of the 1980s. Prior efforts to decentralize the system, the most recent one initiated in 1978, had failed largely because of the opposition of this union.[38] Shying away from the politically charged restructuring implicit in decentralization, the de la Madrid administration attempted to deconcentrate the national ministry to the state level in 1983. The issue of decentralization was back on the government's agenda in 1989, however.

In the first years of the Salinas administration, the ministry of education worked to reassert control over personnel assignments, which had been taken over by the unions at the state level under the prior administration. The first initiative, then, was to reassert ministry control by appointing national administrators to the state level to take over personnel and other administrative responsibilities from the political control of governors and union leaders. Then, Salinas appointed one of his close advisors, the minister of planning and budgeting, to head the ministry of education in January 1992. This move sent a message to the political establishment that the modernizers were determined to expand their reformist efforts to the educational system.

Analysis of the educational system by the team that arrived in January indicated that the system suffered from being overly bureaucratized, politicized, and centralized; that the content of education was not consistent with the new market-oriented and globally competitive Mexico envisioned by the modernizers; and that the teaching profession was poorly developed, remunerated, trained, and respected. Decentralization to state level ministries of education was one effort to respond to this set of problems.

This education reform was announced with little advance notice. Although there were many in the national ministry and the government who thought it important to go slow and build support for decentralization, Minister Ernesto Zedillo and the team he brought with him to the ministry believed that "blitzkrieg" tactics would take both the governors and the union by surprise and limit the extent to which they could mobilize opposition to the change. At least in the short term, they appeared to have been correct in this assessment. In May of 1992, a national agreement on modernizing basic education set the framework for decentralizing the management of education to state level ministries. The ministry of education would continue to set norms and monitor educational performance; the state ministries, however, would take on the responsibility of actually delivering educational services and overseeing staff, including negotiating with the teachers' union.

The agreement between the government, the state governors, and the union ensured that the union would continue to have a national presence. However, with powers of appointment, assignment, and salary determination decentralized to the state level, the focus of union concern and activity would naturally follow, decentralizing the union de facto and limiting its capacity to stymie change at the national level. The budget for education was expanded to ensure increases in teacher salaries and training opportunities as sweeteners for the package. At the state level, decentralization implied that state governors would roughly double the budgetary and personnel responsibilities they had, an increase that many were reluctant to accept. These added responsibilities, in addition to becoming the target of the activities of the teachers' union, led to a cool reception to the initiative. The governors' objections, however, had little impact on the initiative to move ahead, other than to elicit federal assurances of financial and administrative support to help them manage the transition.

To avoid some of the problems encountered in the decentralization of health care, the poorest states were assured that special grants for quality education would be forthcoming as a way of equalizing educational opportunities across states. For politically ambitious governors, the educational reform was presented as an opportunity for them to demonstrate commitment to the Salinas modernization package and to highlight their own political and administrative skills.

The initiative to decentralize education was spurred by the modernizers in the Salinas team, but they were assisted by the widespread sense that the educational system was failing the country. Private universities had burgeoned since the mid-1970s as parents with means sought alternatives to the state-supported university system for their children. Increasing numbers of elite families were electing to send their children to universities and even private secondary schools in the United States or elsewhere. People of more modest means were increasingly dismayed that secondary and university educations from the national school system were not leading to employment for graduates. In addition, reforms in other sectors, such as the ejido, privatization, and trade, encouraged many to believe that change was possible, even in a sector that had experienced repeated failures in this regard. Moreover, the dynamic that surrounded other reform initiatives seemed to affect the resistance of the teachers' union to decentralization. According to one educational reformer, "Even some in the union are supporting us in the decentralization effort because it is clear that the ship is leaving the dock and they realize they need to be on it if they are to remain credible to the government and their members."[39]

Another effort to modernize the educational system was less well received. A major new initiative to affect the content of education was introduced in 1992 through the revision of nationally distributed textbooks. These textbooks had last been revised in the early 1970s and reflected the strongly statist and third world perspective of the administration of Luís Echeverría. The Salinas modernizers were convinced that if the country were to have a future as a newly industrialized country in an expanding global economy, and if the new market-oriented policies were to be successful, more positive attitudes about foreign capital, multinational corporations, the industrialized nations of the north, and less interventionist states had to be inculcated. Existing textbooks erred on all these accounts.

[The textbooks refer to] the world hunger caused by the multinational companies, the evils of foreign investment, the great revolutionary traditions of China, Cuba, and Chile, and the exploitation caused by capitalists and the capitalist systems of the world. You can imagine the problems this creates as we are now trying to encourage foreign investment and move toward a market economy. How confused the students must be! And it is clear that they are not being effectively prepared to play a role in the new economic system that is emerging.[40]

A study team was organized within the ministry of education and work began on an urgent schedule to rewrite the textbooks.

In fact, such urgency and such commitment surrounded the initiative that consultation over the content of the textbooks was significantly truncated. As a result, when the textbooks were introduced in 1992, public response was strongly negative. The modernizers in the ministry of education were accused of improperly presenting the country's history and undermining national culture and sentiment. In particular, reporting of the dictatorship of Profirio Díaz and the protest movement of 1968 was criticized as biased and the history of the Salinas administration was presented in highly favorable terms. Moreover, the lucrative contracts to write and publish the textbooks were awarded with notable lack of transparency. Introduction of a second set of textbooks in 1993 was similarly mishandled.[41] The blitzkrieg tactics, which had worked well in the decentralization initiative, did not have such a positive outcome in the case of the textbooks. In the first case, there was a significant consensus already developed that something needed to be done to improve the way the educational system was organized; in the second case, a consensus in favor of change did not exist nor had it been promoted by the reformers.

In yet another initiative, the Salinas administration attempted to deal with infrastructure deficit in education outside the education ministry. As with the health sector, Solidarity projects added significantly to efforts to expand the availability of infrastructure. Solidarity documents indicate the construction of 16,500 classrooms by 1992 and the supply of equipment to 20,000 schools.[42] In 1992, 7.6 percent of Solidarity's budget was earmarked for education (see Table 6.2). The construction and rehabilitation of large numbers of school buildings directly reduced the social infrastructure deficit that escalated in the 1980s. The implications of Solidarity's activities remained uncertain, however. The newly responsible state ministries of education would differ in their capacities to staff, supply, and maintain the buildings. In addition, parents had been active participants in the Solidarity building projects; the quality of education provided would undoubtedly be enhanced if parents were effective in holding teachers, supervisors, and ministry officials accountable for it.

Providing physical infrastructure

In Mexico, the ministry of communication and transportation was responsible for road building, maintenance, and modernization. As with health and education, government expenditures on the most basic physical infrastructure also was cut back during the 1980s. As with the other sectors also, the boom years of the early 1980s were ones in which public sector spending on roads increased rapidly; they fell precipitously after 1983 (see Figure 6.8). In 1989, expenditures on road construction were one fifth of what they had been in 1982, road maintenance was half of the 1982 amount, although road modernization funding increased by almost a third over the earlier amount. These figures begin to suggest the extent to which austerity cut into the ability of government to provide for the infrastructure necessary to promote economic development in the country.

The Salinas administration attempted two reforms directed toward increasing the efficiency of the country's beleaguered road system. They were aimed at the extremes of the road infrastructure – superhighways connecting large cities and towns, and rural roads. The first initiative built on an innovation introduced under the de la

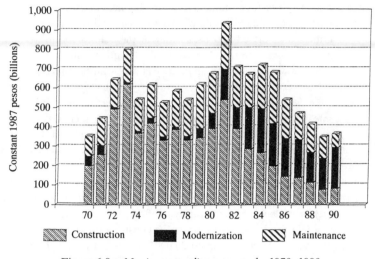

Figure 6.8   *Mexico expenditure on roads, 1970–1990*
Source: Salinas de Gortari (1990: Anexo).

Madrid administration to sub-contract road building and maintenance to the private sector, "concession highways." This initiative focused on the major highways that would be contracted out to private sector firms to build, manage, and maintain in return for the right to collect tolls until investments and profits of a specified amount were recouped. The effort was expanded under the Salinas administration to include more major highways and consciously borrowed from the experiences – both positive and negative – of other countries, particularly Spain, for its design. Solidarity responded to the other end of the spectrum with a large effort to fund the expansion and repair of rural roads. Over 14 percent of its budget in 1992 was channeled toward road building and maintenance projects, providing input into infrastructure and also employment opportunities to meet the short-term costs of adjustment (see Table 6.2). According to program documents, 18,000 kilometers of roads were constructed or rehabilitated in 1989 and 1990.[43] The low-income rural population was the target of the largest part of these efforts to develop local infrastructure and to provide jobs. In this case, the ministry of communication and transportation provided technical assistance, but organization and funding responsibilities passed to Solidarity. In the initiative to add to the country's infrastructure for economic growth – the major highways – the ministry was involved but the initiative itself was undertaken as a way of compensating for the failure of the public sector to meet national needs for building, managing, and maintaining an effective infrastructure of highways.

The 1980s and early 1990s in Mexico witnessed a number of efforts to improve the capacity of the public sector to deliver basic services to the population. In particular, reorganizing the structure of the ministries of education and health and contracting out highway services were innovations directed at improving both efficiency and effectiveness. The task of reforming public sector ministries – many of which had never functioned well – was only begun, however, and it was debatable if the reforms introduced had any measurable impact on the administrative capacity of the state. The most innovative program to address social and physical infrastructure needs in the country, Solidarity, effectively bypassed traditional ministries to mobilize local governments and communities to respond to the crisis of service provision. Their longer-term impact, however, would be determined by the extent to which the ministries at state or national level could respond with trained and effective teachers, effective routine administration, concern for the utility of the services being delivered, and attention to recurrent costs for operations and maintenance.

ADMINISTERING THE PUBLIC GOOD IN KENYA

Kenya's ability to provide basic government services also experienced considerable change during the 1980s and 1990s. Its service delivery systems were modeled on the highly centralized colonial "law and order" administration. As we have seen, policy formulation and management were cabinet and central ministry functions; for long periods, the provincial administration played an important role in carrying out central directives in the regions. Under Moi, the district level of public administration became more important in carrying out central government activities at local levels. Local government was never strong after independence, but its capacities and autonomy declined significantly under the Moi administration.[44]

The provision of public services was made more responsive to local needs than this centralized system suggests, however, through the institution of harambee. Under this system, local communities organized and contributed to the creation of infrastructure for schools, health centers, public sanitation facilities, and roads that the government was then asked to staff and operate. In conjunction with harambee, at least through the early 1980s, the electoral system helped ensure that many local communities received timely government assistance because MPs were under electoral pressure to "deliver the goods."

During the 1980s, Kenya did not experience the deep budgetary cuts that affected public spending in Mexico. In fact, Figure 6.9 indicates that per capita current expenditures grew fairly consistently from the early 1970s through the late 1980s, despite considerable fluctuations in government revenues. Current expenditures as a proportion of GDP grew from approximately 15 percent in the early 1970s to 23 percent in the late 1980s. A considerable amount of this increase in expenditure corresponds to a dramatic growth in the number of officials in Kenya's public sector over the course of the 1970s and 1980s. Table 6.3 indicates that the number of central government employees more than tripled from some 57,000 in 1963 to 191,000 in 1982 and then continued to increase to 274,000 in 1991. While the public sector accounted for 34.2 percent of total wage employment in 1963, it accounted for

Table 6.3 *Kenyan public sector employment (thousands)*

	1963	1982	1991
Central government[a]	57.0	191.2	273.7
Parastatals and majority control by public sector	46.7	128.6	117.3
Local government authorities	60.2	41.3	52.0

[a] In post.

Source: Cohen (1993: 4), based on official government statistics.

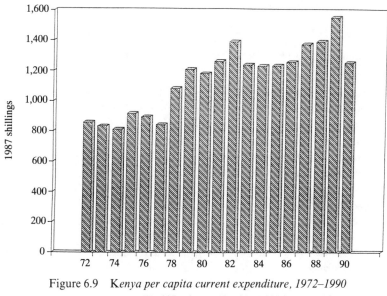

Figure 6.9 *Kenya per capita current expenditure, 1972–1990*
Source: World Bank, *World Tables* (1993).

49.5 percent in 1990.[45] Public sector employment expanded most rapidly in the 1970s, when the annual average growth rate was 8.1 percent; in the 1980s, growth was slower at 6.7 percent, but still considerably above the increase in the population.[46] Moreover, the 1980s expansion added significantly more people to the public payroll because the rate of expansion was building on an ever-increasing base.

A combination of increased numbers of public sector employees and decreased government revenues contributed to budget deficits and greater portions of public expenditures allocated to recurrent expenses, primarily wages, salaries, and operating costs. In 1980, 47.6 percent of the recurrent budget was allocated to wages and salaries; in 1987, 68.5 percent was consumed as wages and salaries.[47] Operating and maintenance budgets suffered corresponding declines. Moreover, salary increases over the decade of the 1980s were generally less than increases in living costs.[48]

Although government budgets continued to expand during the 1980s, this did not necessarily translate into more effective public service provision. According to Sessional Paper No. 1 of 1986, "With salaries absorbing so much of expenditure, there is not adequate provision for complementary resources, such as transport, typewriters, even paper and pencils, that are required to make these officers productive ... Eventually, many services may cease to be offered at all, while officers continue to draw salaries."[49] This helps account for the fact that even though government expenditures increased, complaints mounted about the poor quality of services being delivered to the population. Many were concerned about the failure to use existing human resources effectively by deploying them where their talents were most needed. "The problem is not necessarily the lack of skilled people in government, but of putting them in responsible positions and letting them do what they were trained to do," suggested one analyst.[50]

Several other factors are relevant to exploring the changes in the state's ability to provide for public welfare in the 1980s and 1990s. As indicated in previous chapters, the regional basis of political support for Presidents Kenyatta and Moi differed significantly. When he assumed the presidency, Moi sought to redistribute development resources away from the Kikuyu heartland of the country to other areas. While total expenditures actually increased, they were reallocated regionally so that some provinces were winners while others lost. Corruption, widely believed to have grown to egregious proportions in the latter years of the 1980s and into the 1990s, also diverted resources away from administering the public good.[51] Changes in the capacity to deliver public goods were reflected in the delivery of health, education, and physical infrastructure services, at the same time that government recognized its continuing responsibilities to provide such services.[52]

Delivering public health

Kenya's public health system was traditionally based in the country's forty-one districts, each of which was assigned a chief medical officer and a health management team.[53] District and sub-district hospitals were complemented by more localized health centers that offered primary care services and dispensaries that provided a more limited range of services. Provincial general hospitals offered services to several districts while in Nairobi, the Kenyatta National Hospital provided the highest level of care and was the referral hospital for the entire country. It also generally accounted for about a third of the health budget.

In the early 1990s, eighty-eight hospitals run by the government composed 70 percent of hospital beds; 76 percent of the health centers and dispensaries were government run.[54] From 1963 to 1989, the government provided free medical care in all its facilities, although small fees were assessed for some services. The Kenya National Hospital Insurance Fund (NHIF) financed health care for its 1 million members, but did not address the needs of the vast majority of the population working in the informal sector or in the formal sector at low wages.[55] Moreover, only about half of the rural population had access to health facilities.[56] Despite these deficiencies, indicators of health in Kenya showed a long-term improvement that continued into the 1980s.[57] In 1979, infant mortality was 104 per 1,000 live births; in 1987, it had dropped to 84 per 1,000.[58] Life expectancy increased from fifty-four years to fifty-eight years in the same period.[59] Rates of immunization showed regular improvement, as did the control of a number of endemic diseases.

During the 1980s, health budgets declined relative to other sectors from over 10 percent of current government expenditures in 1980 to less than 6 percent in 1989. The recurrent budget declined by 25 percent in this period.[60] On a per capita basis, 120 shillings was spent on health care in 1980 but less than 85 (constant) shillings in 1989 (see Figure 6.10). Curative care accounted for more than 70 percent of the total ministry of health budget in 1990, with preventive medicine accounting for 3.5 percent of the budget.[61] Throughout the system, complaints increased about poor service delivery, and particularly about the shortage of drugs.

As the economic situation became graver in the early 1990s, the ministry of health suffered cutbacks. For ministry officials, the situation seemed bleak.

We in the ministry of health keep cutting back. Now we are only paying salaries. We have no money for petrol and vehicles, the donors take care of all that. There is no medicine, other than that supplied by donors. We have no development budget and the only projects that are going are those that are one hundred percent funded by donors.[62]

At the same time, however, the sector increased the number of professional personnel at a rate slightly higher than that rate of population growth. In 1978, there was one doctor for every 10,136 Kenyans and one nurse for every 1,077 Kenyans; in 1984, there was one doctor for every 9,970 people and one nurse for every 950 people.[63]

During the late 1980s, the World Bank, other international agencies, and some policy makers began to press for innovations in the health care system that would respond to some of its budget and service delivery problems. As a result of this pressure, the government introduced user fees in December of 1989 at the provincial, district, and health center level. Services provided at the dispensary level were to remain free of charge. While there was not a strong tradition of cost sharing in social service delivery in Kenya, the NHIF did provide an example of a contributory scheme for health care.[64] In addition, the problems of the sector and the pressure from the international agencies engendered greater tolerance for some innovation in the existing system.

The design of the cost-sharing plan was strongly influenced by the World Bank in consultation with USAID, which in turn was actively engaged in discussion with the ministry of health. Discussion of user fees between the international agencies and the ministry were carried on over the course of several months, during which a number of plans were discussed. Eventually, a plan was agreed to and a secret cabinet paper prepared by the international agencies and top officials in the ministry. The cabinet, with strong support from the minister of health, approved the plan in August 1989, effectively adopting a World Bank proposal, but with some downward adjustments

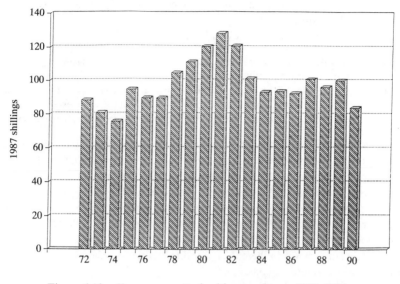

Figure 6.10   *Kenya per capita health expenditure, 1972–1990*
Source: IMF (1992a).

in user fees.[65] According to the plan, standard inpatient and outpatient fees would be assessed and fees for specific services and tests would also derive from a standard schedule. Three-fourths of user fee revenue would be made available to the collecting unit for maintenance, supplies, and upgrading services; the other fourth would go to the district level for investment in preventive health and for distribution to dispensaries, which had no independent source of income. Donor funding was made available for the ministry of health to encourage it to move away from curative toward preventive medicine and away from personnel to non-wage expenditures.

This general plan for reform was passed on to the ministry of health under the assumption that ministry officials would define the process for its administration and develop procedures for fee waivers for low-income clients.[66] In fact, the date set for introduction of the plan gave ministry officials little time to set procedures for fee collection and a system of waivers for indigent patients. Those responsible for its implementation professed no knowledge of the plan until it was officially announced.[67] Moreover, little public notice was given of its initiation. It is not surprising, then, that the introduction of the scheme met with widespread protest and administrative confusion. In practice, it was difficult for local health care professionals and administrators to assess ability to pay; the costs and administrative infrastructure for collecting the fee had not been thought through. In the health centers and hospitals, administrative systems were unclear and enrollment and waiver forms and monitoring procedures were not in place. The rapid introduction of user fees in the health sector had an immediate impact of decreasing outpatient use of hospitals, a trend that was gradually reversed over several months of operation.[68]

Additional problems plagued the user fee initiative. *The Daily Nation* reported that

> General hospitals across the country once notorious for over-crowding now find themselves in the unfamilar position of being deserted. It is not the illnesses which have mysteriously disappeared, it is the assumption that every sick person can afford ksh 20 which was way off the mark. The introduction of cost sharing therefore except in terminal cases, made the common illnesses a luxury. People simply choose not to seek treatment.[69]

Stories and editorials circulated that patients were being held involuntarily in hospitals for non-payment of fees. Analysts and citizens noted that the fee system constrained the ability of the poor, but not the rich, to gain access to health care.[70] Revenues collected amounted to less than the anticipated 5 percent of the ministry's recurrent budget; evidence suggested that most fees remained uncollected because of bureaucratic resistance to the plan. Richer districts were able to collect more revenue and, because it was earmarked for the districts and the facilities where they were collected, health services in these areas benefited more from the user fee experiment than did those in poorer regions.

Protests continued. The president announced a reduction of fees in January 1990 and by August, nine months after their introduction, user fees for outpatient services were discontinued by order of the president, although other fees remained in place. Some analysts argued that riots in July in urban areas heightened the speed with which the unpopular user fees were withdrawn.[71] Unpopularity aside, the innovation was also stymied by the inability of the country's health administration to manage it.

Organizing public education

The budget for educational services in Kenya fared much better than did that for health. Figure 6.11 shows a significant increase in government expenditures on education from the early 1970s. They grew by about 60 percent between 1980 and 1989. Even when corrected for population growth, the country's expenditures on education showed long-term growth (see Figure 6.12). On a per capita basis, the government spent 300 shillings for every Kenyan in 1980 and over 360 (constant) shillings in 1989.[72]

Growth of expenditures was reflected in a larger infrastructure of schools and teachers. The number of primary schools grew almost 40 percent between 1980 and 1988, the number of primary school teachers increased by 52 percent, and the number of primary school students by 30 percent during this period.[73] At the primary school level, the proportion of untrained teachers in the total remained at about 30 percent, while at the secondary level fully 51 percent of teachers were untrained in 1980 and only 39 percent were in this category in 1989.[74] By the end of the 1980s, Kenya was moving toward accomplishing the goal of universal

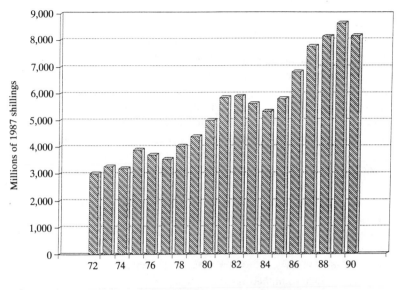

Figure 6.11   K*enya education expenditure, 1972–1990*
Source: IMF (1992a).

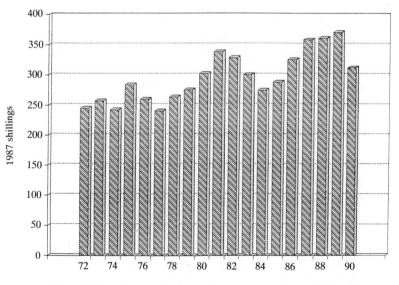

Figure 6.12   *Kenya per capita education expenditure, 1972–1990*
Source: IMF (1992a).

primary education and was also close to achieving parity in the education of boys and girls.[75]

Behind the figures indicating expanded allocations for education are some disturbing trends in the delivery of educational services in the country, however. In 1982, Kenya had a primary school enrollment of 4.1 million students; by 1990, the figure was 5.4 million, and yet a smaller proportion of eligible children was entering school in 1990 than in 1980.[76] As primary enrollments increased, it became more and more difficult to reach groups of unenrolled children – those whose lifestyles were nomadic or semi-nomadic, for example, or street children in large urban areas. Secondary school enrollments continued to lag and dropout rates at all levels were high. Allocation of education's recurrent budget to primary education declined from 64 percent in 1980 to 57 percent in 1990; the proportion expended on higher education expanded from 11 percent to 20 percent of the recurrent budget and secondary education went from 12 percent to 15 percent in that period.[77]

Teacher salaries remained relatively constant and teacher/student ratios declined significantly. The Teachers Service Commission registered 164,000 teachers in 1986; by 1991, there were 219,000 teachers in the system.[78] In this year, personnel costs in the ministry of education were consuming over 81 percent of its budget, and teachers were demanding increases in their salaries.[79] In addition, serious problems existed in the content and quality of education being provided. In 1990, one estimate was that, after discounting expenditures for salaries, emoluments, and infrastructure development, per capita student expenditure for teaching materials was less than two shillings per student.[80]

Not surprisingly, education reform was an important political issue under the Moi government. The introduction of a new system, labeled the 8–4–4, replaced a prior 7–4–2–3 division of primary, secondary, and higher education years. The 7–4–2–3 system offered 7 years of primary education, 4 years of secondary (O levels), 2 years of specialized secondary (A levels), and 3 years of university education. The new system provided 8 years of primary education, 4 years of secondary education, and 4 years of higher education.

Critics of the old system, including those in government, charged that it was too academic and that it failed to prepare students for employment opportunities or to give them proper attitudes about agricultural or self-employment activities. A new system, they argued, was needed to offer Kenyans a more vocationally oriented curriculum. Such a curriculum was expected to encourage the development of skills with greater relevance to the job market and the country's development. The new system was launched abruptly by presidential directive in January 1985. Changes in the curriculum, intended to make education a response to the country's growing employment problem, emphasized job-related and self-employment skills. With the introduction of the new curriculum, students would be expected to study such subjects as home science, woodwork, metalwork, power mechanics, drawing and design, and agricultural science.

Whatever the merits of the 8–4–4 system – and it generated considerable debate – its introduction was plagued by implementation problems. First, vocational education, because of its need for equipment and materials, was more expensive than traditional education. Although educational expenditures were growing over this period, they did not expand uniformly across levels of education and they were destined primarily for salaries rather than equipment and materials. Moreover, the 8–4–4 system envisioned a very broad curriculum, requiring students to master a large number of topics, with teachers often improperly prepared to teach such a range of subjects. In a survey carried out in 1990 among a sample of twenty-three secondary schools in three districts, only 20 percent of 152 teacher/respondents had been trained in the new curriculum.[81] In addition, teachers complained that they were far short of basic requirements for laboratories, equipment, and library materials for the curriculum. A significant number of schools were unable to offer the full range of subjects expected under the new curriculum, despite the fact that students would be tested in them.[82] Both teachers and students reported being overworked by the new curriculum. Perhaps most important, the new curriculum, at least in its initial years, did not seem to be changing attitudes about the desirability of different kinds of employment. Overwhelmingly, secondary students surveyed in 1990 continued to prefer white-collar jobs to vocational and agricultural ones.[83]

Because the new system offered one year less of pre-university preparation than the 7–4–2–3 system, and because of the need to allow university entry to students from both systems during the first year, introduction of the new system had a significant impact on the university system. Intake into the university system in 1987 expanded from the previous year's 3,550 to 8,774. Additional strain was put on the system in 1990, when intake expanded from 7,349 students to 20,174. Moreover, in the more difficult economic conditions of the late 1980s and early 1990s, pressure to increase the number of entrants to universities increased, no matter what the cost in terms of the quality of education received. The long-term policy of providing government employment to university graduates made such pressure inevitable.[84] In addition, the Moi government sought to expand the number of places available to students who had not traditionally benefited from the better educational resources available in the central regions of the country. These factors meant expanding expenditures on higher education.[85]

The introduction of user fees also figured in the Kenya education reforms. Fees for primary education were significantly raised after 1989; boarding school fees for secondary students rose significantly; and universities introduced a modest reduction in terms of the stipends they provided to students. In another effort to deal with the rapidly deteriorating financial and political situation at the national universities, a quasi-governmental commission on higher education was set up to recommend actions to make the university system more self-sustaining and more responsive to the needs of the country. However, despite increasing expenditures, the condition of education in Kenya in the early 1990s remained difficult at best. The reforms of the system actually added to the administrative burden of government, yet insufficient resources were directed toward increasing the sector's capacity to manage it.

Providing physical infrastructure

The most dramatic changes in public expenditures were in the development of physical infrastructure. Figure 6.13 indicates the impact of the coffee boom on the rapid growth of expenditures between 1977 and 1980. After 1982, however, there was a significant six year decline in expenditures on roads. As a result, 1988 expenditures were 58 percent of what they had been in 1980. Spending on roads fell from 10.8 percent of current government expenditures in 1980 to 3.0 percent in 1989.[86] Moreover, with limited funding, there was a significant change in the allocation of funds. Table 6.4 indicates that the percentage of the budget allocated to recurrent expenditures decreased while the percentage expended on new roads grew steadily, reflecting the expansion of physical infrastructure to regions that had not received much attention during the Kenyatta period.[87]

Efforts to deal with the costs of infrastructure and the inherent problem of recurrent costs for maintenance were not absent, however. In 1984, the government initiated a toll system for major highways and gradually expanded it to some fifteen major roads in the country. The tolls were to be allocated directly to maintenance. While the amounts collected did not begin to cover the needs, ministry of finance analysts believed that the introduction of user fees on highways was a major step in the right direction for making the road network more self-sustaining. Similarly, discussion of a gasoline tax had come on to the government's agenda in the 1990s for much the same reason.

The capacity to administer the public good in Kenya declined during the 1980s and 1990s. The number of public sector personnel grew but their salaries declined. The health sector suffered significant reductions in funding and efforts to reform the sector were truncated. Reforms introduced were targeted primarily at resolving the financial constraints on the ministry of health but were not efforts to deal directly with management and organizational constraints. In education, a decade of expansion was coupled with efforts to redefine the content of education. Again, however, the management and organizational needs of the ministry of education were not a direct focus of concern. Road infrastructure in Kenya was hard hit by budgetary constraint; new expenditures went primarily for new roads rather than for the maintenance of the existing road network. While such investments were important in expanding the limited road infrastructure in the country and in bringing greater equity to its distribution, maintenance of existing infrastructure suffered.

In Kenya, political crisis and economic decline robbed many public servants of the incentive to perform effectively. In addition, although difficult to document, many institutional structures were acknowledged to have become dysfunctional as massive corruption and abuse of authority percolated into virtually every interaction. According to many public officials, decision making became more focused on short-term personal advantage as economic and political insecurity increased. And, as in the case of health and education, reforms whose purpose was to improve efficiency and effectiveness fell victim to the inability to meet their implementation requirements.

Table 6.4 *Kenya: development and recurrent expenditure on roads, 1987–1992 (percent of total)*

	1987/1988	1988/1989	1989/1990	1990/1991	1991/1992
Development	65.5	73.8	79.9	78.6	80.2
Recurrent	34.5	26.2	20.1	21.4	19.8

Source: Republic of Kenya (1990, 1991b).

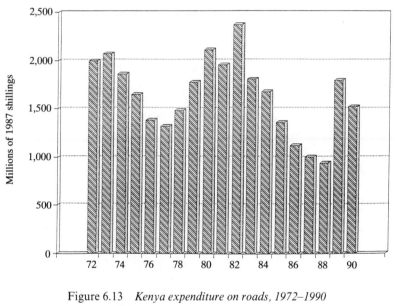

Figure 6.13   *Kenya expenditure on roads, 1972–1990*
Source: IMF (1992a).

CONCLUSION

The ability to carry out basic tasks of government requires well-trained individuals, organizational structures that encourage and reward efficiency and effectiveness, and decision-making perspectives that are medium and long term. In Mexico and Kenya, economic and political crises constrained the ability to fund and deliver public sector services in health, education, and physical infrastructure. In both cases, efforts to redefine delivery systems for these services were introduced, but none were able to compensate for the inability of poorly organized, poorly funded, and poorly motivated ministries to carry out their mandates effectively and efficiently. The administrative capacity of these governments to deliver basic social and physical

infrastructure continued to require sustained attention to human resource development, organizational structures and processes, and concern for the long-term goals
of the countries. There were important innovations in these sectors during the
decade; some led to useful results. Nevertheless, the ability to recreate government to
be more responsive, efficient, and effective continued to elude reformers in both
countries.

7

Responding to society

Capable states must be responsive to citizen needs and demands. They must provide channels for interests to be represented in decision making and in monitoring the behavior of public officials. They must allow for societal participation in the allocation of public resources and the mediation of economic and political conflict. This political capacity differs from institutional capacity in that it deals not with the authoritativeness of broad rules of the game or with their normative content, but with the everyday interactions between citizens and public officials and the ability of civic society to demand access to the state, its officials, and its decision-making processes.

Capable states do not necessarily require democracy, but regimes must be able to receive, process, and satisfy at least some citizen demands for responsiveness, representation, and participation or they will either be short-lived or need to expend considerable resources on coercive activities to remain in power. In fact, states have an inherent interest in acquiring and maintaining political capacity because it is central to their security concerns. In practice, most governments treat the allocation of public resources at least in part as a way of maintaining the social peace among diverse interests in society and the stability and coherence of coalitions supporting the regime or the administration in power.[1]

Beyond a minimal level necessary to maintain public order and safety, however, states may have no inherent interest in responding to societal needs, providing for the representation of interests, or encouraging societal participation in policy or allocative decision making. While particular regimes, political elites, or parties may have commitments to these goals, for many countries, the degree of responsiveness, concern for representation of interests, and willingness to permit participation is determined by the ability of civic society to demand to share political space with the state. Thus, analysis of the political capacity of states shifts the principal focus of inquiry away from the state, the concern of the previous three chapters, to the interaction of state and society, where issues of governance are contested on a daily basis.

The political crises that gripped large numbers of countries during the 1980s were centrally concerned with forcing greater responsiveness, representation, and participation from state institutions and state elites. Civic protests frequently focused on demands that public resources be allocated to assist populations affected by economic decline, external shocks, or adjustment programs. Movements for democratization were principally concerned with demanding channels of representation that allowed for public input into decision making. They also insisted on the right to participate in selecting public officials and in holding officials and institutions accountable for their actions. From the perspective of state elites in many countries, such demands were particularly unwelcome at a time when economic crisis had robbed them of resources traditionally used to respond to or control societal demands and when the authoritativeness of the state itself was under siege.

This chapter focuses on contention over these issues during the 1980s and early 1990s in Mexico and Kenya. To what extent was civic society in these two countries able to make effective claims on the state and to insist on responsiveness, representation, and participation? To what extent were state actors and institutions willing to provide channels for demand making, the representation of interests, and the participation of citizens in decision making and implementation? In Mexico and Kenya, answers to these questions imply a larger one: to what extent were state–society relations in these two authoritarian regimes reconstructed around more open and pluralistic principles of governance? In both cases, central issues of contention between state and society related to how groups mobilized to demand greater responsiveness and autonomy from the state, the extent to which political parties were able to offer new opportunities for the representation of societal interests, and the balance struck between participation and the power of the state to control input into decision making.

CONTESTING GOVERNANCE IN MEXICO

As indicated in Chapter 3, the period between 1985 and 1988 was a time of extensive civic mobilization in Mexico. By this time, it was clear that the PRI and its constituent groups were no longer able to channel, control, and mediate the demands of diverse interests in society. The PRI was fundamentally challenged by the emergence of strong opposition movements. Moreover, traditional class-based organizations were increasingly less important and community- and issue-based organizations became the central actors in contending with the regime. At the same time, long existing and newly organized groups became concerned not only with basic bread-and-butter issues and access to government resources, but also with larger issues of political voice and representation in decision making.

The economic crisis was certainly important in mobilizing such groups, but in general, the agendas they brought to public debate were larger than protest over economic distress. Their concerns involved the rights of citizens to demand that their interests be heard, that they have representation in decision-making arenas, and that they be allowed to participate individually and collectively in political and policy debate. They were, in fact, demanding a fundamental dismantling of the authoritarian system. The response of Mexico's political elites and institutions to these demands indicated considerable concern to strengthen the political capacity of the state while containing demands for greater democracy and accountability.

New voices, demands, and styles of contestation

Civic mobilization during the 1980s and 1990s in Mexico was characterized by the emergence of new forms of civic organization and new ways in which demands for responsiveness were articulated. But Mexico's civic society did not emerge in this period; the country had a long history of urban, rural, and union mobilization stretching back to the revolution.[2] In the 1930s, locally organized groups of peasants and workers, responding to the encouragement of the government of Lázaro Cárdenas, initiated massive efforts to expand syndicates and unions in support of revolutionary goals to redistribute property and social rights.[3] Their efforts culminated in national confederations of organizations mobilized around class-based claims for representation and distribution.

Much of the political history of Mexico in the period after the 1930s is a story of how these organizations and their leaders were gradually but systematically incorporated into the PRI and coopted into the authoritarian system dominated by the president and controlled by the official party. Their rhetoric remained class based, but the demands for social and economic equity were muted through the development of a political machine that traded individual and group favors for political loyalty and conformity. Periodic eruptions of class and local demands by peasants, workers, and localities often achieved attention, but rarely made a dent in the impressive capacity of the regime to incorporate and coopt dissidence.

In 1968, a student movement provided additional evidence that civic society in Mexico had some potential to contest the power of the regime. This movement, seeking to limit the power of the regime to control civic society through cooptation and corporatist structures of representation, laid foundations for the gradual increase of dissent in society.[4] The emergence of independent unionism in the 1970s was another indication of renewed willingness to question the right of the regime to stifle the voices of dissent and the emergence of demands for greater equity and participation. Already by the late 1970s, large and powerful unions such as those representing teachers, automobile, electrical, and mining workers had been challenged when their members demanded changes in leadership in their organizations, greater participation in the affairs of the unions, and less corrupt and cozy relationships with the PRI and the government.[5] In addition, community-based organizations developed greater ability to define local needs, lobby with government for resources, and respond independently to citizen demands. Thus, civic activism in Mexico had political roots in a history of demands for response and representation and limits on the power of the Mexican government and the hegemony of the PRI.

The economic crisis of 1982 combined with this tradition to affect the dimensions of civic protest, the kinds of demands being made on the state, and the style of demand making. The crisis heightened citizen demands for assistance from government and increased skepticism about the ability of the government and the PRI to respond to those needs. As official unions declined in power and influence and became less able to deliver the goods – or even participate in high level discussions within the PRI and the government – and as formal sector employment declined, many workers joined community-based organizations. The middle class, hard hit by high rates of inflation, likewise turned to old and new organizations to respond to the exigencies of daily life and to demand response from government.[6] In October 1983, as many as 2 million participants in a civic strike called attention to the costs of the crisis on households and neighborhoods and demanded government response to the dire situation of average citizens. A similar, but less successful strike in June of the following year made the same point to the government. One Mexican newspaper reported 1,448 demonstrations, strikes, and other kinds of protest activities in the country between 1985 and 1987.[7]

The civic mobilization of the 1980s was most evident in urban areas. Of course, much of the response to the crisis was economic and personal rather than political and organizational. Many households of middle- and low-income urbanites were primarily focused on the economic strategies that allowed them to survive despite high inflation, declining wages, and severe cutbacks in services. In addition, however, significant political mobilization expressed citizen dissatisfaction with the regime. Street committees, neighborhood improvement societies and councils, and citizens' committees burgeoned during this period. By the early 1980s, most cities of the country could boast of an urban popular movement that was affiliated with the National Urban Popular Movement Coordinating Committee (CONAMUP). After the earthquake of 1985, when the government seemed incapable of responding effectively to the emergency, citizens of Mexico City became more actively engaged in local civic action in response to the immediate needs caused by the disaster. After this, CONAMUP and its affiliate organizations made significant progress in demanding response and autonomy from government.[8]

These organizations, composed of residents of squatter settlements and other low-income areas and self-employed workers and retailers, were concerned about land and housing issues and improving urban amenities in their neighborhoods. But they also developed a broader agenda of demands for local autonomy and participation in governing their communities.[9] This agenda was pursued on a practical level by insisting that the demands of citizens for land rights, housing, infrastructure, and urban services be responded to as a right of citizenship and as a result of negotiation with government and authentic self-help efforts rather than the traditional response of clientelist exchanges of favors. The groups also eschewed the traditional mediating role of the PRI and presented demands directly to government.

In the aftermath of the 1985 earthquake, when the government sought to relocate central city residents who had lost their housing, the movement forced it to reorient reconstruction plans to allow them to continue to live in the area and to participate in urban renewal planning. Reconstruction demands also forced a reconsideration of how land would be used and the composition of central city neighborhoods.[10] The urban movement in Mexico City also demanded self-government for the city as a way of increasing citizen input into decision making about the environment in which they lived. Popular elections for mayor was an important issue, as was granting greater power to a newly created representative body, the House of Representatives of the Federal District.[11] Perhaps the most notable form in which the urban popular movements made their interests known to government was in the 1988 election, when the cities voted overwhelmingly against the PRI.

In rural areas, civic mobilization was less widespread. In fact, the elections of 1988 confirmed a long tradition in which the firmest base of electoral support for the PRI continued to come from rural areas, particularly from the poorest regions.[12] And, as in urban areas, response to the crisis by the poorest and most marginal of the country's population was generally centered on economic survival.[13] In particular, increased incidence of labor migration and the diversification of sources of household income were widely practiced adaptations to rising prices for consumer goods, declining wages, and cutbacks in government subsidies and services. In some communities, political response was largely absent or characterized by increased cynicism.[14] Indeed, almost all rural (and most urban) communities could recite numerous instances of fraud, manipulation, and unfulfilled promises that resulted from efforts to make demands on the state or on the PRI. Apathy and cynicism about collective action and protest thus reflected an objective appreciation of the traditional ways in which the political system controlled and coopted citizen input.

Despite a generalized sense of disenfranchisement among Mexico's rural poor and despite the urgency of focusing on short-term economic survival at the household level, rural movements did emerge during the period. The "new peasant movement" was characterized by independence from the corporatist peasant organization, the CNC. A diverse set of organizations sought to define peasant interests in opposition to the rural bosses and corrupt leaders of the CNC and the PRI.[15] They demanded greater autonomy from government, echoing the urban demand for response based on citizenship rights rather than clientelism or patronage. Their manifestoes and debates were replete with denouncements of leadership corruption, manipulation, and bossism. For these organizations, autonomy meant the right to raise issues independent of the CNC and the PRI and to demand accountability from their leaders. Autonomy also meant freedom to continue to exist without government control or subornation.

In addition, these peasant organizations made new kinds of demands. Traditionally, peasant organizations, including the CNC, focused demands on rights to land and the implementation of the agrarian reform of 1917. Both the PRI and the CNC effectively used rights to land as a way of controlling the ejidos and peasant dissidence, ensuring that most peasants would be captive clients of the state, the CNC, and the agrarian reform ministry. Beginning in the 1970s, however, peasants increasingly defined their interests in terms of their roles as producers and consumers. Prices for agricultural commodities, access to markets and credit, development of production infrastructure and basic services, and control over inflation emerged as critical issues in deliberations with government.[16] The change in demands was in part a pragmatic recognition of the limits of agrarian reform to address the problems of rural poverty and marginality. But it was also a recognition of the ways in which peasant communities were affected by the larger national and international economy.

In mobilizing as producers, consumers, and citizens, peasants began to identify interests with other groups in Mexican society that also felt alienated from government and that wanted both autonomy and responsiveness. In the 1970s in Juchitán, Oaxaca, for example, workers, peasants, and students joined in a broad coalition to acquire greater local autonomy and to challenge official corruption, economic decline, and local bossism.[17] In 1981, this coalition won a municipal election; for two years, a leftist coalition occupied the town hall. Members of the Coalition of Workers, Peasants, and Students of the Isthmus (COCEI) demanded fair treatment from government, minimum wage regulation, and an expansion of municipal services. The experience of Juchitán demonstrated the extent to which peasants had come to share concerns with their urban counterparts about the role of the state in dominating local economies and politics.

In other areas as well, peasant movements reflected common interests as producers, consumers, citizens, and wage earners. After 1982, such organizations protested against the impact of the crisis and continued to contest the control of the party and government over their destinies. A national alliance, the National "Plan de Ayala" Coordinating Committee (CNPA), helped provide a focus for diverse regional and local groups and participated with urban counterparts in the civic strikes in 1983 and 1984 to protest against the impact of the crisis.[18] A National Union of Autonomous Regional Peasant Organizations (UNORCA) also sought to present a broad array of common rural grievances to government at the same time it sought to preserve its independence from government.[19] Peasants had clearly come to identify their interests in issues beyond access to land in the 1980s. They had also come to recognize the importance of broad alliances in challenging the power of the regime to encapsulate and control their activities. Evidence from field studies suggests that clientelism and corporatism were no longer effective responses to deal with peasant protest movements.[20]

On January 1, 1994, a rural rebellion in the southern state of Chiapas presented additional evidence of new modes of political interaction. The Zapatista National Liberation Army (EZLN), whose name recalled one of the country's great revolutionary heroes, Emiliano Zapata, gained military control of four towns and captured national and international attention. The EZLN demanded a range of responses from government, including land, jobs, education, social services, and political freedom and justice. This peasant army also called on the government to repeal the North American Free Trade Agreement. A call for an end to exploitation at the hands of voracious landowners and corrupt bosses of the PRI was added to other demands that resonated deeply with citizen groups in the rest of the country. Soon, a broad spectrum of local, regional, professional, and human rights groups took up the banner of the Chiapas rebels. Although they took their name from a revolutionary hero at the outset of the century, the peasants in Chiapas were expressing very modern demands on the political system.

A significant aspect of urban and rural mobilization was a difference in the style of interaction with government. Traditionally, demands made on the government followed a pattern of petitioning in which clientelist networks were invoked to achieve access to officials who had the capacity to respond to citizen needs. Increasingly, citizens demanded to negotiate with government on the basis of citizenship rights; they formed horizontal alliances among themselves and conspicuously refused the temptations of cooptation or clientelistic response. They also resisted the tradition of federating into large national organizations that then negotiated with government on behalf of their membership or, as in many cases, negotiated compromises with their members on behalf of government and the personal interests of their leaders. Instead, the movements that emerged in the 1980s sought to form broad but loose coalitions with other similar organizations. National coordinating committees, such as CONAMUP and CNPA, emerged to formalize these alliances. In seeking to alter traditional relationships between state and citizen, civic organizations often identified and worked with reform-oriented public officials.

Representing civic society

Many of the civic organizations came to believe that an electoral strategy was necessary to achieve more effective response from the regime. The elections of 1988 provided them with this opportunity. These elections presented an unprecedented challenge to the PRI and to traditional forms of political interaction in Mexico as civic organizations actively negotiated with party leaders about the representation of interests within the party. In effect, crisis created a large political space for electoral mobilization. The parties that were most active in attempting to fill this new political space were the National Action Party (PAN) on the right and the Democratic Revolutionary Party (PRD) on the left. The elections and their aftermath provided considerable opportunities to these parties, but also presented them with challenges.

The PAN, founded in 1939, began to develop a greater sense of itself as an effective and independent opposition party in the early 1980s. The party's organizational roots were planted in the soil of opposition to statism and anti-clericalism. It maintained itself over time as a voice of northern regional independence against Mexico City, propounding a creed of religious and educational conservatism, liberal economic principles, and good government. President López Portillo's bank nationalization, strongly objected to by the country's economic elites, strengthened the PAN economically and strategically. Given broader scope for defining its opposition to the PRI, party councils in the 1980s focused on appealing to a larger electorate and a wider geographic support base.[21] This strategy was modestly successful in 1988 when the PAN captured 16.8 percent of the vote for president, 101 congressional seats, and one seat in the senate. In addition, the PAN was successful in capturing some governorships and municipalities from the traditional control of the PRI.

These victories were not easily achieved, nor could they necessarily be sustained. The ideological basis of the PAN conformed closely to the neoliberal agenda of the Salinas administration. After the 1988 election, much of the agenda of PAN's most loyal membership was appropriated by the government; a liberalized economy and a rapprochement with the Catholic Church about religious and educational freedom went far in meeting many traditional PAN demands. Further, the PAN as a political organization remained largely a regional affair with an elitist image. In fact, much of the 1988 vote for the PAN was, in reality, a protest against the PRI.[22] Indeed, none of the leaders presented by the party through the early 1990s had the broad organizational base, resources, or charisma other candidates and parties – particularly the PRI – could count on. In the electoral campaign of 1994, however, the party's candidate made a much stronger showing and for the first time, the PAN appeared to be within striking distance of the presidency when it garnered 26 percent of the presidential vote.

On the left, the PRD threatened the PRI much more in 1988 than did the PAN. This party had its origin in a dissident wing of the PRI and several small parties that formed the National Democratic Front to contest the elections of 1988. During the election, the FDN program emphasized the importance of the unfulfilled social goals of the Mexican Revolution and the responsibility of the state for improving social welfare and cushioning people from the social costs of adjustment. Democratization of the political system and nationalism in foreign policy were also emphasized. Capturing 31.1 percent of the presidential vote by official count, the movement's candidate, Cuauhtémoc Cárdenas, benefited from massive political defection from the PRI as well as attraction to the nationalist, populist, and democratic program of the FDN. It garnered its strongest support in Mexico City, where it captured 50.4 percent of the presidential vote. After the elections, the PRD was formally incorporated as a political party.

The PRD demonstrated its political muscle in 1988, not only at the presidential level but also by capturing 139 seats in the chamber of deputies. Its leadership and allies claimed loudly that Cárdenas had actually won the election and only the electoral fraud perpetrated by the PRI kept the party from Los Pinos, the official residence of Mexico's president. But the party's ability to represent a spectrum of interests in civic society was forestalled in the aftermath of the elections as it demonstrated ineptitude in creating a coherent national organization or program. It was consistently plagued by internal divisions over its platform, organizational structure, and strategy for achieving political power.[23] Indeed, elections after 1988 indicated that the PRD had little widespread appeal.[24] In the 1994 campaign, its platform and leadership failed to arouse sustained citizen interest. The party emerged from the elections with only 17 percent of the vote.

Moreover, as with other opposition parties in Mexico, the PRD was faced with the dilemma of whether to continue to oppose the government or negotiate with it. Cárdenas considered the Salinas government illegitimate and argued for a policy of confrontation and protest; others within the party favored negotiation within congress to achieve some party goals. It also faced a dilemma of whether to focus its attention on building a party structure or on mobilizing support through the civic organizations that had supported it in 1988. In addition, as a party wedded to the notion of expanding democratic government in Mexico, it was faced with demands that internal party councils and nominations to party positions and electoral candidacies follow democratic practices.

In part, the problems faced by the PRD were those of any organization that must invest time and effort in moving beyond its identity as a movement of social protest to an identity as an organized and enduring political party. In addition, however, both the PRD and the PAN shared a significant challenge: the PRI was not an easy opponent to unseat. Whatever its level of national and local disarray, the official party was far stronger as an organization than either the PRD or the PAN. The national organization was centralized and experienced in the arts of electoral mobilization. It had extensive networks of the party faithful and those who had benefited from its largesse and patronage from the national capital all the way down to tiny villages and hamlets. Even in the midst of considerable internal dissention about democratization of the party and the political system and with some of its high-ranking officials under suspicion for investigating political assassinations, the PRI was able to deliver the vote for its candidate, Ernesto Zedillo, more effectively than any of the other parties.

Opposition parties were far from having this kind of an organization.[25] After the euphoria of 1988 passed, many began to question the extent to which voting patterns represented approval of the opposition parties or simply disapproval of the PRI. Party identification remained weak. Both opposition parties needed to organize broadly throughout the country at grassroots levels. The dimensions of this task were clear in contemplating the creation of party structures in some 3,500 municipalities and finding poll watchers for some 88,000 voting sites.[26] Both the PAN and the PRD also needed national organizations with coherent platforms and leaders who could identify a national strategy for campaigns and governance. In the aftermath of the elections of 1988, the failure of the parties to consolidate their positions and move ahead with effective opposition to the PRI was considerable. In particular, the PRD failed to consolidate its electoral strategy and lost significant support in 1994. Moreover, the issue of who would represent civic society continued to be an open question. The civic organizations that acquired new voice in the 1980s tended to be suspicious of political parties, largely because of their experiences with the PRI. They were therefore generally willing to negotiate, but not to subordinate their organizations or interests to those of the parties.

Participation and political power

Civic mobilization, party formation, and electoral representation combined to raise questions about the form in which participation in Mexico's political life would occur. Participation in the PRI had traditionally been organized along corporatist lines that, at least initially, provided for class-based interest representation of workers, peasants, and "popular sectors."[27] As we have seen, interest representation on such bases became increasingly unrepresentative of civic society during the 1980s, as non-class identities emerged as important foci for collective action and protest. Central to the social mobilization of the 1980s and 1990s was a notion of the plurality of interests in society, each of which should be able to seek access to political participation and voice in national, regional, and local decision making. On a more experiential level, the corporatist organizations of the PRI were centrally identified with corruption, bossism, manipulation, centralized control, and lack of effective participation.

Participation through pluralist interest representation was evident in the electoral arena also. Most particularly, it was apparent in the reluctance of civic organizations to incorporate themselves fully into political parties and their insistence that campaigns be pursued on the basis of alliances and overarching coordinating committees rather than through more hierarchical federations and confederations. This resistance, in fact, increased the obstacles to the PAN and the PRD in cementing their electoral gains in more permanent form through deeper commitment to the parties. Thus, not only had loyalty to the PRI become looser, more fluid, and more sensitive to performance, voter commitment to the PRD and the PAN was also affected by the greater insistence on autonomy and pluralism of the new social movements of the period.

The fact that the opposition parties had mounted campaigns that helped destroy the myth of PRI invulnerability widened the potential for the representation of interests in political discussions in the country. In particular, parties and civic organizations alike continued to question and challenge the PRI and the legitimacy of the political system and to press for democratic opening, thus keeping open the space for greater political diversity and debate. Yet, in the early 1990s, modes of participation in the newly conscious political arena were still far from clear.

State response

The capacity of the state to respond to civic demands is part of the ongoing contestation over the political space available for demand making, representation, and participation. In Mexico, the two-sided nature of the governance equation was clear in the period after 1988. The Mexican government and the PRI made concerted efforts to respond to the new activism of civic society, to control it, or to reassert traditional norms for political interaction. Taken together, the varied responses were at times ambiguous and subject to diverse interpretations, in part because political and policy elites in Mexico City were divided over the degree to which democratization should proceed and in part because the government and the PRI were experimenting with a variety of ways of reasserting control over political contestation in the country. Among diverse responses were the effort to reestablish clientelist linkages with society outside the purview of the party, efforts to reform the party, and the tension between ensuring electoral victory and democratic reform.

As we saw in Chapter 4, Solidarity was a major social initiative organized through the president's office until the spring of 1992 when it was incorporated into a new ministry for social development. Between its creation in 1988 and the end of 1993, it invested some 12 billion dollars in local projects and claimed to have encouraged the organization of 150,000 Solidarity committees.[28] Its activities, which spanned economic sectors and levels of government, brought government resources together with local groups to foster development projects, employment, and social services in urban and rural communities. It differed from traditional forms of allocating project resources in that it relied on local communities to contribute funds, labor, or other forms of participation. Solidarity was more than a strategy to deal with the social costs of adjustment, however. In fact, its political impact was probably far greater than its impact on conditions of social welfare in the country.

In prior chapters I argued that the political capacity of states was thrown into question by the scarcity of political goods, including jobs and government largesse, that could be used to cement support for regimes and elites in power. In Mexico, Solidarity provided a means for reclaiming diminished political capacity.[29] It gave political elites renewed ability to allocate resources to local communities and groups in exchange for politically approved behavior. As indicated previously, Solidarity was important in the changing political dynamics in Mexico because its resources were not generally distributed through the party networks and local party officials and bosses, but flowed directly from the president's office to local communities, effectively building support for the president and increasing the extent of presidential control over the political system.[30] According to one of its officials, "[Solidarity] is a new institution for intermediation between state and civic society ... The PRI used to be the most effective way in which people could get access to government goods and services. Now it's [Solidarity]."[31] The program was, in part, a recognition that "Presidents now need to build their own social bases of support. The PRI doesn't do this [anymore]."[32]

Solidarity was effective in stimulating political reform in the sense that it contributed to the breakdown of the corporatist organizations of the PRI and weakened the control of the PRI over the distribution of political goods. In this regard, it assisted in extending the pluralism of political organization in the country. Its independence from the party also emphasized the extent to which party officials needed to consider reform of their internal organizational structures and how to control the activities of the party bosses that were the cause of so much disaffection.[33] In other ways, however, Solidarity reinforced traditional forms of political interaction. Although it placed some emphasis on the local identification of needs and organization of demands, the distribution of resources was generally determined through the time-honored process of top-down decision making. Its operation was even more centralized than the traditional system, which was mediated both by the PRI and by regional and local officials. Decisions about whose demands would be attended continued to be made at the top, strengthening the presidentialism of the Mexican political system.[34]

The political implications of the Solidarity strategy were significant. According to one analyst,

The government designed Solidarity to meet three sets of objectives: (1) to adapt the state's traditional social role to new economic constraints and redefine the limits of its intervention in the context of a neoliberal reform strategy; (2) to diffuse potential social discontent through selective subsidies, accommodate social mobilization through "co-participation," and undermine the strength of left-wing opposition forces by establishing ties with and commitments to popular movements; and (3) to restructure local and regional PRI elites under an increased degree of central control.[35]

Solidarity proved itself to be an effective political mechanism. Results from the August 1991 elections, which restored the PRI to its important two-thirds majority position within the national congress, were credited in part to the inability of the opposition parties to mobilize and consolidate support, in part to the improved economic situation after 1989, and in part to the effectiveness of Solidarity in delivering goods and services to local communities. Within Solidarity, great emphasis was placed on the timely delivery of resources to local communities to counteract the impression that the government did not care about or could not respond to the social costs of adjustment. In effect, Solidarity allowed the government – even in the absence of an effective PRI – to demonstrate that it could still deliver the goods. In this regard, the presidency had, at least temporarily, assumed the role of the PRI in mediating political demands and political conflict.

A second aspect of state response to diminished political capacity was an ongoing effort to reform the party, which was itself deeply divided over this issue. The new guard that was appointed to head the PRI under Salinas was clearly interested in modernizing the party, improving its image, and doing away with the old mechanisms of corporatist controls. As part of the more general coalition supporting the administration, they were identified as the party modernizers. Their view was that reform of the party was central to reestablishing credibility for the government. According to one such official, "The PRI has always been associated with power in Mexico and when it was possible to criticize the government and to react against its power, it was the PRI that people turned against. The elections of 1988 were society's way of punishing the government."[36] The modernizers had support within the government among the technocratic elites who gained such great influence after 1988.

However, while the modernizers held the top positions in the party and set the party's policy goals for the Salinas administration, they were hampered by ambivalence about the extent to which the party should be democratized. Leadership rhetoric emphasized the importance of reform and democratization. Practice, however, indicated continued reliance on lower level party functionaries and activists to carry out party activities and to deliver the vote when necessary. Importantly, within the government, the technocrats' ability to carry out their economic reforms depended to a considerable extent on the party's ability to ensure continued support for the government. Thus, the old guard, identified by the Salinas group as dinosaurs, was not without the ability to resist the young turks. At local and regional levels, party operatives who had for generations delivered the vote in national, state, and local elections, continued in their positions. Their interests lay in maintaining power and access to the allocations of state resources that cemented their positions and ensured PRI electoral victories for generation after generation. It was they who ensured that Salinas, fair or foul, was elected president. And it was they who managed the networks of party loyalists who continued to expect that the PRI would look out for their individual interests.

The struggle for reform resulted in some changes. In 1989, the National Confederation of Popular Organizations (CNOP), which had long represented urban middle- and lower middle-class groups within the party, was replaced by a broader-based organization, the UNE (Citizens in Movement), which sought to incorporate a wide array of non-class citizen and neighborhood movements. In 1990, rules for affiliation with the party were altered to allow individuals and groups not identified with its corporate organizations to join the party and to provide representation for regional organizations of the party.[37] Party conventions and other democratizing reforms were also mandated, although they seemed to have little effect on the practice of selecting candidates or increasing grassroots participation in the party.[38] Some of these reforms were reversed at a party congress in 1993. In addition, some states and localities held primaries to select PRI candidates in 1989 and 1991. Additional efforts were made to strengthen centralized control over state party organizations as a way of undercutting regional bosses who had been closely allied with the hierarchical clientelist system in the past.[39] Some of these initiatives altered the structure and operations of the party, but whether they made it more democratic remained an open question. The 1994 campaign was characterized by political violence – including the assassination of the PRI candidate for president, Luis Donaldo Colosio – and by suspicion that PRI operations instigated it. The campaign also resulted in much more open discussion of rifts within the party.

The reform of the party was related to a third way in which the government responded to the challenge of civic mobilization – reassertion of political control. Electoral reform laws in 1986 and 1990 provided for majority control of the congress, even in the event that the winning party did not win a majority of the votes in multiparty elections. These provisions strongly favored the continued dominance of the PRI in the legislature and, through that control, the dominance of the president. Other changes encouraged the proliferation of small parties contesting at the national level.[40] In addition, electoral fraud, practiced in 1988 and in subsequent congressional and gubernatorial elections, remained a potent weapon for the regime.[41] Despite widespread protest and the high salience given to the issue by the opposition parties and the international press, vote rigging and misreporting of electoral outcomes continued to figure in the strategies used to maintain control over the political system. Similarly, a more open political environment brought allegations and evidence of the use of violence to stifle opposition and to ensure the preeminence of the PRI. During the campaign of 1988, PRD supporters were attacked and two of Cárdenas' political aides were assassinated. In 1990, police and army contingents were used against PRD activists.[42] In 1994, allegations of violence indicated that tensions had escalated within the party. Because of the loss of legitimacy implicit in voter dissatisfaction with electoral procedures and party behavior, government invested enormous financial and political resources in trying to ensure "squeaky clean" elections, even while it continued to use privileged access to the media and state resources to pull in the vote for PRI candidates.

In previous chapters, evidence suggested that the Salinas administration had gone far in attempting to rewrite traditional forms of state–economy relationships in Mexico. The record in terms of recreating state–society relationships is less clear. While the state assumed the leadership of efforts to introduce a new development strategy for the country, it was much more likely to be reacting to social pressures to liberalize the political system. Moreover, within the government there was clear consensus about the need to liberalize the economy, but there were more mixed motives related to political reform. The old system was recognized as corrupt and in many ways bankrupt, but traditional mechanisms of political control and cooptation continued to be important to those in power. The modernizers were dependent on them to achieve their own economic reform agenda.

By the early 1990s, the Mexican state had regained considerable political capacity that it had lost during the 1980s. It had increased its ability to manage day-to-day political interactions and respond to citizen demands through the mechanisms of Solidarity. It had also found ways of mediating conflicts that accepted new, more pluralist modes of participation by linking the president more directly with local communities. But it was less clear that it had accepted new forms of representation, at least those based in the possibility of opposition parties achieving greater power and participation in policy and decision making. A decade of change added up to a considerable opening of the political space for contestation in Mexico, but no clear victory for democratizing the political system.

CONTESTING GOVERNANCE IN KENYA

The debate about responsiveness, representation, and participation was heated and at times violent in Kenya. The 1980s and 1990s witnessed the most extensive civic mobilization in Kenya's post-independence history; the issues of concern centered on fundamental questions of state–society relations. Civic organizations demanded autonomy from the state, a voice in elections, accountability from public officials, representation in policy debate, and institutional controls on violations of laws and norms. These demands were met with resistance, as President Moi attempted to pursue his definition of appropriate relationships between state and society. During the course of the 1980s and early 1990s, demands and resistance to those demands sparked increasing confrontation and a wider mobilization of civic society, expanding to include international actors and an international audience of partisans.

Kenya's debate over issues of governance confirmed the salience of political issues, although economic elites were in part mobilized by a desire to end government mismanagement of the economy.[43] That is, contention was almost exclusively over issues of centralization and abuse of power, rights of citizenship, and autonomy from the control and repression of the state. Civic mobilization was a response to efforts to constrict political space and to widely perceived abuses of customary relationships and rights. The demands of civic society in response to government actions frequently elicited reactions from the government that then sparked further protest and demands. As in Mexico, then, state–society relations in Kenya depended as much on the capacity of civic society to mobilize, protest, and demand as it did on the government's ability – or inability – to respond in ways that promoted effective conflict resolution and responsiveness to societal concerns.

New voices and demands

A variety of voices – largely urban, professional, and middle class – emerged in Kenya demanding greater political space in response to increasing restrictions on the ability of groups and individuals to dissent from government or to carry out activities without being subject to control or threat. As indicated in Chapters 3 and 4, Kenya's political system became increasingly centralized and control oriented in the 1980s under the leadership of Daniel arap Moi. Activities that had traditionally been local and regional, such as harambee and competition for positions within KANU, came increasingly under the purview of the office of the president. KANU increased in political importance at the same time as it became a much more centralized mechanism of political and electoral control. District, provincial, and party officials were increasingly called to account for the pursuit of presidential objectives. And the regulatory, security, and administrative power of the state was increasingly in evidence to investigate and control the activities of groups and individuals. The space for political expression was clearly being narrowed. As these dynamics increased, traditional forms of state–society interaction and accommodation became less frequent and more difficult.

Kenya had a long tradition of civic activism. The Mau Mau rebellion in the 1950s, the independence movement, and the organization of political parties in the 1960s attest to this tradition, as do the extensive local activities organized around harambee. However, from the 1982 coup onward, political insecurity encouraged greater efforts by the Moi government to tighten its control. University students and teachers were among the first to feel the impact of efforts to "progressively block all avenues to alternative political thinking."[44] From that year on, local and international groups began to monitor increases in political detentions and instances of violations of human rights. This narrowing of political space dramatically increased the mobilization of civic society in the 1980s. The ethnic and regional conflicts that had traditionally been played out within patronage networks became more public and widespread. Civic organizations, often led by Kikuyu elites and identified with the old structures of privilege, formed the basis of the opposition movement. As a precursor to wider mobilization, an underground

movement, Mwakenya, emerged in the mid-1980s.[45] It demanded political reform
and social justice, along with some specific measures to improve both urban and
rural economic and social conditions. Because of fear of government retaliation, its
organization, activities, structure, and membership remained secret.[46] The emergence of Mwakenya, however, marks the initiation of more extensive organized
opposition to the Moi government. Reports by Amnesty International of police
torture of its members confirmed the government's response.

Among the first formal organizations of civic society to protest openly against the
encroachment of the state were the churches.[47] As in many other countries, the
churches offered a relatively safe haven for political dissidence under a repressive
government because their moral authority and wide audience allowed them to resist
some encroachment by the regime. In 1986, religious organizations spoke out
against the queuing system for voting which virtually eliminated the secret ballot.
The National Council of Churches of Kenya (NCCK), the peak organization
representing the protestant religious establishment, led the protest against the loss of
political rights. This organization announced a boycott of elections using the
queuing system. Many of its member organizations began to use weekly sermons as
opportunities to protest against government activities and appeal for the expansion
of political freedoms. The national organization promoted these actions at some cost
to itself; several member churches disagreed with the NCCK assuming this visible
political role and left the organization.[48]

The NCCK was a powerful opponent; its capacity to reach large numbers of
people through its constituent denominations and churches, its moral authority, and
the difficulty of taking public action against mainstream religious organizations gave
it even greater national presence than the Law Society of Kenya, another organization that figured prominently in the resistance movement.[49] Its public stance against
the authoritarianism of the government was responsible for garnering further
international support, now in the guise of denominational organizations in other
countries that increased international awareness of the problem and provided
activist Kenyans with some protection from detention or harassment.

Despite the relative safety of the churches, they were not immune from retaliation.
The leaders of the boycott were verbally attacked by KANU politicians in 1987 and
thereafter. Some were jailed for criticizing government and demanding political
reforms and others were charged with being members of the illegal underground,
Mwakenya. In 1990, Anglican Bishop Alexander Muge, an outspoken activist, was
killed in a suspicious accident. Such actions, however, only increased national and
international awareness of growing opposition to government; in particular, international press coverage focused on the role of the churches in the initial stages of civic
mobilization in the country. The queuing system, one-party rule, specific instances of
violations of civic rights, political prisoners, corruption, centralization of power,
ethnic violence – all were denounced by the activists within the NCCK and its
affiliate church organizations. The first – and tentative – demands for multiparty
democracy were aired through the churches in 1990.[50] By that time, the churches, led
by the NCCK, had become the most active of the groups protesting against the state

in Kenya. In the electoral campaign of 1992, the NCCK sponsored two symposia that brought together opposition parties, openly encouraging them to unite against KANU. The Catholic Church joined in open opposition in 1992 through a series of pastoral letters critical of both KANU and the government.[51]

Lawyers were also actively engaged in the emergence of civic opposition to government. Their activities initially focused on efforts to contest laws they deemed unconstitutional or restrictive of civic rights. They protested in particular against a series of acts that constrained freedom of association, legalized preventive detention, and limited freedom of the press.[52] As many legal professionals became more involved in the opposition movement, their concerns came to mirror those of the churches and other groups, focusing on the constriction of political freedoms, the growth of centralized government power, the violation of individual rights, and the inherent abuses of a single-party state. Lawyers were well placed to take on the issue of constitutional law and to speak for a constitution embodying limitations on the power of the state and the personal power of incumbent officials. By training, they were concerned with protecting individual rights vis-à-vis the state and they were practiced in using the institutions of the state to define and enforce rules. They were also part of a new urban professional class that identified itself as such; in doing so, lawyers claimed some autonomy from government to monitor their own professional behavior and claimed a set of professional norms and standards that they believed should be the basis for their own conduct and the conduct of government. During this period, the *Nairobi Law Monthly* became a forum for sharing information within the legal community.

The Law Society of Kenya (LSK) emerged as the central actor in the lawyers' political protest movement in 1987 and 1988. As with the NCCK, however, there were significant divisions within the organization, membership in which was compulsory for lawyers, about the degree to which the organization should "go political." Activists won important leadership positions within the organization in 1987. Its activism became more organized and determined in 1989 and 1990 when several members of the society, encouraged by the government, brought suit against the chairperson of LSK to restrain his public actions and statements against the government. The suit dragged on until 1993, after the chairperson was elected to parliament, when it was withdrawn by the complainants.[53] In its protest activities, the LSK focused largely on using the court system to protect individuals from abuses of government power. In addition, it focused on actions that impinged on the (declining) independence of the judicial system.

Many activist lawyers had been trained abroad and had strong ties to international organizations such as the International Commission of Jurists and universities in other countries. They used these ties to focus international attention on the abuses of government and demands for reform. Despite these international ties, the lawyers were less protected than the clergy. Their leaders were detained, harassed, and denounced by government. In addition to threats and detention of outspoken lawyers and members of the LSK, the government also sought to reduce the autonomy of the profession by creating a unit in the attorney general's office to handle complaints against members of the profession. An effort was made to require lawyers to obtain licenses to practice from government, opening up the potential to deny licenses to those considered to be dissidents.[54] It initiated a move to make membership in the LSK optional rather than compulsory.

While the lawyers focused on the legal system, a number of grassroots organizations were more directly involved in local mobilization. Large numbers of Nairobi residents flocked to support the Green Belt movement, under the leadership of Professor Wangari Maathai, in its 1989 effort to halt the construction of a highrise office building in a public park in the city. This activity was a rallying point for many who had become increasingly angered by the authoritarianism of the government. The assassination of Foreign Minister Robert Ouko in February 1990, in which the top leadership of the government was implicated, sparked not only violence among his ethnic cohort, the Luo, but also brought opposition to the government more fully into the open.[55] In particular, workers in the informal sector in urban areas began to mobilize in support of multiparty elections, particularly after the government moved to suppress their economic activities to control their political behavior.[56]

The Saba-Saba (Seven-Seven) riots, so called because they broke out in Nairobi and several other towns on July 7, 1990, were a culmination of the protest and repression that characterized the relationship between urban activists and the government. Protest music and hand signals emerged as a way of expressing popular discontent with government and with Moi.[57] Mothers of political prisoners established a "freedom corner" in a Nairobi park in 1992 and declared a hunger strike to pressure the government to release those held on political charges.[58] Indicating new bases of affiliation, organizations such as the Green Belt movement, Mothers in Action, Professionals Committee for Democratic Change, the Kenya Chapter of the International Federation of Women Lawyers, and Release Political Prisoners spoke out openly in opposition to government and sought broad alliances with each other and emergent opposition political parties.

The established business community also entered the civic mobilization increasingly in the late 1980s. Opposition by this elite focused less on political repression and the single-party state than on restrictions on business activities and the increasing difficulties of dealing with a public sector that was no longer sympathetic to its role in the economy.[59] These concerns were widely viewed to have political solutions, however, in the introduction of multiparty democracy and restrictions on the arbitrary powers of government. More particularly, the solution was deemed more simply to be that of getting rid of Moi in the presidency. Nevertheless, the range of protest activities available to this sector was relatively small; it had no base for grassroots organization nor did it have much capacity to initiate strikes.

The NGO sector entered the civic protest movement relatively late. The number of NGOs had increased by over 250 percent between 1978 and 1987, according to one count.[60] A large number of these organizations, however, were primarily offspring or clients of international development and philanthropic organizations.[61] As such, they had fairly shallow roots in Kenya. In addition, many NGOs had a long tradition of avoiding political controversy by maintaining that their development-oriented efforts had no relation to politics. Even civic education was avoided as many such organizations concentrated on local projects and acquiring the resources necessary to continue their activities. In this context, the notion of participation was defined very narrowly as involvement in project activities. For these reasons, the NGOs were much more reluctant than the churches to become involved in civic activism.

The activism of the churches, the lawyers, and the civic organizations such as the Green Belt movement and womens' organizations shaped the agendas of the NGOs, however, when the government passed the Societies Act in November 1990. In this act, associations of all kinds were required to register with the internal security office in the office of the president. Registration required extensive information on each organization and reserved for the government the definition of organizational tasks.[62] More than any other, it was this act that politicized the NGOs, forcing them to confront the issue of the rights of such organizations to operate autonomously from government.[63] The NGO response was to protest the terms of the law and to pressure government to postpone and alter its provisions. Through their pressure on government, they managed to delay the initiation of registration significantly, reduce the amount of information that had to be disclosed, and win seats on the government board that was created to oversee the sector. In addition, the increased threat from the regime encouraged them to establish an informal organization, the NGO Forum, to discuss issues and coordinate activities. More generally, they became allied with opponents of KANU and Moi.

Gradually, the organizations involved in the protest against the Moi government's constriction of political space in the country found a vehicle for common effort in demands for multiparty elections. This demand responded to concerns over rights and freedoms in that it promised a means of controlling the power of government. It responded also to concerns about Moi as president and the centralization of personal power in the office of the president because it provided a mechanism to unseat him. It further responded to the increasing authoritarianism of KANU by providing alternative means of expressing political voice and a competitive environment that would make the party more responsive to the people. Finally, the demands for multiparty elections helped focus international attention on a goal with a heightened international profile in the late 1980s and that was concrete enough to garner the support of international agencies involved in discussions of policy reform with the government.

Representing civic society

Resistance to government and demands for a widened political space thus coalesced in a movement for multiparty democracy in 1990 and 1991. Despite his clear opposition to political opening, Moi responded to increased pressure for multiparty elections by appointing a KANU committee to review the issue. In a December 1990 meeting with party leaders, Moi indicated continued strong support for the single-party system, although he was willing to scrap the queuing system for voting. In June 1991, these changes were made official – the queue system was abolished and the one-party system was reaffirmed.[64] At this point, however, bilateral and multi-lateral agencies negotiating economic reform measures with the government entered the debate. At a consultative meeting in Paris in November 1991, they made further financial assistance contingent not only upon economic policy reforms but on political reform.[65] Fast-disbursing aid amounting to 350 million dollars was suspended until reform progress was demonstrated. Within days, Moi announced the repeal of Section 2A of the constitution; multiparty elections would be held in the future.

This announcement was, of course, a major concession to the lenders and the opposition, but it was also a calculated risk on the part of Moi and KANU leaders. At that point, there were no legal opposition parties in existence, nor had there been any organized party opposition since 1969 when the KPU was suppressed. The opposition movement was strong but not centralized and the identity of leaders of potential opposition parties was not clear. It was not until after the repeal of Section 2A that many prominent KANU politicians resigned from the party to join the opposition. Grassroots networks that could be harnessed by party organizers were practically non-existent, and the government maintained considerable power to control campaign organization, media attention, and communication networks. With only a year to organize and with power firmly in government and KANU hands, loss to a widespread but still inchoate opposition was not easily imagined.

The opposition had continued to grow, however. In May 1990, two prominent former KANU politicians, Kenneth Matiba and Charles Rubia, made a public statement in favor of political opposition.[66] In August 1991, dissident politicians created the Forum for the Restoration of Democracy (FORD).[67] FORD offered the best opportunity for a large and united opposition to KANU. Nevertheless, soon after the announcement for multiparty elections, the coalition began to break apart. The Democratic Party, led by Mwai Kibaki, split from the united front in February. This party had a regional basis "supported by stalwarts of the old Kenyatta regime and members of the Kikuyu business elite, as well as the rural population in the northern Kikuyu [areas] ... and among the Embu and Meru to the immediate east."[68] Other FORD leaders demonstrated increasing inability to remain united and eventually two other parties, one led by Kenneth Matiba and Martin Shikuku (FORD-Asili or FORD-A) and one led by Oginga Odinga (FORD-Kenya or FORD-K) were registered to contest in the elections. FORD-A primarily repre-sented southern Kikuyu areas and the central regions of the country, and FORD-K appealed primarily to Luos and across ethnic boundaries to professionals and those with more ambitious policy agendas. Thus, what had begun as a movement to institute multiparty democracy became increasingly a set of parties that represented regional and ethnic interests.

After the elections, a new parliament was sworn in on January 26 and then the president deferred its opening until the end of March for "lack of a government program" to discuss. When it finally convened, the president sought to rebuild a two-thirds majority needed for constitutional amendments by encouraging members to cross the aisle and to change their party affiliation to KANU. In the event that any members chose to accept what was rumored to be a very attractive package of economic and political inducements, a by-election had to be called in the member's district. KANU then actively campaigned for the defector. Initially, this tactic proved to be less successful than anticipated, however, when one by-election turned out the defector. Nevertheless, efforts to encourage defection to KANU continued and increased in effectiveness. Civic protest against such decisions by opposition members mounted also, and those tempted to defect were increasingly reminded that not only might they lose in by-elections but they might be victims of violence and retaliation by disappointed constituents and party organizers.[69] Ethnic clashes continued, increasing the extent to which politics was viewed in zero-sum ethnic terms.

In Kenya, the issue of representing civic society and the ability of diverse interests to set limits on the actions of government posed the same dilemma for the opposition as in Mexico. The new parties had shallow roots in society, they had little or no sense of what being in the opposition in parliament meant, and they lacked effective organizations, platforms, and strategies for contesting future elections. One observer commented that the opposition parties were "not really political parties. They are part of a movement for change, not a way of managing political competition. KANU had people active in every single village in the country and the opposition just wasn't organized to do that."[70] The fact that their constituencies were identified with ethnic and regional loyalties further detracted from their ability to claim to represent a broad spectrum of interests. They were also criticized for their failure to focus on deep problems of poverty and inequality in Kenya.[71]

The parties also suffered from jealousies and divisions that arose from the election process. In fact, one official characterized the parties as "loose coalitions around a strong man, just like KANU."[72] Moi's victory was widely blamed on their inability to work together and field a single candidate during the elections. Their leaders were widely criticized for putting personal economic and political interests above the unifying goal of removing Moi from office. While the churches, the lawyers, the NGO movement, and grassroots organizations emerged from the elections with their reputations largely intact, the same could not be said for the politicians or their parties.[73]

Multiparty elections had brought some important changes to Kenya, however. KANU could not easily contemplate return to its single-party dominance and both the president and the party were required to pay more attention to electoral strategies and means of building broader support in the country. The opposition parties had learned some valuable lessons from their defeat in 1992 and would approach subsequent elections with them in mind. And, civic society had been given a taste for the politics of participation. In a more general sense, the political capacity of the state was significantly undermined by the inability of Moi and KANU to accommodate more effectively to the opposition. Confrontation succeeded confrontation and heightened the sense that the government was incapable of mediating political conflict.

Participation and political power

National and international observers of the elections in December of 1992 were unanimous in noting the impact of the opportunity to participate on citizens in Kenya. They noted the lines that began to form early in the morning of December 29, the miles that rural people traveled to reach polling booths, and the long periods of time that urban and rural voters waited patiently for the opportunity to cast their ballots. Such enthusiasm was no doubt encouraged by the extensive amount of money that changed hands during the campaign and the ethnic loyalties that were called upon, but the act of participation in a multiparty contest – for whatever reasons – had a profound impact. In the end, some 68 percent of registered voters and 53 percent of all those eligible to vote cast their ballots. Election observers witnessed irregularities and mistreatment of illiterate voters, but in general found less fault with the process of voting itself than with the faulty administration of the electoral process and the counting of ballots.

Participation in multiparty elections was clearly a major advance for civic society in Kenya. Opposition representation in parliament was an additional step in the direction of more effective participation. Despite such advances, political power continued to reside in the office of the president after the elections. Government officials, many of whom were widely accused of extensive corruption and abuse of power, continued to hold their positions and to reap the legal and illegal benefits of office with impunity. Efforts to hold them accountable for their actions proved ineffective.[74] Moreover, the opposition political parties demonstrated inability or unwillingness to negotiate and compromise among themselves or with KANU. The specter of ethnic division continued to haunt the prospects for the development of a more democratic political environment.[75] It became increasingly clear to many Kenyans that participation in electoral contests was distant from effective participation in policy discussions and the ability to hold public officials accountable for their actions.

Despite limitations on wider participation in national politics and policy making, there were some reasons to expect continued pressure for political opening. In particular, the role of the press helped widen the scope for participation and brought the issue of corruption and accountability of public officials to much greater public attention. Newspapers like *The Standard* and *The Nation* appeared daily with allegations of abuses of power by the police and by high level government officials. The influential magazine, the *Weekly Review*, covered allegations of fraud and mismanagement in depth, as did the *Economic Review* and a host of other periodicals. While the government moved to suppress some of the more outspoken periodicals, it did not take public actions against well-established ones until 1994. This contributed to what one observer called "the new spring of the press in Kenya."[76]

State response

"Transitions from authoritarian rule are inevitably fraught with uncertainty and danger," wrote two observers of Kenyan politics. "It is not democracy or elections that are so dangerous, but rather the chaos and mayhem that sitting regimes are capable of fomenting in their efforts to squeeze the most out of eroding power monopolies."[77] The response of the Kenyan state to civic society's demands for responsiveness, representation, and participation supports this view unambiguously. At every turn, the response of the state was to repress the emergence of dissent and threats to KANU. In fact, argued one observer, "The government is not really responding to pressure, it is just reacting against it."[78]

During the late 1980s and early 1990s, when the widespread mobilization of civic protest emerged, the government used a variety of methods to repress and curtail questioning of Moi's right to dominate the political landscape. Laws were passed that restricted the ability of groups and individuals to engage in politics and that regulated the activities of organized groups. National security laws were invoked to detain leaders of dissident groups. Violence was used against others. Police reacted brutally to public protests such as the Saba-Saba riots and the hunger strike by the mothers of political prisoners. Restricted access to the media and rights to travel were used to curtail organizational activities. Independent organizations, such as the Central Organization of Trade Unions (COTU) and Maendeleo y Wanawake, a national women's organization, were incorporated by fiat into KANU's structure in 1988 and 1989. And resources were denied to groups and regions engaged in – or suspected of – opposition activities.

During the election campaign, the regime sought to restrict the ability of opposition parties to organize, mobilize votes, and present candidates for elections. Similarly, the ability of these parties to oversee the fairness of the election process itself was constrained. Party leaders, for instance, were not allowed to travel to "national security" areas of the country and permits to hold rallies and meetings were difficult to acquire. The opposition press was threatened and access to the broadcast media was restricted for the opposition. Public officials delayed processes for approving candidates and providing necessary documents. In some cases, they denied the right to register as candidates. The electoral commission was not open to participation by the opposition parties and a variety of difficulties impeded the registration of parties, candidates, and voters.[79] In a response to the electoral threat to KANU, massive amounts of money were printed and used to encourage support for the government party, adding considerably to inflationary trends.[80] Through the use of both legal and illegal methods, the government was able to keep the opposition parties very much on the defensive during the electoral campaign and far from being able to focus on issues, policies, or platforms. In addition, rumors of possible deals with KANU weakened the credibility of opposition leaders.[81]

When ethnic violence flared in late 1991 and 1992, particularly in the areas that bordered Kalenjin homelands, many believed that it was deliberately sparked by KANU hoodlums operating under presidential orders. They alleged that the president was determined to demonstrate that multiparty politics would only incite ethnic violence in the country and lead to "tribal chaos."[82] This belief was supported by the fact that the government made little effort to suppress the violence and that the victims were primarily non-Kalenjins.[83] In what was widely viewed as a cynical manipulation of the political process, Moi and KANU worked to satisfy international and domestic demands for multipartyism at the same time as they sought to demonstrate that they would bring the country to ethnic disaster. By demonstrating this negative consequence of political opening, they would demonstrate that the single-party system was the only alternative for a stable and secure Kenya.[84]

Regime response to the mobilization of civic society was similar during the election process itself. Administrative difficulties, such as ill-prepared polling places, interfered with voting in a number of places when ballots, stamps, registration lists, and staff were insufficient.[85] Some polling stations opened late and some were affected by strikes by clerks protesting that they had not been paid. After the voting, poll watchers observed faulty ballot boxes, substitution of ballot boxes, the disappearance of ballot boxes in some stations, and a variety of other abuses. The pace of vote counting was extremely slow, with the first results made public on 31 December and the results not announced until 4 January.[86] Many charged that fraud had been widely practiced to ensure the president's victory and that of KANU. Nevertheless, international observers, caught between declaring the election fraudulent and encouraging potential civic violence, declared that the elections were flawed but that they generally reflected the will of the people.[87]

After the elections, the response of the state was also unambiguous. An unusual delay in the opening of parliament, the suspension of parliament, inducements to opposition members to cross the aisle, and an increase in harassment of political activists witnessed the extent to which Moi and his political coalition would go to maintain KANU and the power of the office of the president.

CONCLUSIONS

Traditionally, both Mexico and Kenya had well-institutionalized systems for channeling and controlling political activities and using state resources to cement political support for the regime. These systems were concerned primarily with control of societal demands rather than with responsiveness to them. Mexico had developed a highly effective and sophisticated machinery for the cooptation and management of demand making and dissent. If the capacity of civic society to demand responsiveness was limited, however, the state was certainly sensitive to the ongoing need to cement loyalties, garner support, and resolve conflict. During its first decade and a half as an independent state, Kenya's political system ensured somewhat greater responsiveness to societal needs due to party competition for candidate support and harambee. It was a system more sensitive than Mexico's to regional differences and to the importance of power sharing among the "big men." Despite these differences, political institutions and public officials in both countries were traditionally motivated to control and manage demands and dissent rather than to open up more democratic forums for interactions between state and civic society.

In the 1980s, these relatively strong political capacities were under siege; responsiveness, representation, and participation became central issues of great contentiousness. In both countries, day-to-day management of political and economic conflict and demand making were major tasks that public officials were increasingly unable to control. Financial and legitimacy resources reached historically low levels, severely limiting the repertoire of response to societal mobilization around such issues. Neither country had resolved this conflict by the early 1990s. In both cases, the potential for developing more open and responsive political systems depended to a significant extent on the capacity of civic society to force system change, given that state elites continued to be primarily motivated to control and manage citizen demands and participation rather than to open the system to more democratic interactions.

The response of these regimes to civic mobilization clarifies the extent to which the eventual recreation of state–society relations depends on the ability of civic society to press for further reform. Left to themselves, regimes in Mexico and Kenya would primarily seek effective means of political control, not democratization, as a goal. Political capacity, therefore, depends fundamentally on the effectiveness of civic society in demanding responsiveness, representation, and participation. Effective political voice requires civic organizations with leaders who responsibly represent the interests of their membership. They must have ongoing structures and strategies for political presence in decision-making arenas. They need effective communications between leadership and membership and they need to be able to assemble, analyze, and use information that is persuasive in forums for political and policy debate. They must also be able to form alliances across organizations, sectors, and regions in order to develop the presence necessary to overcome the greater financial and coercive resources of the state.

Civic organizations in Mexico and Kenya continued to struggle to achieve these characteristics in the early 1990s. At the same time, political elites and institutions continued to search for and use resources to control the ability of civic society to insist on more open and democratic forms of governance. Thus, in both Mexico and Kenya, the political capacity of national states remained uncertain in the early 1990s. In both cases, civic society demanded that the basic social pact between state and society be renegotiated and rewritten. In both cases, political leaders and parties attempted to respond in ways that provided them with leverage to determine the scope and nature of that pact.

8
States of change

States vary in their ability to make positive contributions to economic and political development. They also vary over time in their capacity to manage essential tasks of development. And they vary along distinct dimensions of capacity for contributing to development. In previous chapters, I considered the extent to which the economically and politically difficult period of the 1980s and 1990s was a watershed for states in Latin America and Africa. A series of exogenous and endogenous shocks severely affected the ability of state leaders and institutions to mediate economic and political conflict. In many countries, the combined impact of economic and political crisis undermined institutional, administrative, and political capacities, even while it encouraged increased technical capacity.

At the same time, however, the crises of the 1980s and 1990s destabilized preexisting relationships among state, economy, and society in ways that opened up opportunities for redefining critical linkages among them. By undermining the viability of established development strategies and policies, weakening the coalitions of support for such public actions, discrediting prevailing ideas about the appropriate role of the state in development, encouraging new interests and groups to develop, and enhancing demands for participation and responsiveness, the period was historic in the sense of opening up possibilities for significant change. In the midst of difficulties, then, states in Latin America and Africa also experienced moments in which new departures seemed possible.

In Mexico, the most prolonged and severe economic crisis since the decade of the 1930s provided a context in which two presidential administrations were forced to grapple with such basic questions as the definition of a national development strategy and of the role of the state in economic development. Political dissent and demand making demonstrated to both administrations that traditional forms of state–society interaction could no longer ensure political stability. They were forced to attempt to reestablish state dominance through new forms of relationships between citizens and the state. So extensive were the resultant changes that the 1980s and 1990s may well be regarded as historically significant as the 1930s for setting the bases on which state–economy and state–society relations would be constructed for subsequent decades.

By the early 1990s, public officials in Mexico had been successful in introducing a new model of economic development for the country, one that exposed the country's industrial and agricultural sectors to greater international competition and that significantly reduced the extent of direct government intervention in the economy. A new ideology of development focused less on nationalist themes and more on the exigencies of global interdependence, less on historical uniqueness and more on competitive advantage, less on the paternal and developmental state and more on the market and its effective regulation. A new coalition of interests became wedded to this vision of a new Mexico. Politically, the corporatist nature of the political system was undermined and civic society was much less willing to accept the strong arm of the state. New interests were empowered through the introduction of a new development model, but how those interests would be organized for political representation and pressure remained unclear. Opposition parties had greater potential to challenge the PRI, but the PRI demonstrated considerable capacity to revive and survive while organizational and mobilizational challenges remained extensive for opposition parties. Civic society achieved increased capacity to influence the state, but its staying power in the face of the political resources available to the regime was as unclear as the future of new interest groups and opposition parties. New state–society relationships continued to be in creation in the early 1990s.

In Kenya, the nature and origin of crisis differed from Mexico. Initially more dramatically political than economic, it was a crisis set in motion by concerted efforts to alter the beneficiaries of state policies and create alternative sources of economic and political power. The coalition of interests that had benefited under Kenyatta was undermined by deliberate use of state policies and presidential prerogatives. But the success of the effort to restructure the bases of power was stymied, in part by the resilience of the old coalition and in part by the gradual deterioration of economic conditions that had permitted the squandering of state resources in a search for political support. As a result, political and economic crises became increasingly interconnected. By the early 1990s, embedded relationships among state, economy, and society had been significantly undone. The period encapsulating their undoing was an important moment in the history of the country.

The destruction of the means through which the state traditionally related to the market and to civic society was not matched by their resolution into new and durable patterns, however. A formerly dominant coalition was marginalized from the management of state institutions and the benefits of state policy. But the colonization of the state and its policies by new groups and interests was counter-productive in the sense that it seriously impinged on the country's economic viability and political stability. Political power became significantly more centralized and personalized, but in the process the state became more vulnerable to contestation over regime design, incumbency, policy, and practice. KANU became more like the PRI in its heyday as an instrument of political control, but much less national than the PRI in its support base. In 1993, the clearest way to describe the future of state–economy and state–society relations in Kenya was to argue that they were ambiguous.

BECOMING CAPABLE

In Mexico, in Kenya, and in large numbers of other countries that experienced economic and political crises in the 1980s and early 1990s, the eventual definition of durable state–economy and state–society relations would depend on the extent to which states themselves proved able to develop characteristics essential to effective economic and political development. Becoming capable was thus a central challenge for large numbers of governments.

Each of the dimensions of state capacity considered in previous chapters – institutional, technical, administrative, and political – embodies distinct challenges, however. Crisis exposed the extent to which states need to be able to assert authoritative and legitimate rules of the game for economic and political interactions. In many countries, these crises had a devastating effect on the explicit rules and informal norms that mediated among state, economy, and society. If economic development and political peace were to be reestablished, institutional capacity would have to be reconstructed. Reconstruction could not be accomplished on the basis of the old rules and norms, however. New models for economic development and new rules for political interaction and accountability had to be developed and consensus generated that they should in fact set the terms of economic and political interaction. The challenge to state leaders and institutions, then, was to find means to reestablish both authoritativeness and legitimacy in ways that incorporated the consent of the national and international economic actors and groups in civic society who would be subject to new rules and norms. It was thus a dual challenge – to generate more appropriate rules and also to establish their broad acceptance. The process through which new rules are negotiated and defined is thus as important as their content.

The crises of the 1980s and 1990s placed great pressures on states to refashion macroeconomic policies and to manage the economic variables that set the context for development to take place. The technical ability of states was under siege from the international financial institutions that used extensive leverage and conditionality to force economic policy changes and from domestic groups exhausted by inflation, economic stagnation, declining real wages, and no hope in sight. As a result of these pressures, those with skills to redesign economic policy achieved increased visibility and influence in many countries. The era of economic crisis was in many ways also the era of the technocrats. Technical input into national policy making was determined in part by the availability of those with technical skills, but more by the extent to which they were given access to decision-making arenas. The challenge to political leaders and institutions, then, was first to attract technocratic elites and then to establish them in positions of influence. More than other dimensions of state capacity, increasing technical capacity was derivative of the political choices and preferences of state leaders.

Almost everywhere, crisis forced governments to retrench on budgets and programs. Many of the functions affected were those that would have a direct impact on the ability to promote economic and social development. States that had in prior periods assumed major roles for the provision of social and physical infrastructure for development were increasingly unable to deliver the goods. Their inability to do so may well have contributed to increasing political disaffection for governments in power. At the same time that crisis undermined the administrative capacity of many states, the demands for services increased because of the impact of economic dislocation. The challenge to state leaders and institutions, then, was to develop ways to do more with less. This challenge was a difficult one to respond to, given that for many countries, administrative capacity had never been well developed, particularly for social infrastructure. The response to diminished ability to deliver the goods necessary for economic and social development required innovative ideas, restructured institutions, and altered notions of public sector–private sector responsibilities. It also required long-term efforts to reshape norms and incentives for bureaucratic behavior and institutional activities. Of the four dimensions of state capacity considered, reconstructing administrative capacity was not only the most mundane, but also the most resistant to timely solution.

Among the most exciting dynamics of the 1980s and early 1990s was the revitalization of civic society in many countries. To an extent far greater than in earlier periods, groups in civic society organized and demanded more from their governments, not only in terms of tangible economic benefits but also in terms of greater participation, input into national and local decision making, and autonomy from state control. These demands frequently coalesced in movements for democratic government and basic human rights. The mobilization of civic society coincided with a period in which politicians and regimes – many of whom had traditionally relied on state resources to manage and control dissent – found themselves without the means to dominate political space and to close off arenas for contestation. Even as both politicians and regimes struggled to assert or maintain their traditional positions, civic organizations sought to occupy a larger political space and to maintain their autonomy from government. The challenge for this dimension of state capacity was primarily for civic society. To what extent could such groups maintain their autonomy and capacity to demand participation and responsiveness? To what extent could they form alliances with more democratic elements within the state and with other civic organizations? To what extent could they survive and build the civic capacity that would increase state capacity? Bringing greater political capacity to states in Latin America and Africa, then, depended to a considerable extent on the capacity of civic society to confront the power of the state, to colonize political space for demand making, and to insist on participation and responsiveness over the longer term.

Case studies of Mexico and Kenya have documented these challenges. These countries were selected in part to reflect the problems faced by many countries in their distinct regions. In Mexico, the depth of the economic crisis mirrored in many ways the extent of the deep and sustained impact of debt and structural dislocations in many other countries in Latin America. In Kenya, the nature of the political crisis and the role of ethnicity in national politics suggested some of the most intransigent problems affecting large numbers of other African countries. These cases also shared important characteristics – traditionally strong and interventionist states, civilian authoritarian regimes, highly presidentialist structures of government, and inclusive political parties whose principal role was to mediate conflict and mobilize regime support. They were countries that had relatively strong states within their regions, relatively strong economies until the 1980s, and relatively well-organized civic societies. They also had relatively well-developed political institutions. There were considerable differences in the experiences of the two countries, however. In Mexico, the most insistent crisis was economic; the political crisis was extensive also, but was exacerbated by the economic conditions that affected ordinary citizens in a myriad of negative ways. In Kenya, the most insistent crisis was political; the economic crisis that emerged most fully in the early 1990s had been brewing for many years but grew worse as political conditions ensured that it would not be attended to. The nature of the crises that affected these two countries affected leadership goals and institutional responses.

In both countries, the institutional capacity of the state declined to historically low levels in the 1980s. Even while coercive activities of the state may have increased, particularly in Kenya, its authoritativeness and legitimacy were under siege. In this situation Mexico made significant efforts to establish new rules to regulate the interaction of the state and the economy and to reassert presidential power over the political system. The state clearly took the lead in defining the rules, but remained dependent on the acquiescence of economic actors and social groups to ensure that its actions were authoritative and legitimate. In Kenya, the focus of attention was in attempting to restructure the relationship between state and society in terms of the rules and norms regulating political interactions. In this case, the state also assumed the initiative but was at times forced to cede their definition to domestic and international interests outside the state. In building consensus on the introduction of new rules and norms for economic and political interaction, Mexico was noticeably more successful than Kenya.

Mexico and Kenya differed most clearly in terms of the technical capacity of the state. In Mexico, technocrats achieved historically high levels of influence and input into policy decision making. In Kenya, the influence of the technocrats waned as policy decision making fell increasingly under the influence of rent-seeking politicians. More clearly than with other dimensions of state capacity, technical capacity derived from leadership interest and objectives, and these in turn were shaped by the nature of the crisis that was paramount to political leadership.

In both countries, administrative capacity suffered under the impact of economic crisis and resultant budget constraint. Particularly in Mexico, resources expended on health, education, and roads were drastically cut back after a period of considerable expansion during the oil boom years. In Kenya, resources for health and roads faltered, but educational expenditures expanded considerably. In both countries, the salaries of public officials were affected, as were job security and the perquisites of public sector employment. At the sectoral level, there were innovations in the management of social and physical infrastructure delivery and positive responses to efforts to do more with less. Few of these initiatives effectively addressed the basic difficulty of improving administrative behavior, reforming organizations, and restructuring delivery systems, however. Even where such innovations provided models for more effective performance, it would be considerable time before their impact would be felt by needy populations. Implementation remained the weak link even in states undergoing fundamental reform.

Mexico and Kenya were also similar in the extent to which politicians and political institutions faltered in their ability to control the level of dissent and demand making in their societies. The history of the political capacity of the state in these two countries is told in terms of basic contention over the right and ability of civic society to have greater input into policy decision making, control over public officials, and greater autonomy to make political and economic decisions as citizens. It is also a history of political elites divided over the extent to which democratization should proceed and frequently seeking to limit – through cooptation, electoral manipulation, and repression – the countervailing power of civic society. In both cases, reestablishing the political capacity of the state would be defined primarily by the ability of civic society to resist cooptation, manipulation, and repression and the capacity of political elites to refashion the resources that gave them such dominance over civic society in the past. Efforts to reestablish political capacity may well provide stimulus to increase institutional, technical, and administrative capacities. The ability to respond to these challenges is mediated by political leadership and institutions.

THE TASK OF POLITICAL LEADERSHIP

Individuals do make a difference in terms of what happens in the political and economic life of countries. In many developing countries, political leaders play particularly important roles.[1] They often inherit the institutional underpinnings of states whose past experiences in economic development and nation building had given them a central place in defining national development objectives, controlling the means of coercion, and determining the relationship between citizens and government. In many cases, limited capacity for interest representation increased the ability of central government, and its leadership, to set policy goals. In Africa in particular, the first generation of nationalist leaders left a legacy of centralized leadership and personal influence over political styles. In many countries also, traditions of authoritarian rule highlight the position of national political leadership.

In practice, of course, the power of political leaders is often severely limited by the very weakness of state institutions, a condition that was exacerbated by deep and sustained crisis. Particularly in weak authoritarian and newly established democratic regimes, the high visibility of national leadership was contradicted by the weak underpinnings of power. Mexico and Kenya, however, had relatively strong states, civilian authoritarian regimes, strongly entrenched presidentialist systems, and historically effective mechanisms for political support building. As a consequence, political leaders had considerable potential to assume the lead in restructuring economic and political relationships. In neither case, of course, was the capacity to affect the course of national development unconstrained. Nevertheless, the cases of Mexico and Kenya suggest that the role of political leadership is critical, particularly under conditions of crisis.

Prior chapters indicate that leaders in Mexico and Kenya had considerable capacity to determine objectives for national development. In Mexico, these objectives amounted to a vision of a transformed state and economy and a society that interacted in new ways with the state. This vision, which had its origins in the professional training and experiences of a group of individuals who reached high level positions under the administration of Miguel de la Madrid, was fully articulated under the administration of Carlos Salinas. The vision emerged in the ideology of modernization – a code word for a transformed set of relationships among state, economy, and society as well as for a political coalition of those who supported the vision, or at least identified it with the winning side in disputes over the nature, direction, and scope of economic and political change. Through the articulation of this vision, government officials, political elites, and economic interests were informed of the likely direction of government policies and of a revised definition of the country's development strategy. Perhaps most important, the vision provided a mechanism for identifying and bringing together a coalition of interests in support of new policies and the new strategy.

In Kenya, President Moi's more populist objectives set the tone for his presidency and for the changes that occurred under it. From the outset, but particularly after 1982, his objectives were to bring new groups into the political arena and use state policies as a way of empowering them economically. Much of this unarticulated vision was related to his own desire to maintain support and remain in power by gradually marginalizing the economic and political elites and ethno-regional beneficiaries of the Kenyatta era and replacing them with his natural ethno-regional support groups and elites. To do so, he used the slogan of Nyayo!, altered the role of the political party, and made opportunities in government and business more available to those who had not been central beneficiaries of the Kenyatta era. It may be stretching a point to call this a vision, but it is clear in the history of the period that Moi had both political and economic objectives and that he infused government and party behavior with a style that responded to his own set of goals.

Political leadership is also critical in the task of coalition building. Policies are influenced by the economic power of interests and coalitions of support for those in power. But the cases of Mexico and Kenya indicate that in periods of crisis, when the power of old coalitions becomes disorganized and new interests emerge, these new interests, by themselves, do not alter policies. Rather, they are sought out and organized by political actors – whether these are in government or the opposition. Often, the vision articulated by such leaders is the element that attracts new interests and encourages them to support policies and development strategies. In moments when the hold of prior beneficiaries over policy weakens, the opportunity to attract new coalitions around alternative policy directions increases.[2]

This was most clear in Mexico. President Salinas used his modernizing vision to attract a coalition of technical and professional elites, export-oriented industrialists and agriculturalists, and financial sector elites in support of his presidency and policies. Attempting to attract a coalition of supporters was not a risk-free enterprise by any means, but it was central to the president's ability to pursue the extensive policy changes that occurred under his watch. In many cases the interests already existed – those who were fed up with the rhetoric of the politicians, the stagnant and protected economy, the lack of access to international markets, the excessive intervention and regulation of the state – but they were not effective as a political voice until given form and visibility through presidential leadership.

President Moi's coalition-building efforts were more basic and more difficult. His traditional support base lay with the ethno-regional groups whose empowerment he championed. Indeed, his ability to remain president was bound to his success in sharing greater economic and political power with this coalition. The interests existed before the president sought to bring them into more central political and economic roles. Their actual access to power, however, lay with the decisions made by Moi and actions taken by him. Thus, the programs that distributed government resources more widely, the centralization of presidential power, the gradual transformation of KANU into an instrument of centralized control, and redefinition of opportunities for rent seeking were discrete presidential acts that brought his people more centrally into relationships of power with the government. The problem, of course, was that his natural coalition was a minority one, whereas Salinas had defined a coalition of interests that had the potential to become a majority. Moi's coalition was primarily defined by region and ethnicity; Salinas' primarily by beliefs and behavior. Thus, while Salinas could hope that many would declare themselves on the side of the modernizers, once it became clear that the modernizers were in the ascendance, Moi was forced to increase coerciveness once the natural limits of his coalition were reached.

Political leaders also have extensive capacity to appoint high level officials and grant or deny them access to decision-making arenas. In most political systems, and certainly in Mexico and Kenya, powers of appointment available to presidents are extensive. In selecting ministers and sub-ministerial appointees, advisors, governors, provincial commissioners, and others, presidents have considerable power to determine degrees of influence in government. There are, of course, limitations on powers of appointments, set by the need to represent different interests or provide representation to coalition leaders. Laws, parliamentary make-up, and the availability of suitable candidates for influential positions also constrain choices. But even where the powers of appointment are more constrained – in the case of Kenya compared to Mexico, for example – it is clear that political leaders control access to the inner circles that provide political and policy advice. In addition, political leaders can create new units in government and reorganize existing ones. They can also set up management systems that provide multiple or minimal points of access. Decisions made about who will fill particular positions, who will have access, how the executive will be organized, and how management is exercised are critical ingredients in promoting vision and empowering coalitions.

The use of appointments and executive powers was clearly at the heart of the Salinas strategy for policy change. His cabinet appointments, heavily weighted in favor of those trained in neoclassical economics who had a consistent and common perspective on the causes of the country's ills and the remedies for those ills, gave full testimony to his policy preferences. So, too, did appointments of large numbers of technocrats at more subordinate levels of government, the appointment of a chief of staff of similar perspectives, the creation of a formal economic cabinet, and the creation of technical units within ministries to study possible policy changes. Equally important was the access that the technocrats were given to decision-making arenas. Technocrats not only managed the most important ministries and met regularly and frequently with the president, the technical units created at sub-cabinet levels had direct access to the office of the president and often to the cabinet and president. The style of decision making and the language of discussion further increased the influence of the technocrats in government. In similar ways, the president used access to reward those who were willing to support new policy directions and to punish those within government who were reluctant to support the modernizers. The way in which new units were created, the access given to sub-cabinet technocrats, and the support provided them by presidential fiat helped insulate the technocrats as they interacted with others in government and the party.

In Kenya, presidential appointments and reorganizations were equally important in promoting the objectives of the administration. President Moi continued the practice of appointing ministers and deputy ministers from a range of ethnic groups and regions, but allocated more positions to his own coalition partners. Even more important in terms of his objectives, access to the president was, over time, constricted more and more to those in whom he had confidence. This was so much the case that he was widely accused of cronyism and a popular pastime was identifying membership in his kitchen cabinet. Access was restricted and the capacity to influence presidential decisions became more critical the more power became centralized in the office of the president. In terms of the organization of government, Moi continued a tradition set by Kenyatta of centralizing power in the national government and then increasing the centralization of power in the office of the president. The style and content of the policies articulated by the Kenyan government differed greatly from those established in Mexico, but the mechanisms for setting the tone of presidential leadership and providing access to power were similar.

The tone of political leadership is important in inspiring confidence in the direction and coherence of public policies. If the task of policy change is to set conditions for renewed economic growth and encourage investment, the domestic private sector, foreign capital, and international financial agencies must have relative confidence that the policies themselves are sound and that they will actually be implemented and sustained. The articulation of a vision, the appeal to particular coalitional partners, and the use of presidential appointments and organizational powers are all important in sending messages about the soundness and durability of policies. Clearly other factors are important – the size and potential of the economy, the history of prior policy regimes, geopolitical importance, prior investments – but in both cases, political leaders were effective in sending signals that indicated some change in the nature and direction of policy.

In Mexico, the signals were unambiguous in content and reiterated signals that were initially sent by the prior administration. For the first two years of the Salinas administration, however, it was not clear that the president and his supporters had the capacity to carry out the reforms they were deciding upon and proposing. Over time, however, and with the assistance of improved economic conditions, the coherence and political viability of the message was important in inspiring domestic and international investors and the international financial agencies to take a risk in Mexico. In fact, Mexico became something of a darling of international investors and financial institutions in the early 1990s.

In Kenya, the signals were more ambiguous. On the one hand, the Kenyan government responded to international agency pressures to reform policies and focus on macroeconomic management until the mid-1980s. The economy continued to perform reasonably well, particularly in comparison to the performance of most other African countries. On the other hand, the use of presidential appointments, the increasing centralization of power, and the identity of those who had most access to the president gradually increased doubt among domestic and international investors and the international agencies that the Kenyan economy could continue to grow. By the late 1980s, investor and international agency confidence in the policy objectives of the Kenyan government had been significantly undermined, adding to already burgeoning economic problems. By that time, the signals about what was occurring in government in terms of presidential objectives, coalitions, and appointments were much less ambiguous and much more objectionable to domestic and international economic interests.

THE INFLUENCE OF POLITICAL INSTITUTIONS

Presidents in Mexico and Kenya would not have been able to assume such a large role in the politics of crisis and innovation if they had not been provided with a range of powerful resources as a result of the structure of political institutions in their countries. The presidency, the bureaucracy, and the party were critical institutions in increasing their power and allowing them to shape government agendas and change the direction of policy and practice. In both cases, the capacity of individuals to take advantage of political and policy space during periods of crisis was related to the extent of the resources available to them to assert leadership.

The presidency provided incumbents in Mexico and Kenya with a legacy of extensive powers that had been accumulated over prior decades. In addition to the formal powers of office, which included the capacity to appoint government officials even at regional and local levels and powers over the organization of executive authority, they also had informal powers that derived from their positions as head of political parties and incumbents in positions imbued with institutional charisma and public visibility. Although these powers existed and had been used by previous incumbents, they were latent and contentless. That is, they could be mobilized or ignored, used skillfully or poorly, and imbued with ideological content or left ambiguous depending on the skills and preferences of presidential incumbents.

In Mexico, Salinas followed a long tradition of extensive utilization of presidential powers to shape national policy and influence political behavior. He had the advantage of assuming office in the midst of a full-blown crisis which had weakened the hold of existing interests over policy and their access to positions of influence. He was disadvantaged, however, in assuming office under questionable electoral circumstances and at a time when presidential and state legitimacy had reached historically low levels. That he was able to introduce such extensive changes during his incumbency is testimony to his skill in using the resources made available to him as president – powers of appointment, government structure, policy initiation, leadership of the party, allocation of resources, public visibility, international attention. These resources were not newly created, but they were used with unusual commitment to particular policy goals.

These presidential resources were critical in allowing Salinas to give concrete evidence that he was serious about the vision of a modernized and internationally competitive Mexico. This in turn allowed him to give coherence to an as yet inchoate coalition of interests that supported economic liberalization. They allowed him to move rapidly and publicly against symbols of the old order such as powerful union bosses, governors, and party officials. Such actions enabled him to increase his international visibility and credibility and to negotiate more effectively with international financial agencies. The resources of the presidency also allowed him to reassert presidential power, mediate conflicts through the allocation of positions and resources, and rebuild electoral support through the judicious use of government largesse. The Salinas presidency thus provides a telling example of the mobilization of presidential power and its infusion with ideological and policy content.

In Kenya, the powers of the presidency were equally impressive and almost as fully mobilized to enhance the power of the incumbent. On assuming office in 1978, Moi was in a weak position. He became president on the death of a widely revered and skillful political leader. Influential segments of the coalition of interests that supported Kenyatta had attempted to alter the constitution so that Moi could not assume the presidency on Mzee's death or resignation. He was identified as a political insider but one who came from an ethnic and regional background that was distinct from the dominant coalition. In addition, KANU had been kept weak under Kenyatta. Despite these impediments, Moi was as skillful as Salinas in taking advantage of the presidential powers available to him to increase his presence in national politics. He used powers of appointment and access to alter the nature of provincial administration, subordinate ministers to the office of the president, alter the constitution, provide disadvantaged regions with greater allocations of public resources, and centralize KANU as a mechanism of political control. The more limited potential for coalition formation may have slowed and made more ambiguous the assertion of presidential power, but it was certainly clear enough by the mid-1980s to inspire heightened opposition. Moi also used the resources available to him as president to assert greater direct control over the police and army and then to use the state security apparatus to impose his authority, a strategy that ultimately backfired.

In both countries, the bureaucracy was important in efforts to restructure the state and redefine state–economy and state–society relationships. In both cases, the state bureaucracy was centralized and had penetrated relatively deep into both economic and social relationships. It was the center of design and implementation of national policies for economic and social development. It also had developed a tradition of sensitivity to presidential leadership. At the same time, however, there were significant divisions within the state apparatus between those who supported the policy directions of the president and those who preferred to see the political and policy traditions of the past maintained. In fact, much of the action in attempting to restructure state–economy and state–society relations occurred within the public bureaucracy.

In Mexico, the bureaucracy was a principal arena in which policy battles were undertaken. In the case of economic liberalization, individual ministries, agencies, or units were among those that had the most to lose. As we saw in the cases of deregulation and agrarian property rights, the modernizing technocrats focused primary attention on the bureaucratic apparatus. Conflict resolution, coalition formation, and support building – activities generally associated with political parties and interest groups at a societal level – were activities played out within the state in Mexico also. In such conflicts, the use of presidential powers and influence appeared to have been critical. The nature of recruitment to public office was important in enabling the president to colonize critical ministries early and effectively. This provided the basis for further successes in altering power and ideological positions. The limits to presidential power to restructure state–economy and state–society relationships seemed to have been most clear in terms of the administrative capacity of the state. Ministries given responsibilities for designing and implementing social welfare policies and providing physical infrastructure limited the delivery power of government, however much they were exhorted to reform, restructure, or innovate. In Mexico as elsewhere, presidents had greater powers to design and initiate policy but much more limited capacity to ensure its implementation, particularly in cases requiring extensive administrative action.

In Kenya, the bureaucracy was particularly important for restructuring political relationships and the interaction of state and society. In particular, the bureaucracy played a central role in the relationship of the center to the periphery in Kenya. Through the civil service structure that provided for provincial and district administration of central government policy, local arenas became more subject to central control just as central ministries became more subject to presidential control. The apolitical traditions and professionalism of the civil service were undermined under the Moi presidency, but those that remained firmly supported the centralization of power and policy leadership in the government. As in Mexico, however, the limits of governmental and presidential power were faced in efforts to implement policies.

The poor delivery of health, education, and infrastructure projects was not substantially altered, suggesting that some aspects of bureaucratic behavior are more resistant to change than others.

Political parties in Mexico and Kenya were also critically important to initiatives to restructure state–economy and state–society relations. Both countries had parties that had enjoyed a near monopoly on political power for long periods of time. In both cases, the principal functions of the parties were to provide support for the government, mobilize the electorate for periodic elections, mediate conflicts, particularly at regional and local levels, and distribute government largesse with an eye toward conflict resolution and political support building. Traditionally, neither party had been centrally involved in setting policy directions for government. In both cases, the parties provided an arena for regionally powerful strongmen to assert control over local politics, local party bosses, and the distribution of political and economic resources at local levels. By the mid- and late 1980s, both parties were under attack by growing opposition to economic disarray and political malfeasance.

In Mexico, the party presented a dilemma to the politicians and the technocrats. It offered a large, well-organized – if seriously tarnished – machine for mobilizing electoral support for candidate Salinas in 1988 and for a return of a two-thirds majority to congress in 1991. At the same time, its image and legitimacy were debased and its ranks were full of the Salinas-styled dinosaurs who clearly wished to continue the politics of clientelism and patronage that gave them power. The response to this dilemma was three-fold. In initiatives to redefine or reassert state hegemony over civic society and to provide greater power to the president to carry out his agenda of restructuring state–economy relations, the party was circumvented as much as possible. The government and its policies were more clearly differentiated from the party and its composition and resource allocation and conflict resolution activities were increasingly taken on by the president's office. In this way, the elections of 1991 were interpreted more as a vote for Salinas than for the PRI. A second strategy was to attempt to reform the party to help it gain legitimacy within a more competitive electoral context. Presidential power was used to staff the ranks of the party, particularly at national policy levels, with those who were identified with the presidential line of modernization. The party was also restructured to diminish its corporatist organization that gave such power to top level leaders of unions and confederations. But this strategy was constrained by the third strategy of allowing PRI operatives to use traditional methods to turn out the vote and win elections that were critical to the policy goals of the administration.

In Kenya, KANU was clearly central to the political restructuring that occurred under Moi. The party itself changed as the effort to entrench new interests in power proceeded. Its leadership became more responsive to the president and its local organizations more controlled by top party leaders and ultimately the president. The centralization of presidential power had as a principal mechanism the centralization of political control by the party, reversing the tradition established by Kenyatta. The party was also a clear protagonist in the redefinition of politics in Kenya. Section 2A of the constitution was the focal point around which the opposition to Moi and to

KANU coalesced and the introduction of multiparty elections in 1992 were a moment in which the composition of KANU changed significantly through the defection of a number of its prominent leaders. Control over the party gave the president considerable leverage to pursue his agenda, but also led to mounting opposition to his power.

POLITICAL CHANGE AND POLICY REFORM

This book is about the politics of change. The changes considered – of ideas, policy directions, policy coalitions, government personnel – did not just happen. They were engineered, negotiated, contested, and strategized about by political leaders, public officials, economic interests, and civic organizations. Political leaders and institutions are frequently held to blame for the failure of efforts to introduce more effective relationships among state, economy, and society. And indeed, the case of Kenya contributes to conventional wisdom that politicians and power are at the heart of problems of economic and political development. This book suggests, however, that politics is also central to the effective pursuit of development. Engendering a shared vision of the future, building coalitions of interests, mobilizing electoral support, attracting talented people to public service, encouraging responsiveness to public needs, and mediating conflict in the interest of political stability – these are all tasks that are essential to promoting economic and political development and they are ones traditionally assumed by political leaders and institutions.

Compared to many other countries, political leaders in Mexico and Kenya were in a particularly advantageous position to shape directions of change. They benefited greatly from the legacy of centralized and authoritarian political institutions, even when these institutions were unusually vulnerable because of economic and political crisis. Leaders in more democratic environments faced many of the problems of diminished state capacity as did those in Mexico and Kenya but with far less control over important political resources.

Where democratic institutions were newly introduced in countries with histories of political instability, leaders faced a particularly risky and constrained environment for change.[3] They were challenged to negotiate new rules of the game for economic and political interactions without the security of compliant legislatures and weakly organized opposition parties. In all likelihood, they would have to negotiate more and work harder and longer to build and maintain consensus around new definitions of the rules. They would be equally affected by the loss of administrative capacity and less able to mandate innovative ways to respond to basic social and economic needs. They would also be attempting to rebuild political capacity in a more politically competitive environment, where the strength of civic organizations and opposition parties would be greater. Only in the case of strengthening technical capacity would democratic leaders have access to resources similar to their counterparts in Mexico and Kenya. As a result, change in state–economy and state–society relations in democratic contexts might be slower to emerge and less thoroughgoing in content than in established authoritarian systems.

However, the case of Kenya is instructive here because it points to the essential vulnerability of authoritarian systems. Political systems in Mexico and Kenya are inordinately dependent on the skills and perspectives of their political leaders. That dependence can destroy the viability of the system and seriously undermine the bases for economic development if those who emerge at the top of the regime are unwise, venal, or seeking short-term political and economic advantage. In such systems, there are few checks on the powerful, at least until civic society is organized sufficiently to demand greater accountability and responsiveness. When and if this occurs, civic society can deny institutional and political capacity to the state and increase the potential for regime change. Fully capable states may therefore be most likely to emerge and persist where civic society is capable of contesting the state and its leadership.

Notes

1. CHALLENGING THE STATE: A DECADE OF CRISIS

1 Other regions experienced economic and political crises during this period also, most notably Eastern Europe and the states of the former Soviet Union. However, I focus on the experiences of Latin America and Africa because they are most central to concerns about economic and political development and because I believe the nature and impact of crises on state–economy and state–society relations had much in common across these two regions.

2 World Bank (1990:16). The first figures refer to an average for all developing countries, as classified by the World Bank.

3 Widner (1992a:1) notes that about half of sub-Saharan countries moved significantly toward political liberalization, largely between 1989 and 1992.

4 Krasner (1984:240) distinguishes between "periods of institutional creation and periods of institutional stasis. The kinds of causal factors that explain why a set of state structures is created in the first place may be quite distinct from those that explain its persistence over time. New structures originate during periods of crisis ... But once institutions are in place they can assume a life of their own ... The causal dynamics associated with a crisis of the old order and the creation of a new one are different from those involved in the perpetuation of established state institutions." For many countries, the 1980s and early 1990s were a period of institutional creation.

5 I define states in the tradition of Weberian analysis as sets of institutions that claim "the monopoly of the legitimate use of force within a given community" (Weber 1946:78). Victor Azarya (1988:10) usefully amends the Weberian definition by explaining that the state is "distinguished from the myriad of other organizations [in society] in seeking predominance over them and in aiming to institute binding rules regarding the other organizations' activities, or at least to authorize ... the other organizations to make such rules for themselves." In this book, I distinguish states from regimes and administrations, but not from governments, which I use as a generic term.

6 See Young (1988) and Bright and Harding (1984) for discussions of defining characteristics and interests of states as adapted for this book. Callaghy (1986:31) emphasizes the extent to which African states are only partially autonomous because they are weakly institutionalized and authoritative. See also Chazan, Mortimer, Ravenhill, and Rothchild (1992: Ch. 2). Bright and Harding (1984:4) explain differences in state power and autonomy; states "are the institutional and ideological

products of historically specific processes structuring power relations in a society." Grindle (1986) and Grindle and Thomas (1991) develop the concept of state interests and consider explanations of public policy that focus on the activities of state elites.

7   Bright and Harding (1984:4).

8   I am building on a definition of regimes used by Collier (1979: 402–403).

9   By state elites, I refer to individuals in positions of official authority who have responsibilities for policy making and implementation. These elites thus encompass both political and bureaucratic officials such as presidents, prime ministers, elected representatives, high level civil servants, regional political and administrative leaders (i.e., state/provincial governors and representatives, district commissioners), and technical advisors to these officials. In countries with a single or historically dominant political party (such as the PRI in Mexico and KANU in Kenya), I also include their high level national and regional leadership because of their close affiliation with official state elites. By political institutions, I refer primarily to institutions such as the presidency, political parties allied to the regimes in power, and state agencies that become active in politically important ways through the distribution of resources or the propagation of politically relevant symbols.

10   Such issues are considered in Evans, Rueschemeyer, and Skocpol (1985); Grindle (1986); Grindle and Thomas (1991); Hamilton (1982); Migdal (1988); Nordlinger (1981); and Skocpol (1979). For useful discussions of this literature; see Colburn (1990a); and Krasner (1984).

11   Useful discussions of state capacity and economic and political development are found in Bratton (1989); Callaghy (1986); Evans (1992); Haggard and Moon (1983); Le Vine (1989); Migdal (1988); Sandbrook (1986); Wade (1990); and Wunsch and Olowu (1990).

12   Both Weberian and Marxian definitions of the state assume that states are capable of exerting control over social and economic interactions (see Chapter 4 n. 2). More recent literature in both traditions has not only asked "Who controls the state?" but also, "Is the state capable of exerting control?" See, for examples, Jackson (1987); Jackson and Rosberg (1982); Migdal (1988); and Rothchild and Chazan (1988).

13   Well-known work on the issue of government failures includes Bhagwati (1978); Colander (1984); Krueger (1974); Lal (1984); and Srinivasan (1985). For discussions, see Killick (1989); Meier (1991); and Weaver and O'Keefe (1991). See also World Bank (1984a).

14   Much of the discussion of economic development in the 1980s can be read as a profound critique of the interventionist or developmentalist state. See especially Colander (1984) and other citations in n. 13.

15   In economics, see Buchanan, Tollison, and Tullock (1980); and Harberger (1984). In political science, see Bates (1981); and Ames (1987). See Grindle (1991a) for a critique.

16   See especially Killick (1989).

17   See Killick (1993); Boeninger (1991); and World Bank (1991a:128–147). For an application of this perspective at the sectoral level, see Timmer (1991).

18   See, for examples, North and Thomas (1973); and Williamson (1985). For a discussion, see Bardhan (1989).

19   See Amsden (1989); Gereffi and Wyman (1990); Montgomery and Rondinelli (1990); and Wade (1990).

20   Concern with the relationship between state capacity and development can be found

in earlier literature in economics and political science. Gunnar Myrdal (1968) developed the notion of soft and hard states, while early work in political development stressed the importance of state capacity to extract resources, regulate behavior, allocate resources, and utilize symbols of national identity (Almond and Powell 1966; Huntington 1968).

21 For examples, see Fowler (1991); Fuentes and Frank (1989); Herbst (1990); Escobar and Alvarez (1992).

22 See Barkan and Holmquist (1989); Bratton (1989); Chazan (1988a); and Lemarchand (1989).

23 These theoretical questions are often concerned with the organization of civic society and how efforts in collective action express political aspirations, contest issues of ideology, leadership, and policy, and demand response and resources from state agencies. Running through much of this work is a debate over the basis for collective action in political society, pitting economistic rational choice perspectives against communitarian views of why individuals come together in political associations and engage in social action (Olson 1965; Sandel 1984; Tilly 1985; and Walzer 1980).

24 See Karl (1990); Nef (1988); and O'Donnell, Schmitter, and Whitehead (1986a, 1986b).

25 See, for examples, Joseph (1990); Karl (1986); Levine (1988); Stephens (1989); and Widner (1992a).

26 See Castells (1983); Cohen (1985); Escobar and Alvarez (1992); Foweraker and Craig (1990); McAdam, McCarthy, and Zald (1988); Offe (1985); and Touraine (1985).

27 See Bright and Harding (1984); and Eckstein (1989).

28 See Foweraker and Craig (1990); Hellman (1992); Hornsby (1991).

29 See, for example, Rothchild and Chazan (1988).

30 See, for example, Roemer and Jones (1991).

31 This point is made in Silverman (1990). See also Fals Borda (1990).

32 See, for example, Hyden (1990); and Wunsch and Olowu (1990). See also Bratton (1989). For a discussion of the relationship of the organization of civic society to democratic government, see Putnam (1993).

33 See Boeninger (1991); Hopkins (1990); Joseph (1990); and Ndulu (1986).

34 The idea of a "market friendly" state that is institutionally, technically, administratively, and politically able to set conditions for economic growth and social stability appears in Boeninger (1991); Hopkins (1990); Hyden (1990); Israel (1990); and World Bank (1991a). Callaghy (1989) refers to this as "embedded liberalism." See also Killick (1993).

35 See Migdal (1988).

36 See Malloy (1989). See also Sheahan (1987); and Dornbusch and Edwards (1991).

37 See Grindle and Thomas (1991), especially Chapter 2.

38 A significant difference between Mexico and Kenya is the organization of the public service. Mexico has an open appointive system for recruiting middle and high level public servants, while Kenya follows the British model of a career civil service that is clearly differentiated from political careers. Some convergence in the actual functioning of the public services has probably occurred over time as Mexico's recruitment and promotion processes have increasingly emphasized professional and technical criteria, while in Kenya the strong differentiation between politicians and administrators has weakened with increased use of political criteria in recruitment and promotion.

39   For Mexico, see Loaeza (1988); and Fox (1993); for Kenya, see Fowler (1991); and Widner (1992b).
40   The term is taken from Reich (1988).

2. CRISIS AND THE STATE: EVIDENCE FROM LATIN AMERICA AND AFRICA

1   The eight countries in Latin America accounted for 87 percent of the population in that region and 91 percent of total regional GDP in 1990. The eight African countries accounted for 51 percent of total regional population and 53 percent of GDP in the same year. The sixteen countries were chosen in part because of their regional importance but also because the most consistent and reliable longitudinal data exist for them.
2   World Bank (1992:30). See also Cornia, Jolly, and Stewart (1987).
3   Felix (1990:733). See also Cardoso and Helwege (1992); Lustig (1990).
4   Lancaster (1991:1–2).
5   Tokman (1989:1067).
6   Bourguignon, de Melo, and Morrisson (1991:1947). In Costa Rica, real wages declined by nearly 35 percent during an economic recession between 1979 and 1982 (Gindling and Berry 1992:1599).
7   Bourguignon, de Melo, and Morrisson (1991:1500).
8   Sheahan (1991:10).
9   Lambert, Schneider, and Suwa (1991:1566–1567).
10   Milimo and Fisseha (1986:27).
11   These figures underreport the incidence of riots and strikes, as only those considered newsworthy by the international press are counted here.
12   See especially Chazan (1988a) on Africa. On Latin America, see Eckstein (1989); Fals Borda (1990); Foweraker and Craig (1990).
13   Naim (1991:10n), for example, comments that at the time of the Venezuelan riots of 1989 "the police ... lacked the manpower, the equipment, the training, and the organizational capacity to react to the situation ... Many years of budget cuts had left the force with insufficient capacity to provide a city of 5 million inhabitants the police services it needed." See also Herbst (1992:21).
14   Summers (1991:3).
15   World Bank (1989:22). Approximately 4 million were officially recognized as refugees; 12 million were displaced persons.
16   The nineteen countries are Argentina, Bolivia, Brazil, Chile, Colombia, Costa Rica, Cuba, Dominican Republic, Ecuador, El Salvador, Guatemala, Haiti, Honduras, Mexico, Nicaragua, Panama, Paraguay, Peru, and Venezuela. Haiti's experiment with popularly elected leadership ended in a coup in 1991. In 1992, the countries in which the military continued to play key roles were Panama, Paraguay, Peru, El Salvador, Honduras, Guatemala, Nicaragua, and Cuba.
17   Regimes recognizing multiparty competition in 1980 were in power in Botswana, The Gambia, Madagascar, Mauritius, Senegal, and Zimbabwe.
18   In 1992, newly recognized multiparty competition was to be found in Benin, Congo, Côte d'Ivoire, Gabon, Kenya, Togo, and Zambia. Niger was in the process of negotiating a regime transition in 1992.
19   Central planning was widely espoused in the 1950s and early 1960s as important to

development and import substitution was widely advocated in previous decades. Moreover, rising levels of debt in the 1970s and early 1980s were encouraged by international economic conditions.

20 See Fajnzylber (1990); Gereffi (1991).
21 Grindle (1986:Ch.4).
22 See Gereffi (1991); O'Donnell (1973); Sheahan (1987).
23 Bates (1981:Part I).
24 Interest rates, based on LIBOR minus the US GDP deflator, were negative for 1975, most of 1976, and part of 1977; for the period 1974–1979, they averaged 0.97% (World Bank 1990:15).
25 Calculated from World Bank, *World Tables* (1993).
26 Data reported in this paragraph are taken from IMF (1992:764–767).
27 See Callaghy (1989); Haggard and Kaufman (1992); Kahler (1989).
28 See especially Stepan (1971) for an analysis of the reasoning behind the Brazilian coup of 1964. See O'Donnell (1979) for the impact of the erosion of the legitimating formulas of bureaucratic authoritarian regimes.
29 See especially Fitch and Fontana (1991); Karl (1990); O'Donnell, Schmitter, and Whitehead (1986a).
30 For discussions of the movement toward democracy in Latin America, see Colburn (1990b); Fox (1993); O'Donnell, Schmitter, and Whitehead (1986a). On the movement toward democracy in Brazil, see Hagopian (1990); Rochon and Mitchell (1989); on Peru, see McClintock (1989).
31 See Fals Borda (1990); Dix (1991); Eckstein (1989).
32 See Sandbrook (1986) for a discussion of neopatrimonialism in Africa.
33 See van de Walle (1992) on elite defections.
34 Sandbrook (1986:322) argues that "The greater the regime's dependence on mercenary support ... the greater is its vulnerability to disaffection in the event of an economic downturn."
35 See van de Walle (1992).
36 See Young (1992:22); Robinson (1992).
37 Fowler (1991:63). See also Barkan and Holmquist (1989).
38 Diamond (1988:26).
39 Herbst (1992:9–19). See Huntington (1991).
40 See Linz and Stepan (1978); O'Donnell (1973).
41 See Bennett and Sharpe (1985); Grindle (1977); Hamilton (1982).
42 See Berry, Hellman, and Solaún (1980); Karl (1986); Winson (1989).
43 Callaghy (1986:31, 34).
44 Mazrui (1983:293). Hirschmann (1991:1680–1681) writes of numerous constraints on the power of the African state; "ethnic groups, religious societies, professional associations, 'second economy' and smuggling networks, a sometimes unpliable peasantry, foreign donors, foreign bankers and investors" are among the limiting factors he points to.
45 Sandbrook (1986:321). See also Bratton (1989).
46 In fact, Jackson and Rosberg (1982) argued, such states were kept in existence only because of a set of international conventions recognizing their sovereignty and international legal status. International law worked to guarantee the integrity of national borders, even though such borders bore little relationship to national realities, reflecting only colonial happenstance and convenience. See also Jackson (1987).

47 Sandbrook (1986:27); Jackson (1987:519, 528–529). See also Wunsch and Olowu (1990); Chabal (1986).
48 See Sandbrook (1986:330–331); Wunsch (1990); Hirschmann (1991:1680–1681); Hyden (1990); Bratton (1989); Chazan (1988b).
49 See Chazan (1988b:126–127).
50 Herbst (1992:19).
51 Sandbrook (1986:329).
52 See especially Migdal (1988) on the power of local and regional "strongmen."
53 See Williamson (1990).
54 Gereffi (1991); Gereffi and Wyman (1990); Winrock International (1991).
55 Dornbusch and Edwards (1991); World Bank (1981, 1984a, 1986, 1989a).
56 See especially Aguirre (1992); Colombi (1992); Domínguez (1993); Malloy (1989); Naim (1991:19).
57 Sigmund (1990:16).
58 Aguirre (1992); Crane (1992). See Grindle and Thoumi (1993).
59 See Grindle and Thoumi (1993).
60 See Gulhati (1990); Ndulu (1986); Paul, Steedman, and Sutton (1989).
61 One study argued, with respect to Zaire, that "demand for analysis comes not from Zairois decision makers but rather from donors. Indeed, negotiations with donors are the main focal points of analysis and information gathering" (Nelson, Biggs, Gordon, Mann, and Widner 1991:38). Another study found "a large implicit demand for skilled economists, especially macroeconomists, not only for the management and monitoring of stabilization and structural adjustment programmes, but also for the negotiation of these programmes with the IMF and the World Bank [and other donors]" (Pegatienan 1990:14).
62 Nelson, Biggs, Gordon, Mann, and Widner (1991). In Nigeria, the incidence of malaria, cholera, measles, tuberculosis, malnutrition, and other diseases increased (Popoola:1993:96).
63 Nelson, Biggs, Gordon, Mann, and Widner (1991:33, 49).
64 Olowu (1991); Nelson, Biggs, Gordon, Mann, and Widner (1991); Njobvu (1992).
65 Olowu (1991:48, 57); Ajayi (1990:27).
66 Njobvu (1992).
67 Saidi (1992).
68 See Adepoju (1993); Bourguignon, de Melo, and Morrisson (1991:1500); Meller (1991).
69 González Block (1991); Frenk (1989); Langer, Lozano, and Bobadilla (1991).
70 Grosh (1991:51).
71 The World Health Organization indicates that 62.5 percent of the world's HIV infected adults are African (*New York Times*, March 7, 1993:E4).
72 See Reimers (1990, 1991a, 1991b).
73 Grosh (1991:40); Hommes (1990:205).
74 Reimers (1990:547).
75 Grosh (1991:49); Reimers (1990:543).
76 Grosh (1991:49, 62).
77 Bowen (1991:51).
78 Lambert, Schneider, and Suwa (1991:1564, 1567).
79 Fadayomi (1993:99).
80 Naim (1991:42).

81 Chew (1990:1013).
82 Chew (1990:1004).
83 Chew (1990:1004).
84 Lambert, Schneider, and Suwa (1991:1564, 1566).
85 Olowu (1991:51).
86 Mutahaba, Baguma, and Halfani (1993:87–88).
87 A civil service census in Tanzania revealed that 6,054 of 303,000 workers (2%) were "ghost" workers whose salaries were presumably being drawn by others (Olowu 1991:53).
88 Chew (1990:1009).
89 Chew (1990:1010).
90 See Mutahaba (1989); Naim (1993).
91 See for examples Ames (1987); Bratton and van de Walle (1992); Grindle (1977, 1980); Herbst (1990); Kimenyi (1989); Rothchild and Foley (1988).
92 Herbst (1990:957). See also Bowen (1991).
93 See Fals Borda (1990:115).
94 Foweraker (1990:8).
95 See especially Bates (1981).

3. CRISIS AND BREAKDOWN IN MEXICO AND KENYA

1 Hansen (1971), Vernon (1964), and Reynolds (1970) provide excellent analyses of the "Mexican Miracle" and its deficiencies during this period.
2 Hansen (1971:42); World Bank (1983a:151).
3 UNDP (1990:135).
4 World Bank (1983a:191).
5 Grindle (1977:80), based on census data.
6 Hansen (1971:74–76).
7 See, for example, Cornelius (1975); Grindle (1977).
8 Grindle (1977) analyzes the linkages among the party, the bureaucracy, and presidential leadership. See also Bailey (1988).
9 Grindle (1977: esp. Ch. 3).
10 Dissent was not unknown, of course. The country experienced a wave of labor unrest in the late 1950s, rural guerrilla movements in the 1960s, and extensive student protests in the late 1960s.
11 For a review, see Bazdresch and Levy (1991).
12 For a comparison of Mexico's industrialization strategy with those of Brazil, South Korea, and Taiwan, see Gereffi (1991). The weakness of second phase import-substituting industrialization (ISI) in Mexico is discussed on p. 244.
13 See Grindle (1977) for an analysis of this policy dilemma.
14 Bazdresch and Levy (1991:235).
15 See especially Bazdresch and Levy (1991:237–246).
16 Central government employees: Estados Unidos Mexicanos (1972) and INEGI (1984); public enterprises: Lustig (1992:104) and Bazdresch and Levy (1991:242).
17 In 1973, Mexico was a net oil importer. By the mid-1970s, high international liquidity linked to an abundance of petrodollars encouraged high rates of international borrowing. See Lustig (1992:Ch. 1).
18 Bazdresch and Levy (1991:236).

19 Bazdresch and Levy (1991:247).

20 Bazdresch and Levy (1991:248).

21 See Lustig (1992:Ch. 2) for a detailed review of the government's policies in response to the crisis. For an insider's explanation of the reforms adopted, see Aspe (1993).

22 Beristain and Trigueros (1990:154–155).

23 Government officials under López Portillo expected that the bank takeover would increase the capacity of the state to control the economy. "Ironically, by breaking the traditional veto power of business in the policy-making process, the bank nationalization raised the political risk discount and created a new disincentive to invest locally and for the long term" (Maxfield 1989:216).

24 See Sheahan (1991).

25 Although non-oil exports increased in 1983 and 1984, oil accounted for 60.1 percent of total exports in 1985 and 26.2 percent of government revenues.

26 For a discussion of the early days of the pact and what led up to it, see Whitehead (1989). See also Beristain and Trigueros (1990:160–162).

27 See PACTO (1987). Pedro Aspe, who was to become minister of finance in late 1988, played a central role in orchestrating the pact. According to Golob (1993:45), he took the Spanish and Israeli experiences as models for designing the Mexican agreement.

28 See Bazdresch and Levy (1991:253). See also Maxfield (1989:221–223).

29 See Davis (1992).

30 See Maxfield (1989:217–221); Davis (1992:665).

31 See *El Excelsior* (Mexico City) January 6, 1992, Financial Section, p.1, for a discussion of the economic "winners" in policy reforms.

32 Davis (1992:664–666). She argues that this condition was particularly true of the National Confederation of Transformation Industries (CANACINTRA), which represented small and medium domestic firms.

33 Maxfield (1989:223).

34 See Davis (1992:660).

35 See especially Middlebrook (1989).

36 See de la Garza Toledo (1991). See also Collier (1992).

37 Middlebrook (1989); see also Middlebrook (1991).

38 Davis (1992:662).

39 See Meyer (1989:326). Electoral wit focused considerable attention on the "electoral alchemy" that produced a PRI victory. Indeed, six days elapsed between the end of voting and the announcement of the winners and a number of fortunately timed power outages added to skepticism about the honesty of the vote.

40 See López Monjardín (1991); Fox and Gordillo (1989).

41 Meyer (1989:326–327).

42 This is particularly well documented in Loaeza and Stern (1987).

43 See Foweraker (1989).

44 For a review, see Klesner (1991a).

45 See Leys (1975); Widner (1992b) for analyses of these political and institutional bases.

46 See Bevan, Collier, and Gunning (1993); Lofchie (1989).

47 World Bank (1983a:150).

48 Prior to the land resettlement carried out by the newly independent government, less than one half of one percent of the population, the Europeans, owned almost a

quarter of the agricultural land (Lofchie 1989:140). The Swynnerton Plan of the 1950s set the stage for post-independence land and agricultural policy by providing for individual title to land, allowing for land consolidation, and lifting the ban on African production of coffee, the principal export crop. Lofchie argues that the government's resettlement and land registration schemes, which favored land distribution on an individual basis to more prosperous farmers and did not favor the wholesale distribution of European land, was "one of the most difficult acts in African political history" (1989:149). See also Leys (1975:Ch. 3); Bates (1989).

49 Between 1960 and 1970, annual inflation averaged 1.6 percent. World Bank (1983b:15).

50 The phrase is from Young (1982). See Hilderbrand (1992:333–336). Gordon (1990:5) refers to Kenya as "probably sub-Saharan Africa's most successful effort at inward looking and public sector-led development."

51 The average for sub-Saharan Africa was 51 percent in the same year. Only South Africa, Botswana, Swaziland, Lesotho, Madagascar, Zambia, and Zaire had higher rates (UNDP 1992:129, 176).

52 UNDP (1992:129, 176).

53 *Weekly Review*, December 9, 1988:25.

54 Barkan (1992:168–173); Mutahaba (1989:119).

55 "Parliament ... does provide a linkage – if not exactly representation of interests – between the people of the country and the national government. Members of Parliament are expected to provide benefits to their constituencies, and if they do not, they are turned out of office. Thus, the linkage role is predominantly a patronage one; but the fact that the patrons can be easily replaced gives the constituency some leverage over their responsiveness" (Hilderbrand 1992:328). Throup (1989:37) indicates that "the average MP has remained in the National Assembly for only 7.2 years since 1963, and until 1979 most members were defeated when they stood for re-election."

56 Rothchild and Foley (1988) characterize African political regimes as either "hegemonial exchange" or "bureaucratic centralist" systems. The first is characterized by coalitions of regional and ethnic notables held together by the distribution of public largesse; the latter is characterized by a coalition of national political, ethnic, and bureaucratic elites held together by ideological conformity and authoritarian leadership. As it emerged in the 1960s and 1970s, Kenya – and KANU – corresponded closely to the hegemonial exchange typology. Rothchild and Foley (1988:246) refer to Kenyatta's "elite cartel" and "grand coalition." For a useful assessment of the development of KANU and its relationship to presidential power, see Widner (1992b).

57 See Barkan (1992:169).

58 See Throup (1989); Mutahaba (1989:119).

59 See Mueller (1984) for a case study of the demise of the KPU.

60 Hilderbrand (1992:329). The Kikuyu coalition was formed of the largest ethnic groups – Kikuyu, Kamba, and Luo – in alliance with the Embu, Kisii, and Meru peoples. These groups represented about 60 percent of the population and the most economically advantaged regions. It is important to note that there were deep rifts within this coalition and more generally, political loyalties never fully coincided with ethnic identities.

61 The country's first constitution was amended within a year of independence to alter

its provisions for federalism. The first amendment to the constitution changed the structure of government by setting up the office of the president and giving the incumbent the right to appoint the vice-president, cabinet ministers, permanent secretaries, the police commissioner, controller, and auditor general. The second amendment abolished the independent revenue base of the regions and increased presidential control over the judiciary. Subsequent amendments further strengthened the center vis-à-vis the regions and the presidency vis-à-vis other governing institutions. See Chapter 4.

62 Widner (1992b:1).

63 Widner (1992b:70).

64 See Barkan (1987). The government estimates that harambee "has provided capital equalling between 4 and 10 percent of Government's actual expenditures" (Republic of Kenya 1986:29). Barkan and Holmquist (1989:359–360) estimate there were 15,000–20,000 harambee organizations by the late 1980s. Fowler (1991:54) puts their number at 26,000.

65 Barkan (1987).

66 Barkan (1992: 172–173).

67 Mutahaba (1989:122–123).

68 Mutahaba (1989:10).

69 See especially Barkin and Holmquist (1989) for a description of how the system worked under Kenyatta.

70 Widner (1992b:24).

71 The assassinations of Luo leader Tom Mboya in 1969 and Kikuyu leader J.M. Kariuki in 1975 have been linked to the threat they posed to the hegemony of the "family" of rich Kikuyu that controlled government.

72 Throup (1989:59).

73 See Widner (1992b:Ch. 4). Moi ran unopposed for president; competition centered on the allocation of resources among regions and districts – and therefore among ethnic groups. Moi's ethnoregional coalition was based among the Kalenjin, Luhya and Mijikenda, and a variety of small nomadic groups. Together they composed about 40 percent of the population.

74 See especially Throup (1989).

75 Widner (1992b:130).

76 See especially Widner (1992b) on this process. See also Throup (1989).

77 The most prominent of these welfare societies was GEMA, the Gikuyu, Embu, and Meru Association, which represented the interests of wealthy Kikuyu closely allied to the Kenyatta "family" of associates and relatives.

78 The motivations of those involved in the "August Disturbances" are not clear; both economic and political grievances are said to have been important and the Kikuyu and Luo identity of the coup leaders support the view that ethnic tensions played an important role in the conflict. As many as three coup plots are thought to have been planned. See especially Throup (1989:64–67). See also Currie and Ray (1985).

79 Leonard (1991:176–177); Throup (1989:64–67).

80 Barkan (1992:180) notes that "Regime policy and procedure became less predictable as Moi expressed increased distrust of those who did not follow the Nyayo line. With uncertainty came both fear of the president and sycophancy to ward off his suspicion." See also Barkan and Chegge (1989).

81 See Barkan (1992:187).

82 Many Kenyans came to believe that Moi and his supporters stimulated ethnic violence as a way of demonstrating the political infeasibility of a multiparty system and to increase the police power of government. See *Weekly Review*, April 9, 1993.

83 Press reports indicated 1,000 deaths and some 50,000 people displaced by late 1992. See Barkan (1993).

84 Barkan (1992:191–192).

85 See Widner (1992b:167).

86 Barkan (1993:11).

87 See Widner (1992b:Ch. 6).

88 See *Weekly Review*, January 8, 1993:16–17.

89 One observer of Kenyan politics referred to the cronies who surrounded Moi as a "vampire elite." Interview, January 21, 1993.

90 Barkan (1992:186).

91 Hilderbrand (1992:362–363). See also Bates (1989) and Lofchie (1989).

92 For an economic analysis of external shocks on the Kenyan economy, see Bevan, Collier, and Gunning (1990:Ch. 5); see also Mwega and Kabudo (1993).

93 This assessment is traced in Hilderbrand (1992:Ch.6).

94 Gordon (1990:15–17). See Chapter 5.

95 See Hilderbrand (1992:354, 374–378); see also Leonard (1991:212–213).

96 Hilderbrand (1992:353).

97 See Republic of Kenya (1986). The authorship of the paper by technocrats in the ministry of finance and foreign advisors, however, creates some doubt about Moi's commitment to its substance.

98 See Cornelius, Gentleman, and Smith (1989:36–45).

4. IMPOSING STATE AUTHORITY

1 See especially Migdal (1988); Azarya (1988); Bratton (1989:408–409).

2 The notion of control is well embedded in the work of the founders of the two main traditions in modern social science, Karl Marx and Max Weber. For both, states are sets of institutions that organize coercion in society and monopolize the legitimate use of violence. Marxians and neo-Marxians are primarily concerned with how dominant classes or class fractions use the apparatus of the state and the ideology of state legitimacy to enhance their economic power and to suppress the countervailing claims of subordinate classes. Weberians, on the other hand, leave open the question of whose interests are served by the coercive power of the state, focusing instead on the powerful civil and military bureaucracies that assume the primary functions of control and administration in the modern state.

3 North (1990:6).

4 Myrdal (1968).

5 See North (1990); Azarya (1988).

6 Basáñez (1993:109), reporting data from a *Los Angeles Times–Prospectiva Estatégica* national survey carried out among 1,487 respondents in September 1989. See Smith (1989:408).

7 Interview, Mexico City, January 7, 1992.

8 Three to five years might be needed to acquire a license for commercial fishing, for example (Lustig 1992:110).

9 Interview, Mexico City, June 16, 1992.

10 Interview, Mexico City, June 16, 1992.
11 Interview, Mexico City, June 16, 1992.
12 Sectors were placed on the agenda for study in a variety of ways. Members of the team often initiated studies on their own or at the suggestion of their team leader. At times, private sector interests would complain of a regulatory environment that affected them and alert the team. In other cases, they received presidential or ministerial directives about what sectors they should focus on. In fact, according to all the officials who were interviewed in this office, there was no systematic strategy for selecting what was to be considered subject to deregulation.
13 During interviews I conducted with officials in the office of deregulation in 1991 and 1992, the deregulation of the transport sector was clearly regarded as a successful effort. I draw on these interviews and on a 1994 case study by Mark Williams for the following discussion of the process of deregulation.
14 Williams (1994:43).
15 See Lustig (1992:107–111).
16 Interview, Mexico City, June 16, 1992.
17 The agrarian reform was first legislated in 1915 and then incorporated into the constitution as Article 27. The purpose of the reform was to ensure peasant access to land and the restitution of lands legally and illegally denied to peasant communities after a series of liberal reforms in the mid-1850s, the 1880s, and 1890s.
18 In the early 1980s, policy changes made it possible for ejidos to rent out both land and labor. Sale of ejido land continued to be prohibited. In practice, a large informal rental market had developed over the years as a way of circumventing the legal constraints.
19 Hansen (1971:33).
20 In the 1920s, an ejidal bank had been established, and under Cárdenas, a number of institutions were created to provide goods and services to ejido communities.
21 See Table 3.2.
22 See Grindle (1986) for a discussion of the bifurcation of Mexico's agricultural sector. See especially Yates (1981) for a critique of the ejido system as an economic institution.
23 The following description is based on interviews with participants in the planning process.
24 Interview, Mexico City, June 22, 1992.
25 Interview, Mexico City, January 19, 1992.
26 Interview, Mexico City, June 16, 1992.
27 Interview, Mexico City, January 19, 1992.
28 Interview, Mexico City, January 19, 1992.
29 See Chapter 5.
30 Interview, Mexico City, June 24, 1992.
31 Interview, Mexico City, January 20, 1992.
32 Many disputes existed regarding the external boundaries of ejidos; internally, conflicts would be massive as only about 2,000 of 28,000 ejidos were clearly demarcated into individual plots. See Fox (1992:1–2).
33 See Bailey (1988) on the tension between the technocrats and the politicians in Mexico. See also Chapter 5.
34 Garrido (1989:422–426) characterizes the powers of Mexican presidents as constitutional (formal), metaconstitutional (informal powers as head of the party, legislative

leader, and chief of government and party appointments), and anticonstitutional (powers that cannot be controlled because of lack of checks and balances in the system). Traditionally, the Mexican president could set policy directions with little fear of rejection and act as an ultimate authority on electoral matters, in selecting his successor, governors, mayors, and legislators. See also Bailey (1988:31).

35 See Collier (1992:137).

36 Interview, Mexico City, January 10, 1992. See Chapter 7 for additional discussion about reforming the PRI.

37 Initially known widely as PRONASOL, this program was, by the early 1990s, widely referred to as Solidarity. I have used the term Solidarity throughout this book. Research on the political and economic implications of Solidarity is found in Cornelius, Craig, and Fox (1994a).

38 The National Solidarity Program will be dealt with in greater detail in Chapters 6 and 7. See also Dresser (1991). Solidarity's institutional heritage is linked to an earlier program, COPLAMAR, which attempted to address the social and economic needs of the country's marginal areas and groups.

39 In 1992, Solidarity became part of a newly established ministry, the ministry of social development, SEDESOL.

40 Cornelius (1993:35–36). See Molinar and Weldon (1994:139–141) on the contribution of Solidarity to the electoral outcome.

41 See Muigai (1993).

42 Muigai (1993:14).

43 Eleven of these amendments were made to the original constitution. In 1969, these amendments were consolidated in a new constitution. Kenyatta's government introduced five additional amendments; Moi's government introduced eleven amendments between 1979 and 1992, ten of which were adopted by early 1993.

44 Interview, Nairobi, January 11, 1993.

45 Muigai (1993:14).

46 Some were also introduced for very personal reasons. For example, the 15th amendment, introduced under Kenyatta, gave the president the right to pardon those found guilty of election violations. The constitutional change was inspired by the president's desire to pardon a close friend of such a violation.

47 See Muigai (1993:11).

48 See Muigai (1993) and Widner (1992b:145).

49 Opposition was also mounted to a number of other constitutional amendments, such as the right of the presidency to determine the tenure of judicial and public service officers. In 1991, opponents were successful in overturning parts of the constitution related to appointments and tenure of some public officials.

50 See Chapter 7.

51 *The Nation*, Nairobi, June 14, 1993:1.

52 See especially Mutahaba (1989).

53 Kenya's experience with various forms of decentralization is described in Cohen and Hook (1987). See also Leonard (1991:204–209) on District Focus. Barkan and Chegge (1989) present a political analysis of District Focus. See also Smoke (1993:20–22).

54 Cohen and Hook (1987).

55 Smoke (1993:20).

56 Leonard (1991:203–204).

57 District Focus provided that the DDCs would have an executive committee and several substantive committees, such as for agriculture, land, and security, to facilitate their work. They were also provided with a planning unit for technical assistance.

58 Cohen and Hook (1987:84).

59 See Barkan and Chegge (1989).

60 Interview, Nairobi, June 16, 1993.

61 Leonard (1991:206).

62 Leonard (1991:207).

63 Interview, Nairobi, June 18, 1993.

64 According to one observer, Moi was astute in understanding the implications of District Focus. "Policywise, he bought quickly into things like 'food self-sufficiency,' 'arid and semiarid lands,' and District Focus because all offered the possibility of redistributing resources to his region and his coalition. He has a basic instinct to see what's in it for him in all policy, even if he is not very conversant with policy. At a political level, he understands it." Interview, Nairobi, June 18, 1993.

65 Oyugi (1990:50). See also *Weekly Review*, April 2, 1993:8–9.

66 This pattern conforms to the "ritual dances" that Callaghy (1989:129) identifies as characteristic of the interaction between international financial institutions and governments when governments lack the desire or capacity to promote difficult economic reforms.

67 See Grosh (1991) for a description and analysis of the parastatal sector.

68 Republic of Kenya (1991a:19).

69 The Commission on Government Expenditure was chaired by the governor of the central bank, Philip Ndegua, who had chaired the 1979 Committee on Review of Statutory Boards. This earlier committee was also highly critical of the inefficiency and mismanagement of the state enterprises. Barbara Grosh (1991) points out that such accusations were true for some, but not all, parastatals. Some, in fact, performed well along several dimensions.

70 Gordon (1990:16–17).

71 A previous structural adjustment program, agreed to in 1980 by the World Bank and the government, sought similar ends and was regarded largely as a failure.

72 Gordon (1990:14–19).

73 Gordon and Spooner (1992:13).

74 See especially Gordon and Spooner (1992) on the objectives of grain market policies.

75 Hilderbrand (1992:375).

76 See Republic of Kenya (1991a).

77 *Weekly Review*, Nairobi, May 21, 1993:20.

78 Republic of Kenya (1991a:21).

79 *Economic Review*, September 13–19, 1993:4.

80 Formerly the Maize Marketing Board and then the Maize and Produce Board. In 1980, this latter was merged with the Wheat Board of Kenya to form the NCPB.

81 Gordon and Spooner (1992:3).

82 Gordon and Spooner (1992:5).

83 Gordon (1990:20).

84 Gordon (1990:34).

85 *Weekly Review*, March 29, 1993:17; *Economic Review*, September 13–19, 1993:4–7.

86 Gordon and Spooner (1992:22).

87 Grosh (1991:155–165).
88 Interview, June 18, 1993.
89 Gugerty (1993:7).
90 Interview, June 19, 1993.
91 Interview, June 18, 1993.
92 North (1990:3).

5. MANAGING THE ECONOMY

1 In 1989, the World Bank estimated that there were up to 100,000 expatriate technical advisors working in the public sector in sub-Saharan African countries (1989a:181). See also Cohen (1992).

2 See especially World Bank (1983a). In the analysis of the East Asian "success stories," and despite a vigorous debate over the origin of those successes, there is little corresponding debate about the importance of state management of macro-economic affairs over long periods of time.

3 See, for example, Hall (1989); Reich (1988).

4 See, for example, Grindle and Thoumi (1993); Malloy (1989).

5 The examples of deregulation and rural property rights, considered in Chapter 4, are relevant here.

6 The use of the term technocrats refers to such individuals, that is, technically trained individuals whose official roles require them to use professional expertise to carry out their responsibilities. Cleaves (1987:88) defines technocrats as "specialists with public sector jobs that require advanced knowledge and training."

7 Two public officials in Mexico expressed their own commitment to the public sector by noting the challenge of helping contribute to important policy changes in the country. "Creative people like to be where things are happening, where they can be creative," commented one. Another indicated the importance of "being where the action is." "In this ministry, there must be at least 30 PhDs. The excitement of being in government won't last for these well-prepared technical types. It is extremely exciting right now because they are at the center of decision making and bringing about major changes in government and the role of the state in the economy. But at some point, it will be time to consolidate and they will find it much more attractive to be in the private sector." Interviews, Mexico City, June 16, 1992. In contrast, Kenya's public officials were apparently much less engaged in resolving critical problems in the early 1990s. "You go to many ministries these days and you find permanent secretaries reading novels ... There are many qualified people here. They can develop all the scenarios and options you want. But they are not used." Interview Nairobi, January 11, 1993. "The civil service does not pay well compared to outside and there is a real brain drain after investing in training. But those who remain ... are not being asked difficult questions. They are given trivial issues to deal with." Interview, Nairobi, January 19, 1993.

8 *The Economist*, December 14, 1991:19, quoted in Golob (1993:4). *The Economist* goes on to report that "According to Mexico City gossip, cabinet ministers who do not have doctorates in economics from the best American universities turn up for meetings with young sidekicks who do."

9 The new model would have been much more difficult to introduce, however, without

major efforts at stabilization and initial structural adjustment efforts under the de la Madrid administration.

10 See Golob (1993); Centeno and Maxfield (1992). In Mexico, this group was referred to by some as the "tecnocracia salinista."

11 Centeno and Maxfield (1992:74).

12 On the process of increasing the numbers and influence of the technically skilled in government, see Smith (1986); Centeno and Maxfield (1992); Camp (1985); and Bailey (1988).

13 "In this respect, the six-year procession often resembles a national game of musical chairs in which the same actors may reappear in different positions; new players are freely admitted, however, and the number of chairs may be enlarged to accommodate some of them. Those who fail to find a chair and must leave the game do so knowing they have the possibility of reentering it at a later date" (Grindle 1977:43). In general, the politically ambitious tend to prefer positions within government to positions within the party or the legislature because they provide greater access to power, much larger scope for influencing public policy, and more prestige.

14 See Grindle (1977:Ch. 3).

15 See especially Smith (1979); Centeno and Maxfield (1992).

16 This point is made in Centeno and Maxfield (1992).

17 Interview, Mexico City, January 7, 1992.

18 Cleaves (1987:96). Data for the Salinas cabinet as of January 1989, Unidad de la Crónica Presidencial (1992).

19 Centeno and Maxfield (1992:66–68). The sample included all officials at the general director level or above. General directors are ranked just below ministers and vice-ministers.

20 See Golob (1993) for a discussion of the importance of deferring to the president. See Smith (1979) for an analysis of the rules of the game for the politically ambitious of Mexico. Camp (1985) and Centeno and Maxfield (1992) also discuss the political requisites for high level positions.

21 Interview, Mexico City, January 13, 1992.

22 The term technopols is used by Domínguez (1993) and others who participated in a research project on the role of technical experts in high level decision making in Latin America in the 1980s and 1990s. The use of various labels for those who combine political and technical skills and those who combine political and professional experiences is discussed in Centeno and Maxfield (1992) and Smith (1986). My use of the term "technocrat" in this chapter assumes that those with technical training who rise to positions of influence will almost necessarily have demonstrated important political skills also. When Alejandro Foxley, Chile's minister of finance with a PhD in economics from the University of Wisconsin, was asked how he would define "technopol," he responded in the following manner. "I would define it two ways. First is the realization that to do a good technical job in managing the economy you have to be a politician. If you do not have the capacity to articulate your vision, to persuade antagonists, to bring people around on some unpopular measure, then you are going to be a total failure ... Economists must not only know their economic models, but also understand politics, interests, conflicts, passions – the essence of collective life. For a brief period of time you could make most changes by decree; but to let them persist, you have to build coalitions and bring people around. You have to be a politician" (Domínguez 1993:50).

23 See Grindle (1977:Ch. 4).
24 See Cordera and Tello (1981) for the nationalist vision. For the more market-oriented view, see Aspe (1993). For a discussion, see Bazdresch and Levy (1991).
25 The nationalization of the banks in 1982 was widely regarded as a victory for the nationalists.
26 Interview, Mexico City, January 9, 1992. For a similar perspective, see Córdoba (1991:31).
27 See Golob (1993) on the influence of foreign graduate training at Harvard, MIT, Yale, University of Chicago, Stanford, and elsewhere.
28 Salinas de Gortari (1992:6–7), my translation.
29 See Grindle and Thomas (1991:Ch. 4).
30 Four other specialized cabinets – agriculture, social development, foreign affairs, and national security – were established, all to be coordinated by a special office in the presidency. See *Diario Official*, June 5, 1992:3–6.
31 This move was expected to address the finance ministry's "lack of legal authority over government expenditures" (Silva-Herzog 1988:15); see also Bailey (1980).
32 Interview, Mexico City, January 7, 1992.
33 Interview, Mexico City, June 21, 1992.
34 Interview, Mexico City, June 16, 1992.
35 Interview, Mexico City, January 7, 1992.
36 The ministry of finance, the ministry of planning, and the central bank were consistently at the center of policy making for economic development. The identities of the two ministries were alternatively merged and separated. The ministry of finance and the ministry of economic planning and development had separate identities until they were merged in the ministry of finance and planning in 1976. They were divided into the ministry of finance and the ministry of economic planning and community affairs in 1978 and the title of the latter reverted to ministry of economic planning and development in 1980. Another merger of the two ministries occurred in 1983, and then another division in 1985 that resulted in the ministry of finance and the ministry of planning and national development (Cohen 1991:21–52. This paper was published in shorter version in 1992 in *Public Administration and Development*, Vol. 12:493–510).
37 Leonard (1991:69); see also Court (1984).
38 See especially Mutahaba (1989); Hyden (1984).
39 The following table indicates average wage earnings per employee in private sector and public sector occupations. For additional data, see World Bank (1983b:66). See also Leonard (1984:163) and World Bank (1991b).

Kenya: average wage earnings per employee (KL)

	1972	1975	1981	1986
Private sector				
Agriculture	94.1	115.6	237.9	373.1
Mining	259.3	401.3	412.0	546.3
Manufacturing	377.0	489.8	834.5	1,270.5
Construction	324.8	411.0	1,114.7	957.1
Trade, restaurants, and hotels	469.6	575.0	1,132.9	1,573.5
Transport, communications	458.6	619.1	1,781.7	1,710.6

Table cont				
Finance, insurance	858.1	962.5	547.9	2,375.7
Community, other services	198.7	265.4	—	891.5
Total private sector	247.9	326.2	688.2	1,029.8
Public Sector				
Central government	300.0	424.9	901.2	1,233.5
Parastatal bodies	326.8	391.7	852.8	1,610.4

Sources: World Bank (1983b:66); Mills (1988:16).

40   See Cohen (1991:12).
41   Cohen (1991:9).
42   Cohen (1991:8–11).
43   Cohen (1991:16).
44   Leonard (1991:Ch. 4).
45   Leonard (1991). David Court (1984) explores how the nature of the educational system in Kenya encouraged increasing inequalities in society. In politics, these inequalities translated into differences between the "haves" of the Kenyatta coalition and the "have nots" of the Moi coalition.
46   Leonard (1991:218). See Chapter 4 of Leonard's useful book for a good analysis of the links between the development vision and the personal interests of the technical and political elite.
47   See Leonard (1991) for an exploration of the careers of these officials. See Gordon (1990:16) for a discussion of their influence between 1982 and 1986. Throup (1989) includes Charles Njonjo and Mwai Kibaki on the list of influential technocrats.
48   For a discussion of the influence of these foreign advisors, see Cohen (1991).
49   Leonard (1991) discusses numerous incidents in which access to the president was the key factor in initiatives to alter policy or institutional structures. He also demonstrates how high level managers formed coalitions and facilitated access for each other.
50   See Gordon (1990:13, 15–16).
51   Gordon (1990).
52   *Weekly Review*, March 27, 1992:3–8, chronicles the activities of one of Moi's closest associates, Nicholas Biwott.
53   Leonard (1991:271). Leonard is referring not just to the technocrats, but to the bulk of Kikuyu senior officers who dominated the civil service.
54   Leonard (1991:271).
55   Interview, Nairobi, January 19, 1993. "Power is highly centralized at the top and technocrats are diffused in government. We can all do analyses. We can write reports and lay down all the issues and options. No one will stop you from doing this and being a good technocrat in this regard. But it all depends on who reads the report." Interview, Nairobi, January 11, 1993. Another observer noted that "Most of the technocrats understand the policy reforms and the reasons for them. But they lack the insulation necessary to make their case to the decision makers." Interview, January 11, 1993.
56   George Saitoti, minister of finance, minister of planning, and vice-president under Moi, was a good example. With a degree in mathematics and a prior career as a university professor, he had been identified with the technocrats in the mid-1980s. By the early 1990s, however, he was deeply implicated in financial scandals and not

noticeably influential in promoting sound economic policies. Simon Nyachae, one of the public sector managers whose life is explored by Leonard (1991), became minister of agriculture, livestock, and marketing under Moi in 1993. His leadership of this important ministry was noted for failure to pursue consistent policies and for lack of insulation from the political claims of Moi, his cronies, and his principal constituents.

57 Interview, Nairobi, January 11, 1993.

58 Foreign advisors had, since independence, played important roles in Kenyan policy making. See Leonard (1991:262–264). The important Sessional Paper No. 1 of 1986 was largely written by foreign advisors, supported and reviewed by the Kenyan technocrats.

59 Interview, Nairobi, January 7, 1993.

60 Cohen (1991: 12–13).

61 Cohen (1993:17).

62 Interview, Nairobi, January 11, 1993. See Cohen (1991:13) for additional discussion of underemployment among Kenyan officials.

63 Cohen (1991:12).

64 *Weekly Review*, January 22, 1993:5. See also *Finance*, January 19, 1993.

6. ADMINISTERING THE PUBLIC GOOD

1 See the discussion of the changing views about adjustment over the "long haul" in Nelson (1989).

2 For an analysis of the impact of the crisis on income and social welfare indicators, see Lustig (1992:Ch. 3).

3 Based on World Bank and IMF data used for analysis in Chapters 2 and 3.

4 Lustig (1992:80–81).

5 Lustig (1992:80–81). The corresponding rate of decline for overall programmable expenditures was 29.2 percent.

6 Lustig (1992:69).

7 Based on World Bank and IMF data used for analysis in Chapters 2 and 3.

8 Soberón, Frenk, and Sepúlveda (1986:678).

9 Langer, Lozano, and Bobadilla (1991:210).

10 Salinas de Gortari (1990: Anexo).

11 Lustig (1992:84–85). IMSS covered an average of 41.9 percent of the population and ISSSTE covered an average of 8.8 percent of the population during this period.

12 González Block (1991:67–68).

13 Langer, Lozano, and Bobadilla (1991:200).

14 Langer, Lozano, and Bobadilla (1991:204).

15 World Bank, *World Tables* (1991).

16 Langer, Lozano, and Bobadilla (1991:200–201, 213). The authors consider possible defects in the data related to methods of collection and analysis.

17 Programa Nacional de Solidaridad (1990:42).

18 Langer, Lozano, and Bobadilla (1991:197); de Lara Rangel (1987).

19 Interview, Mexico City, January 8, 1992.

20 Interview, Mexico City, January 20, 1992.

21 Interview, Mexico City, January 8, 1992. Research institutes also reported increased budgetary support. According to one official, this was because "We needed increased information and research precisely then, to try to understand and respond to the

impact of the crisis." Increased research funding is also a reflection of the increased presence and influence of technically trained personnel in the sector.

22 Prior reforms within the health care system had attempted to decentralize some functions while retaining central ministry control; the new reforms sought to give the states greater autonomy to set policy and manage the system, reserving the role of setting standards and norms for the central ministry.

23 Soberón, Frenk, and Sepúlveda (1986:673). Prior to decentralization, a relatively small proportion of the ministry of health budget was passed on to the state level. In 1980, for example, 40 percent was directed to the state level.

24 González Block (1991:73). In practice, the ministry of health also emphasized deconcentration over devolution of authority, at least until the mid-1980s.

25 González Block (1991).

26 González Block (1991).

27 González Block (1991:86). "In fact, the state governments did not want effective devolution of financial responsibility. Despite fiscal and administrative reforms to shore up revenues, the states' shares of federal appropriations were still meager, and what did come in was inefficiently applied. The states' own tax base, meanwhile, remained weak. Financial devolution would have given them more responsibility than they were prepared to handle" (González Block 1991:78).

28 González Block (1991:75).

29 Programa Nacional de Solidaridad (1992:3–4).

30 Interview, Mexico City, January 7, 1992.

31 Salinas de Gortari (1990: Anexo). The total figure includes adult and other non-traditional forms of education.

32 Based on World Bank and IMF data used for analysis in Chapters 2 and 3.

33 About two-thirds of Mexican states also had a parallel state system of schools, but this system was all but overwhelmed by the size of the national system.

34 Interview, Mexico City, June 19, 1992.

35 Salinas de Gortari (1990: Anexo).

36 Interview, Mexico City, June 21, 1992.

37 Street (1993:13).

38 See Pérez Arce, 1990.

39 Interview, Mexico City, June 18, 1992.

40 Interview, Mexico City, June 16, 1992.

41 See *New York Times*, August 30, 1993:A9.

42 Programa Nacional de Solidaridad (1992:2).

43 Programa Nacional de Solidaridad (1990:n.p.).

44 See Smoke (1993) on the diminishing power of local authorities over time.

45 See Cohen (1993:4). Republic of Kenya (1991b:229). Cohen reports that the public sector accounted for 49.6 percent of total wage employment in 1991.

46 Republic of Kenya (1992a: Appendix 3, p.85). A number of factors contributed to the expansion of the civil service, ranging from increased demand for services due to population increase and a gradually increasing role of government in the economy, to political concerns about unemployed school leavers and the use of public sector employment to reward political loyalty. See Cohen (1993:5–9).

47 Mills (1988:23).

48 Cohen (1993:10).

49 Republic of Kenya (1986:32).

50 Interview, Nairobi, January 12, 1993.
51 See, for example, *Weekly Review*, July 9, 1993:16–18. One official reflected the rising disgust many felt about corruption. "We all pay taxes and fees and we are getting tired of wondering where the money is going. It is certainly not going to fix the roads or improve conditions of life in Kenya ... It is ending up in corrupt officials' pockets." Interview, Nairobi, January 7, 1991.
52 Republic of Kenya (1986:24).
53 Kenya also has an extensive system of private and voluntary (missionary and non-governmental organization) hospitals and clinics.
54 Republic of Kenya (1992b).
55 Republic of Kenya (1992b:8).
56 Republic of Kenya (1992b:4).
57 Overall dimensions of mortality and morbidity were no doubt affected by the large role of the NGO sector and the missions in the provision of health care, particularly for the low-income population.
58 UNICEF (1988:44).
59 UNICEF (1988:44).
60 Republic of Kenya (1992b:6).
61 Dahlgren (1990:70).
62 Interview, Nairobi, April 7, 1993. See Mwega and Kabudo (1993).
63 UNESCO (1980, 1987). Other data indicate 1 doctor per 10,107 people in 1979, 1 doctor to 7,482 people in 1984, and 1 doctor to 7,542 people in 1987. Nurses were 1 to 1,144 in 1979; 1 to 1,139 in 1984; and 1 to 1,004 in 1987. See UNICEF (1988:55). The distribution of health professionals was heavily skewed toward urban areas, with urban areas averaging 1 doctor per 1,600 population and the remotest area of the country (Turkana) with 1 doctor per 160,000 people.
64 The process of negotiating the new plan is explored in Dahlgren (1990).
65 Dahlgren (1990:71–73).
66 In fact, the ministry had limited input into the decision-making process and was provided with little information about how to manage the user fee process. When the ministry asked for a thirty-day delay in introducing the system to enable its officials to develop an effective system for implementation, the request was denied (Interview, Nairobi, April 7, 1993).
67 Interview, April 7, 1993. See Karanja Wa Mbugua (1993:13).
68 Republic of Kenya (1992b:8–9).
69 *The Daily Nation*, editorial, January 12, 1990, quoted in Dahlgren (1990).
70 Dahlgren (1990:78–80).
71 Interview, Nairobi, April 7, 1993.
72 Based on World Bank and IMF data used for analysis in Chapters 2 and 3.
73 UNESCO (1980–1993). Text figures are based on the following data:

	1980	1988
Primary schools	10,255	14,288
Primary teachers	102,489	155,694
Primary students	3,930,991	5,123,581
Students/teacher	38	33

The number of secondary school teachers increased by 52 percent between 1980 and 1987; the number of secondary students increased by 30 percent between 1980 and 1988; the ratio of teachers to students was 1:25 in 1980 and 1:21 in 1987.

74   Republic of Kenya (1992a:Appendix 5).
75   In 1988, the World Bank reported a primary school enrollment of 94 percent; boys made up 52 percent of the total number of students, girls 48 percent. See World Bank (1988:Ch. 5).
76   Republic of Kenya (1991b:185). On the intake proportion, see Barber (1991:7).
77   Barber (1991:3).
78   Republic of Kenya (1990:48, 1991b:40).
79   World Bank (1991b:51). See *Weekly Review*, July 9, 1993:18–19.
80   Barber (1991:11).
81   Kibera (1993:17).
82   Kibera (1993:18).
83   Kibera (1993:21).
84   The employment of university graduates by government was deeply ingrained, amounting to "a contract with society." Interview, Nairobi, April 7, 1993.
85   Barber (1991:3,18).
86   Based on World Bank and IMF data used for analysis in Chapers 2 and 3.
87   In addition, the expansion of new roads under the Moi government may be related to the greater potential to benefit personally from government investments. According to some officials, pressure for increasing investment in new constructions came, not from those seeking better services, but from those seeking a cut of the government pie through the contracting system.

7.   RESPONDING TO SOCIETY

1   This is a major point made in Grindle (1980).
2   See especially Knight (1990).
3   See especially Craig (1990) for an analysis of the mobilization of rural interests during the 1930s and the legacy of this form of civic activism.
4   For a discussion of the links between 1968 and the 1980s, see Cornelius, Gentleman, and Smith (1989). See also Knight (1990).
5   See especially Pérez Arce (1990) on the dissident movement within the national teachers' union.
6   See Loaeza and Stern (1987).
7   *La Jornada*, May 5, 1988, reported in Aziz Nassif (1989:94).
8   See especially Ramírez Saiz (1990) on CONAMUP. On urban organizations more generally, see Bennett (1992).
9   Ramírez Saiz (1990:234).
10   Ramírez Saiz (1990:240–241).
11   The mayor of Mexico City is appointed by the president and serves on the national cabinet. The city's laws and regulations are set by the national congress.
12   Klesner (1991b:15, 25).
13   See especially Grindle (1991b).
14   Grindle (1991b:139–144).
15   See especially Fox (1992, 1993).
16   See especially Fox and Gordillo (1989).

17   Rubin (1987) provides a useful analysis of the events of Juchitán.

18   See Carr (1986) on the National "Plan de Ayala" Coordinating Committee.

19   See Fox and Gordillo (1989:152–155).

20   See Harvey (1990).

21   Cornelius (1993:21).

22   Klesner (1991a:153–154).

23   Cornelius (1993:30–31). The PRD was, in fact, an alliance of parties and movements of the left during and after the 1988 elections.

24   Cornelius (1993:31).

25   See Klesner (1991a).

26   Klesner (1991a:151); Cornelius (1993:33). Cornelius reports that only 60 percent of polling places had watchers from opposition political parties in 1988.

27   Popular sectors were identified largely as urban middle-, lower middle-, and lower-class groups who were not unionized. The National Confederation of Popular Organizations (CNOP) was one of the three constituent pillars of the PRI.

28   Cornelius, Craig, and Fox (1994b:8).

29   One observer commented, "The PRI started out with pork and with spoils. In the 1970s, it ran out of pork with the end of land to distribute and jobs to create and big investments. But it still had spoils. But then in the 1980s, it ran out of spoils and pork." He suggested that the "pork" was now being supplied by Solidarity. Interview, Mexico City, January 15, 1992.

30   Cornelius, Craig, and Fox (1994b:12).

31   Interview, Mexico City, June 24, 1992.

32   Interview, Mexico City, January 13, 1992

33   Dresser (1991:2) argues that Solidarity strengthened the party by providing new sources of patronage. My research, however, indicates that the party was able to take advantage of the new clientelism at the local level only if it adopted practices that supported the modernization of the party. See Bailey (1994:97).

34   Bailey (1994).

35   Dresser (1991:1–2). See also Bailey (1994); Dresser (1994).

36   Interview, Mexico City, January 10, 1992.

37   Cornelius (1993:40).

38   Cornelius (1993:41).

39   A government official indicated how the reformers within the party were proceeding. "[The head of the party] is important. He controls resources and he uses them against governors who want to go on playing the old game. The message is clear, play along with the new rules and the new people in power, or you won't get resources from the party for building political support." He indicated that in such cases, the party drew on Solidarity resources. Interview, Mexico City, January 13, 1992.

40   See Cornelius (1993:43–45). Klesner (1991b) discusses the electoral reforms in terms of "preemptive reform." He characterizes a 1977 reform of the electoral system which made it easier for small parties to register and contest elections as "a classic divide-and-conquer strategy" (p. 7). Over the longer term, however, such reforms may in fact have strengthened the capacity of opposition parties to challenge the PRI.

41   In a *Los Angeles Times* poll after the 1988 election, 2 percent of those who voted for the PRD and 11 percent of PAN voters said they believed the PRI won the election fairly. Interestingly, only 50 percent of PRI voting respondents believed their party won the election fairly. See Klesner (1991b:Table 17).

42 See Cornelius (1993:33).

43 Holmquist and Ford (1992:100–101).

44 *Society*, December 30, 1991:14.

45 See Widner (1992b:177–178).

46 The organization was accused of promoting "oathing," a practice initiated under the Mau Mau movement in the 1950s. The Mwakenya movement was widely discussed, but little is known of its actual activities. See Widner (1992b:175).

47 *Weekly Review*, June 19, 1992:3–10, provides a series of articles on the activism of the churches. See also the same periodical for May 22, 1992:12–13.

48 This was characterized as "an acrimonious debate about whether to withdraw into the spiritual concerns or whether the churches should be concerned with where we are standing" (Interview, Nairobi, January 22, 1993). See *Weekly Review*, June 19, 1992:5–7, for a discussion of dissent within the NCCK.

49 Widner (1992b:190–193).

50 Widner (1992b:192).

51 *Weekly Review*, March 27, 1992:20–21.

52 Widner (1992:188).

53 Interview, Nairobi, June 17, 1993.

54 According to one legal activist, "The government said it was a form of taxation. But this would have meant that any district commissioner could deny anyone a license for whatever reason." Interview, Nairobi, June 17, 1993.

55 Scotland Yard implicated a close associate of the president, Nicholas Biwatt, in the murder. Moi assented to his imprisonment but then released him.

56 Widner (1992b:192–194).

57 On the riots and increasing discontent, see *The Economist*, July 14, 1990:42.

58 *Weekly Review*, March 6, 1992:3–7.

59 "Appointment of close associates [of Moi] to key economic posts led to use of political criteria in the allocation of critical licenses and even in access to bank loans and foreign exchange. Second, meritocratic personnel policies were difficult to maintain because of interference in the hiring and firing of employees. Third, State House succeeded in manipulating the political process in order to secure new rules that promoted the private business interests of the president and his associates. For example, when Moi acquired bakery businesses, existing bakeries discovered that they faced new rules, quickly legislated, to limit their selling range to Nairobi and to eliminate the competition they would have provided to the president's own enterprises in other areas" (Widner 1992b:179).

60 Fowler (1991:54).

61 In what follows, I draw from the insightful comments of Kingston T. Kajese of January 22, 1993 and April 5, 1993. At the time, he was program officer of the Ford Foundation in Nairobi.

62 "In essence, the government saw a murky pond it wanted to fish in and instead of fishing with a hook to see whether the fish would see the bait, it simply threw dynamite into the pond to kill the bloody lot. This was how it decided to get rid of the Green Belt movement and the NCCK." Interview, Nairobi, January 22, 1993.

63 "This strategy of throwing dynamite raised an international outcry and in the process of resisting the legislation, the NGOs became more and more politicized. They found a political voice." Interview, Nairobi, January 22, 1993.

64 See Barkan (1992:183).

65 Kenya was the first African country to become the subject of political conditionality. See *The Economist*, November 30, 1991:42, for a discussion of the Paris meeting. The US ambassador, Smith Hempstone, played a leading role in encouraging the use of such conditionality. In May 1990, he began to join the issues of foreign assistance and democratic opening. Later, an initiative was undertaken in parliament to declare him *persona non grata*. See *Society*, December 30, 1991:17–22. See also Kuria (1991a, 1991b).

66 See especially Widner (1992b:174–177).

67 FORD limited its leadership cadre to avoid the necessity of having to register with the government under the Societies Act and to avoid a violation of the Section 2A of the constitution that declared KANU the only legal party. See Barkan (1993:13).

68 Barkan (1993:15).

69 A close observer of Kenyan politics reported on the "street talk" about government machinations in June 1993. "Efforts to encourage defection from opposition are rising in price. You can get 200,000 shillings for agreeing to have tea with the president. You can get 5 million shillings if you cross over. Those who cross over have to stand for election, and KANU ensures them their salary for the full term so even if they lose the election, they are set ... One new opposition MP ... reported being met at the bus stop by political and KANU operatives who whispered in her ear, made offers, heckled her, and harassed her. At the same time, it is increasingly dangerous to defect ... It could get you beaten and killed." Interview, Nairobi, June 16, 1993.

70 Interview, Nairobi, January 7, 1993.

71 Holmquist and Ford (1992:100).

72 Interview, Nairobi, April 6, 1993.

73 See Holmquist and Ford (1992:106–108).

74 One estimate is that corruption enriched some individuals by some 300 million dollars in 1992 alone. Another estimate indicated that ending corruption might add as much as 2 percent to GDP. See Barkan (1993:10). On corruption in government, see *Weekly Review*, March 27, 1992:3–11; July 9, 1993:16–18.

75 See Barkan (1993:26–27).

76 Interview, Nairobi, January 22, 1993.

77 Holmquist and Ford (1992:98).

78 Interview, January 11, 1993.

79 The International Republican Institute, one of the organizations involved in monitoring the elections, concluded that as many as 3 million eligible Kenyans were not allowed to vote because of a flawed registration process.

80 Barkan (1993:20) indicates that the money supply increased by 40 percent in the last three months of 1992.

81 Barkan (1993:17).

82 See Barkan (1993:16–17) for a summary of the role of Moi and KANU in the violence. He reports that some 1,000 people died as a result of this ethnic violence and some 50,000 people were driven from their homes. Other estimates place the number of deaths at 400 and 1,200 (Holmquist and Ford 1992:103). A coalition of opposition groups implicated the government.

83 Holmquist and Ford (1992:103). See also *Weekly Review*, April 9, 1993:9–10.

84 Barkan (1993:16).

85 International Republican Institute (1992).

86　Barkan (1993:21).

87　One observer reflected that "The voting was rigged. But more important, the whole system is rigged. It is rigged in favor of some who can campaign and some who can't, who can go where for what purpose, and who can advertise and who can't." Interview, Nairobi, January 11, 1993.

8. STATES OF CHANGE

1　The reasons for the extensive role of political leaders in developing countries are presented in Grindle and Thomas (1991:Ch. 3). For an interesting case study of leadership and economic reform, see Naim (1993). See also Ascher (1984).

2　See Waterbury (1992:192–194).

3　Grindle and Thoumi (1993).

References

Adepoju, Aderanti, ed. 1993 *The Impact of Structural Adjustment on the Population of Africa*. London: United Nations Population Fund.

Aguirre, Juan Manuel 1992 "Economic Policy Making in Chile." Personal correspondence, Cambridge, MA.

Ajayi, S. Ibi 1990 "Graduate Training in Economics in Nigeria and Ghana." Special Paper no. 6. Nairobi, Kenya: African Economic Research Consortium.

Almond, Gabriel A., and G. Bingham Powell, Jr. 1966 *Comparative Politics: A Developmental Approach*. Boston: Little, Brown and Company.

Ames, Barry 1987 *Political Survival: Politicians and Public Policy in Latin America*. Berkeley: University of California Press.

Amsden, Alice 1989 *Asia's Next Grant: South Korea and Late Industrialization*. New York: Oxford University Press.

Ascher, William 1984 *Scheming for the Poor: The Politics of Redistribution in Latin America*. Cambridge, MA: Harvard University Press.

Aspe, Pedro 1993 *Economic Transformation the Mexican Way*. Cambridge, MA: MIT Press.

Azarya, Victor 1988 "Reordering State – Society Relations: Incorporation and Disengagement." In *The Precarious Balance: State and Society in Africa*, ed. Donald Rothchild and Naomi Chazan. Boulder, CO: Westview Press.

Aziz Nassif, Alberto 1989 "Regional Dimensions of Democratization." In *Mexico's Alternative Futures*, ed. Wayne A. Cornelius, Judith Gentleman, and Peter H. Smith. San Diego: Center for US – Mexican Studies, University of California.

Bailey, John 1980 "Presidency, Bureaucracy, and Administrative Reform in Mexico: The Secretariat of Programming and Budget." *Inter-American Economic Affairs* 34, no. 1:27–60.

1988 *Governing Mexico: The Statecraft of Crisis Management*. London: MacMillan Press.

1994 "Centralism and Political Change in Mexico: The Case of National Solidarity." In *Transforming State – Society Relations in Mexico: The National Solidarity Strategy*, ed. Wayne A. Cornelius, Ann L. Craig, and Jonathan Fox. San Diego: Center for US – Mexican Studies, University of California.

Barber, Gerald A. 1991 "Adjustment of Education Sector Policy at a Time of Financial Restraint." Technical Paper 91–03. Nairobi: Ministry of Planning and National Development, Republic of Kenya.

Bardhan, Pranab 1989 "The New Institutional Economics and Development Theory: A Brief Critical Assessment." *World Development* 17, no. 9:1389–1395.

Barkan, Joel D. 1987 "The Electoral Process and Peasant – State Relations in Kenya." In *Elections in Independent Africa*, ed. Fred M. Hayward. Boulder, CO: Westview Press.

1992 "The Rise and Fall of a Governance Realm in Kenya." In *Governance and Politics in Africa*, ed. Goran Hyden and Michael Bratton. Boulder, CO: Lynne Rienner Publishers.

1993 "Kenya: Lessons from a Flawed Election." *Journal of Democracy* 4, no. 3 (July): 85–99.

Barkan, Joel D., and Michael Chegge 1989 "Decentralizing the State: District Focus and the Politics of Reallocation in Kenya." *Journal of Modern African Studies* 27, no. 3:431–453.

Barkan, Joel D., and Frank Holmquist 1989 "Peasant – State Relations and the Social Base of Self-Help in Kenya." *World Politics* 41, no. 3:359–380.

Basáñez, Miguel 1993 "Is Mexico Headed toward its Fifth Crisis?" In *Political and Economic Liberalization in Mexico: At a Critical Juncture?*, ed. Riordan Roett. Boulder, CO: Lynne Rienner Publishers.

Bates, Robert H. 1981 *Markets and States in Tropical Africa*. Berkeley: University of California Press.

1989 *Beyond the Miracle of the Market: The Political Economy of Agrarian Development in Kenya*. Cambridge: Cambridge University Press.

Bazdresch, Carlos, and Santiago Levy 1991 "Populism and Economic Policy in Mexico." In *The Macroeconomics of Populism in Latin America*, ed. Rudiger Dornbusch and Sebastian Edwards. Chicago: University of Chicago Press.

Bennett, Douglas C., and Kenneth E. Sharpe 1985 *Transnational Corporations versus the State: The Political Economy of the Mexican Auto Industry*. Princeton: Princeton University Press.

Bennett, Vivienne 1992 "The Evolution of Urban Popular Movements in Mexico between 1968 and 1988." In *The Making of Social Movements in Latin America: Identity, Strategy and Democracy*, ed. Arturo Alvarez and Sonia E. Alvarez. Boulder, CO: Westview Press.

Beristain, Javier, and Ignacio Trigueros 1990 "Mexico." In *Latin American Adjustment: How Much Has Happened?*, ed. John Williamson. Washington, DC: Institute for International Economics.

Berry, Albert, Ronald G. Hellman, and Mauricio Solaún, eds. 1980 *Politics of Compromise: Coalition Government in Colombia*. New Brunswick, NJ: Transaction Books.

Bevan, David, Paul Collier, and Jan Willem Gunning 1990 *Controlled Open Economics: A Neoclassical Approach to Structuralism*. Oxford: Clarendon Press.

1993 *Agriculture and the Policy Environment: Tanzania and Kenya*. Paris: Organization for Economic Cooperation and Development.

Bhagwati, Jagdish N. 1978 *Foreign Trade Regimes and Economic Development: Anatomy and Consequences of Exchange Control Regimes*. Cambridge, MA: Ballinger.

Boeninger, Edgardo 1991 "Governance and Development: Issues, Challenges, Opportunities and Constraints." Paper prepared for the World Bank Conference on Development Economics, Washington, DC, April 25–26.

Bourguignon, François, Jaime de Melo, and Christian Morrisson 1991 "Poverty and Income Distribution during Adjustment: Issues and Evidence from the OECD Project." *World Development* 19, no. 11:1485–1508.

Bowen, Merle L. 1991 "Mozambique and the Politics of Economic Recovery." *The Fletcher Forum of World Affairs* 15, no. 1:45–55.

Bratton, Michael 1989 "Beyond the State: Civil Society and Associational Life in Africa." *World Politics* 41, no. 3:407–430.

Bratton, Michael, and Nicolas van de Walle 1992 "Toward Governance in Africa: Popular Demands and State Responses." In *Governance and Politics in Africa*, ed. Goran Hyden and Michael Bratton. Boulder, CO: Lynne Rienner Publishers.

Bright, Charles, and Susan Harding 1984 "Processes of Statemaking and Popular Protest: An Introduction." In *Statemaking and Social Movements: Essays in History and Theory*, ed. Charles Bright and Susan Harding. Ann Arbor: University of Michigan Press.

Buchanan, J.M., Robert D. Tollison, and Gordon Tullock, eds. 1980 *Toward a Theory of the Rent-Seeking Society*. College Station: Texas A&M University Press.

Callaghy, Thomas M. 1986 "Politics and Vision in Africa: The Interplay of Domination, Equality and Liberty." In *Political Domination in Africa*, ed. Patrick Chabal. Cambridge: Cambridge University Press.

1989 "Toward State Capability and Embedded Liberalism in the Third World: Lessons for Adjustment." In *Fragile Coalitions: The Politics of Economic Adjustment*, ed. Joan M. Nelson and contributors. New Brunswick, NJ: Transaction Books.

Camp, Roderick 1985 "The Political Technocrat in Mexico and the Survival of the Political System." *Latin American Research Review* 20, no. 1:97–118.

Cardoso, E., and A. Helwege 1992 "Below the Line: Poverty in Latin America." *World Development* 20, no. 1:19–38.

Carr, Barry 1986 "The Mexican Left, the Popular Movements, and the Politics of Austerity, 1982–1985." In *The Mexican Left, the Popular Movements, and the Politics of Austerity*, ed. Barry Carr and Ricardo Anzaldría Montoya. La Jolla: University of California at San Diego, Center for US – Mexican Studies.

Castells, Manuel 1983 *The City and the Grassroots*. London: Edward Arnold.

Centeno, Miguel Angel, and Sylvia Maxfield 1992 "The Marriage of Finance and Order: Changes in the Mexican Political Elite." *Journal of Latin American Studies* 29, Part I (February):57–85.

Chabal, Patrick 1986 "Introduction: Thinking about Politics in Africa." In *Political Domination in Africa*, ed. Patrick Chabal. Cambridge: Cambridge University Press.

Chazan, Naomi 1988a "Patterns of State – Society Incorporation and Disengagement in Africa." In *The Precarious Balance: State and Society in Africa*, ed. Donald Rothchild and Naomi Chazan. Boulder, CO: Westview Press.

1988b "State and Society in Africa: Images and Challenges." In *The Precarious Balance: State and Society in Africa*, ed. Donald Rothchild and Naomi Chazan. Boulder, CO: Westview Press.

Chazan, Naomi, Robert Mortimer, John Ravenhill, and Donald Rothchild 1992 *Politics and Society in Contemporary Africa*. Boulder, CO: Lynne Rienner Publishers.

Chew, David C. 1990 "Internal Adjustments to Falling Civil Service Salaries: Insights from Uganda." *World Development* 18, no. 7:1003–1014.

Cleaves, Peter S. 1987 *Professions and the State: The Mexican Case*. Tucson: University of Arizona Press.

Cohen, Jean L. 1985 "Strategy or Identity: New Theoretical Paradigms and Contemporary Social Movements." *Social Research* 52, no. 4:663–716.

Cohen, John M. 1991 "Expatriate Advisors in the Government of Kenya: Why They Are There and What Can Be Done About It." Cambridge, MA: Harvard Institute for International Development, Development Discussion Paper No. 376.

1992 "Foreign Advisors and Capacity Building: The Case of Kenya." *Public Administration and Development* 12, no. 5:493–510.

1993 "Importance of Public Service Reform in Africa: The Case of Kenya." Unpublished manuscript, Harvard Institute for International Development, Cambridge, MA.

Cohen, John, and Richard Hook 1987 *District Development Planning in Kenya.* Cambridge, MA: Harvard Institute for International Development, Development Discussion Paper No. 229.

Colander, David C., ed. 1984 *Neoclassical Political Economy: The Analysis of Rent-Seeking and DUP Activities.* Cambridge, MA: Ballinger Publishing Co.

Colburn, Forrest D. 1990a "Statism, Rationality, and State Centrism." *Comparative Politics* 20, no. 4:485–492.

1990b *Prospects for Democracy in Latin America.* Princeton: Center for International Studies, Princeton University.

Collier, David 1979 "Glossary." In *The New Authoritarianism in Latin America,* ed. David Collier. Princeton: Princeton University Press.

Collier, Ruth Berins 1992 *The Contradictory Alliance: State – Labor Relations and Regime Change in Mexico.* Berkeley: University of California, International and Area Studies Series.

Colombi, Pedro 1992 "Economic Policy Making in Argentina." Personal correspondence, Cambridge, MA.

Cordera, Rolando, and Carlos Tello 1981 *Mexico – La disputa por la nación: perspectivas y opciones del desarrollo.* Mexico: Siglo Veintiuno Editores.

Córdoba, José 1991 "Diez lecciones de la reforma económica en Mexico." *Nexos* 14 (February): 31–48.

Cornelius, Wayne A. 1975 *Politics and the Migrant Poor in Mexico City.* Stanford: Stanford University Press.

1993 "Mexico's Incomplete Democratic Transition." Paper presented at the 34th Annual Convention of The International Studies Association, Acapulco, Mexico, March 23–27.

Cornelius, Wayne A., and Ann L. Craig 1991 *The Mexican Political System in Transition.* San Diego: Center for US – Mexican Studies, University of California.

Cornelius, Wayne A., Ann L. Craig, and Jonathan Fox, eds. 1994a *Transforming State – Society Relations in Mexico: The National Solidarity Strategy.* San Diego: Center for US – Mexican Studies, University of California.

1994b "Mexico's National Solidarity Program: An Overview." In *Transforming State – Society Relations in Mexico: The National Solidarity Strategy,* ed. Wayne A. Cornelius, Ann L. Craig, and Jonathan Fox. San Diego: Center for US – Mexican Studies, University of California.

Cornelius, Wayne A., Judith Gentleman, and Peter H. Smith 1989 "The Dynamics of Political Change in Mexico." In *Mexico's Alternative Political Futures,* ed. Wayne A. Cornelius, Judith Gentleman, and Peter H. Smith. San Diego: Center for US – Mexican Studies, University of California.

Cornia, Giovanni Andrea, Richard Jolly, and Frances Stewart 1987 *Adjustment with a Human Face: Protecting the Vulnerable and Promoting Growth.* New York: Oxford University Press.

Court, David 1984 "The Education System as a Response to Inequality." In *Politics and Public Policy in Kenya and Tanzania*, rev. edn., ed. Joel Barkan. New York: Praeger.

Craig, Ann L. 1990 "Legal Constraints and Mobilization Strategies in the Countryside." In *Popular Movements and Political Change in Mexico*, ed. Joe Foweraker and Ann L. Craig. Boulder, CO: Lynne Rienner Publishers.

Crane, Catalina 1992 "Economic Policy Making in Colombia." Personal correspondence, Cambridge, MA.

Currie, Kate, and Larry Ray 1985 "State and Class in Kenya – Notes on the Cohesion of the Ruling Class." *Journal of Modern African Studies* 22, no. 4:559–593.

Dahlgren, Göran 1990 "Strategies for Health Financing in Kenya – The Difficult Birth of a New Policy." *Scandinavian Journal of Social Medicine* 46, Suppl.:67–81.

Davis, Diane E. 1992 "Mexico's New Politics: Changing Perspectives on Free Trade." *World Policy Journal* 9, no. 4 (Fall/Winter):655–671.

de la Garza Toledo, Enrique 1991 "Independent Trade Unionism in Mexico: Past Developments and Future Perspectives." In *Unions, Workers and the State in Mexico*, ed. Kevin J. Middlebrook. San Diego: Center for US–Mexican Studies, University of California.

de Lara Rangel 1987 "El impacto económico de la crisis sobre la clase media." In *Las clases medias en la coyuntura actual*. Mexico, DF: Centro de Estudios Sociológicos, Colegio de México.

Diamond, Larry 1988 Introduction to *Democracy in Developing Countries: Africa*, ed. Larry Diamond, Juan J. Linz, and Seymour Martin Lipset. Boulder, CO: Lynne Rienner Publishers.

Dix, Robert H. 1991 "Latin American Democracy 1960–1990." Unpublished manuscript.

Domínguez, Jorge 1993 "Technopols: Ideas, Leaders, and their Impact on Freeing Politics and Freeing Markets in Major Latin American Countries in the 1980s and 1990s." Paper presented for the Harvard Workshop on Technopols in Latin America, April 16.

Dornbusch, Rudiger, and Sebastian Edwards, eds. 1991 *The Macroeconomics of Populism in Latin America*. Chicago: University of Chicago Press.

Dresser, Denise 1991 *Neopopulist Solutions to Neoliberal Problems: Mexico's National Solidarity Program*. San Diego: Center for US–Mexican Studies, University of California.

   1994 "Bringing the Poor Back In: National Solidarity as a Strategy of Regime Legitimation." In *Transforming State-Society Relations in Mexico: The National Solidarity Strategy*, ed. Wayne A. Cornelius, Ann L. Craig, and Jonathan Fox. San Diego: Center for US–Mexican Studies, University of California.

Eckstein, Susan, ed. 1989 *Power and Popular Protest: Latin American Social Movements*. Berkeley: University of California Press.

Economic Review (Nairobi) 1990–1993 Various

The Economist Various.

Escobar, Arturo, and Sonia E. Alvarez, eds. 1992 *The Making of Social Movements in Latin America: Identity, Strategy and Democracy*. Boulder, CO: Westview Press.

Estados Unidos Mexicanos 1972 *IX censo general de población: Resumen general*. Secretaría de Industria y Comercio, México, D.F.

Evans, Peter 1992 "The State as Problem and Solution: Predation, Embedded Autonomy, and Structural Change." In *The Politics of Economic Adjustment*, ed. Stephan Haggard and Robert R. Kaufman. Princeton: Princeton University Press.

Evans, Peter B., Dietrich Rueschemeyer, and Theda Skocpol, eds. 1985 *Bringing the State Back In*. Cambridge: Cambridge University Press.

Fadayomi, T.O. 1993 "Nigeria: Consequences for Education." In *The Impact of Structural Adjustment on the Population of Africa*, ed. Aderanti Adepoju. London: United Nations Population Fund.

Fajnzylber, Fernando 1990 *Unavoidable Industrial Restructuring in Latin America*. Durham, NC: Duke University Press.

Fals Borda, Orlando 1990 "Social Movements and Political Power: Evolution in Latin America." *International Sociology* 5, no. 2:115–127.

Felix, David 1990 "Latin America's Debt Crisis." *World Policy Journal* 7, no. 4:733–772.

Finance (Nairobi) 1990–1993 Various.

Fitch, Samuel J., and Andres Fontana 1991 "Military Policy and Democratic Consolidation in Latin America." Paper prepared for the XVI International Congress of the Latin American Studies Association, Washington, DC, April 4–6.

Foweraker, Joe 1989 "Popular Movements and the Transformation of the System." In *Mexico's Alternative Political Futures*, ed. Wayne A. Cornelius, Judith Gentleman, and Peter H. Smith. San Diego: Center for US–Mexican Studies, University of California.

1990 "Popular Movements and Political Change in Mexico." In *Popular Movements and Political Change in Mexico*, ed. Joe Foweraker and Ann L. Craig. Boulder, CO: Lynne Rienner Publishers.

Foweraker, Joe, and Ann L. Craig, eds. 1990 *Popular Movements and Political Change in Mexico*. Boulder, CO: Lynne Rienner Publishers.

Fowler, Alan 1991 "The Role of NGOs in Changing State–Society Relations: Perspectives from Eastern and Southern Africa." *Development Policy Review* 9, no. 1:53–84.

Fox, Jonathan 1992 "Democratic Rural Development: Leadership Accountability in Regional Peasant Organizations." *Development and Change* 23, no. 2:1–36.

1993 *The Politics of Food in Mexico: State Power and Social Mobilization*. Ithaca, NY: Cornell University Press.

Fox, Jonathan, and Gustavo Gordillo 1989 "Between State and Market: The Campesinos' Quest for Autonomy." In *Mexico's Alternative Political Futures*, ed. Wayne A. Cornelius, Judith Gentleman, and Peter H. Smith. San Diego: Center for US–Mexican Studies, University of California.

Frenk, Julio 1989 "Salud y Crisis Económica." *Nexos*, no. 16:35–36.

Fuentes, Marta, and Andre Gunder Frank 1989 "Ten Theses on Social Movements." *World Development* 17, no. 2:179–191.

Garrido, Luís Javier 1989 "The Crisis of Presidencialismo." In *Mexico's Alternative Political Futures*, ed. Wayne A. Cornelius, Judith Gentleman, and Peter H. Smith. La Jolla: University of California at San Diego, Center for US–Mexican Studies.

Gereffi, Gary 1991 "International Economics and Domestic Policies." In *Economy and Society: State of the Art*, ed. Neil J. Smelser and Alberto Martinelli. Newbury Park, CA: Sage Publications.

Gereffi, Gary, and Donald Wyman, eds. 1990 *Manufacturing Miracles: Paths of Industrialization in Latin America and East Asia*. Princeton: Princeton University Press.

Gindling, T.H., and Albert Berry 1992 "The Performance of the Labor Market during Recession and Structural Adjustment: Costa Rica in the 1980s." *World Development* 20, no. 1:1599–1616.

Golob, Stephanie R. 1993 " 'Making Possible What Is Necessary': Pedro Aspe, the Salinas Team, and the Next Mexican Miracle." Unpublished paper, Department of Government, Harvard University.

González Block, Miguel Angel 1991 "Economic Crisis and the Decentralization of Health Services in Mexico." In *Social Responses to Mexico's Economic Crisis of the 80's*, ed. Mercedes Gonzalez de la Rocha and Agustín Escobar Latapí. San Diego: Center for US-Mexican Studies, University of California.

Gordon, David 1990 "The Political Economy of Economic Reform in Kenya." Paper prepared for the Center for Strategic and International Studies, Washington, DC.

Gordon, Henry, and Neil Spooner 1992 "Grain Marketing Reform in Kenya: Principle and Practice." PAM Papers. Egerton University, June.

Grindle, Merilee S. 1977 *Bureaucrats, Politicians, and Peasants in Mexico: A Case Study in Public Policy*. Berkeley: University of California Press.

 1986 *State and Countryside: Development Policy and Agrarian Politics in Latin America*. Baltimore: Johns Hopkins University Press.

 1991a "The New Political Economy: Positive Economics and Negative Politics." In *Politics and Policy Making in Developing Countries: Perspectives on the New Political Economy*, ed. Gerald M. Meier. San Francisco: ICS Press.

 1991b "The Response to Austerity: Political and Economic Strategies of Mexico's Rural Poor." In *Social Responses to Mexico's Economic Crisis of the 1980s*, ed. Mercedes Gonzalez de la Rocha and Agustín Escobar Latapí. San Diego: Center for US–Mexican Studies, University of California.

Grindle, Merilee S., ed. 1980 *The Politics of Policy Implementation in the Third World*. Princeton: Princeton University Press.

Grindle, Merilee S., and John W. Thomas 1991 *Public Choices and Policy Change: The Political Economy of Reform in Developing Countries*. Baltimore: Johns Hopkins University Press.

Grindle, Merilee S., and Francisco Thoumi 1993 "Muddling toward Adjustment: The Political Economy of Economic Policy Change in Ecuador." In *Political & Economic Interactions in Economic Policy Reform*, ed. Ann O. Krueger and Robert H. Bates. Cambridge, MA: Blackwell Publishers.

Grosh, Barbara 1991 *Public Enterprises in Kenya: What Works, What Doesn't, and Why*. Boulder, CO: Lynne Rienner Publishers.

Gugerty, Mary Kay 1993 "Privatization and Public Enterprise Reform: The Case of 'Strategic Parastatals' in Kenya." Unpublished paper, J.F. Kennedy School of Government, Harvard University.

Gulhati, Ravi 1990 "Who Makes Economic Policy in Africa and How?" *World Development* 18, no. 8:1147–1161.

Haggard, Stephan, and Robert R. Kaufman, eds.1992 *The Politics of Economic Adjustment*. Princeton: Princeton University Press.

Haggard, Stephan, and Chung-In Moon 1983 "The South Korean State in the International Economy: Liberal, Dependent, or Mercantile?" In *The Antinomies of Interdependence*, ed. John Ruggie. New York: Columbia University Press.

Hagopian, Frances 1990 " 'Democracy by Undemocratic Means'?" *Comparative Political Studies* 23, no. 2:147–170.

Hall, Peter A. 1989 Introduction to *The Political Power of Economic Ideas: Keynesianism across Nations*, by Peter A. Hall. Princeton: Princeton University Press.

Hamilton, Nora 1982 *The Limits of State Autonomy: Post-Revolutionary Mexico.* Princeton: Princeton University Press.

Hansen, Roger 1971 *The Politics of Mexican Development.* Baltimore: Johns Hopkins University Press.

Harberger, Arnold C. 1984 "Economic Policy and Economic Growth." In *World Economic Growth*, ed. Arnold C. Harberger. San Francisco: Institute for Contemporary Studies.

Harvey, Neil 1990 "Peasant Strategies and Corporatism in Chiapas." In *Popular Movements and Political Change in Mexico*, ed. Joe Foweraker and Ann L. Craig. Boulder, CO: Lynne Rienner Publishers.

Hellman, Judith Adler 1992 "The Study of New Social Movements in Latin America and the Question of Autonomy." In *The Making of Social Movements in Latin America: Identity, Strategy and Democracy*, ed. Arturo Escobar and Sonia E. Alvarez. Boulder, CO: Westview Press.

Herbst, Jeffrey 1990 "The Structural Adjustment of Politics in Africa." *World Development* 18, no. 7:949–958.

1992 "The Dilemmas of Explaining Political Upheaval: Ghana in Comparative Perspective." Paper prepared for the Colloquium on the Economics of Political Liberalization in Africa, Harvard University, March 6–7.

Hilderbrand, Mary Ellen 1992 "Crisis, Constraints, and State–Society Relations: The Politics of African Adjustment in the 1980s." PhD dissertation, Department of Government, Harvard University.

Hirschmann, David 1991 "Women and Participation in Africa: Broadening the Scope of Research." *World Development* 19, no. 12:1679–1694.

Holmquist, Frank, and Michael Ford 1992 "Kenya: Slouching toward Democracy," *Africa Today* 39, no. 3: 97–111.

Hommes, Rudolf 1990 "Colombia." In *Latin American Adjustment: How Much Has Happened?*, ed. John Williamson. Washington, DC: Institute for International Economics.

Hopkins, Raymond F. 1990 "The Role of Governance in Economic Development." Paper prepared for the Task Force on Development Assistance and Cooperation (Agriculture 2000), November 14–15.

Hornsby, Ann 1991 *Pushing for Democracy in Columbia: Non-Profit Challenges to Dependence on the State.* PhD dissertation, Department of Sociology, Harvard University, September.

Huntington, Samuel P. 1968 *Political Order in Changing Societies.* New Haven: Yale University Press.

1991 *The Third Wave: Democratization in the Late Twentieth Century.* Norman, OK: University of Oklahoma Press.

Hyden, Goran 1984 "Administration and Public Policy." In *Politics and Public Policy in Kenya and Tanzania*, rev. edn., ed. Joel Barkan. New York: Praeger.

1990 "Reciprocity and Governance in Africa." In *The Failure of the Centralized State: Institutions and Self-Governance in Africa*, ed. James S. Wunsch and Dele Olowu. Boulder, CO: Westview Press.

IMF (International Monetary Fund) 1992a *Government Financial Statistics*, Washington, DC.

1992b *International Financial Statistics*, Washington, DC.

INEGI (Instituto Nacional de Estadística Geografía e Informática) 1984 *Participación del sector público en el producto interno bruto de México 1975–1983.* Mexico City: INEGI.

International Republican Institute 1992 "Final Report on December 1992 Kenya Elections." Washington, DC.

Israel, Arturo 1990 "The Changing Role of the State: Institutional Dimensions." Working Paper No. 495 (August). Washington, DC: Country Economics Department, World Bank.

Jackson, Robert H. 1987 "Quasi-States, Dual Regimes, and Neoclassical Theory: International Jurisprudence and the Third World." *International Organization* 41, no. 4:519–549.

Jackson, Robert H., and Carl Rosberg 1982 "Why Africa's Weak States Persist: The Empirical and the Juridical in Statehood." *World Politics* 35, no. 1:1–24.

Joseph, Richard, ed. 1990 *African Governance in the 1990s.* The Carter Center, Emory University.

Kahler, Miles 1989 "International Financial Institutions and the Politics of Adjustment." In *Fragile Coalitions: The Politics of Economic Adjustment*, ed. Joan M. Nelson and contributors. New Brunswick, NJ: Transaction Books.

Karanja Wa Mbugua, J. 1993 "Has Targeting Worked in the Health Sector?" *DPMN Bulletin* 1, no. 3:12–13.

Karl, Terry 1986 "Petroleum and Political Pacts: The Transition to Democracy." In *Transitions from Authoritarian Rule: Latin America*, ed. Guillermo O'Donnell, Philippe C. Schmitter, and Laurence Whitehead. Baltimore: Johns Hopkins University Press.

1990 "Dilemmas of Democratization in Latin America." *Comparative Politics* 23, no. 1:1–21.

Kibera, Lucy W. 1993 "Vocationalising Kenya's Secondary School Curriculum: Career and Educational Aspirations of Boys and Girls." Working Paper no. 490. Institute for Development Studies, University of Nairobi.

Killick, Tony 1989 *A Reaction too Far: Economic Theory and the Role of the State in Developing Countries.* London: Overseas Development Institute.

1993 *The Adaptive Economy: Adjustment Policies in Small, Low-Income Countries.* Washington, DC: EDI.

Kimenyi, Mwangi S. 1989 "Interest Groups, Transfer Seeking, and Democratization: Competition for the Benefits of Government Power that May Explain African Political Instability." *American Journal of Economics and Sociology* 48, no. 3:339–349.

Klesner, Joseph L. 1991a "Challenges for Mexico's Opposition in the Coming Sexenio." In *Sucesion Presidencial: The 1988 Mexican Presidential Election*, ed. Edgar W. Butler and Jorge A. Bustamente, Boulder, CO: Westview Press.

1991b "Modernization, Economic Crisis, and Electoral Realignment in Mexico." Paper prepared for the XVI International Congress of the Latin American Studies Association, Washington, DC, April 3–6.

Knight, Alan 1990 "Historical Continuities in Social Movements." In *Popular Movements and Political Change in Mexico*, ed. Joel Foweraker and Ann L. Craig. Boulder, CO: Lynne Rienner Publishers.

Krasner, Stephan D. 1984 "Approaches to the State: Alternative Conceptions and Historical Dynamics." *Comparative Politics* 16, no. 2:223–246.

Krueger, Anne O. 1974 "The Political Economy of the Rent-Seeking Society." *American Economic Review* 64, no. 3:291–303.

Kuria, Gibson Kamau 1991a "Confronting Dictatorship in Kenya." *Journal of Democracy* 2, no. 4:115–125.

1991b "Human Rights and Democracy in Africa." *The Fletcher Forum of World Affairs* 15, no. 1:23–36.

Lal, Deepak 1984 "The Political Economy of Predatory State." Discussion Paper 105. Washington, DC: Development Research Department, World Bank.

Lambert, Sylvie, Harmut Schneider, and Akiko Suwa 1991 "Adjustment and Equity in Côte d'Ivoire:1980–86." *World Development* 19, no. 11:1563–1576.

Lancaster, Carol 1991 "Journeys without Maps." *The Fletcher Forum of World Affairs* 15, no. 1:1–8.

Langer, Ana, Rafael Lozano, and José Luis Bobadilla 1991 "Effects of Mexico's Economic Crisis on the Health of Women and Children." In *Social Responses to Mexico's Economic Crisis of the 1980s*, ed. Mercedes Gonzalez de la Rocha and Agustín Escobar Latapí. San Diego: Center for US–Mexican Studies, University of California.

Lemarchand, Rene 1989 "African Peasantries, Reciprocity and the Market: The Economy of Affection Reconsidered." *Cahiers d'Etudes Africaines* 113, no. 24:33–67.

Leonard, David K. 1984 "Class Formation and Agricultural Development." In *Politics and Public Policy in Kenya and Tanzania*, rev. edn., ed. Joel Barkan. New York: Praeger.

1991 *African Successes: Four Public Managers of Kenyan Rural Development*. Berkeley: University of California Press.

Levine, Daniel H. 1988 "Paradigm Lost: Dependence to Democracy." *World Politics* 40, no. 3:377–394.

Le Vine, Victor 1989 "The State of the State in Africa." *Africa Today* 36, no. 2:55–56.

Leys, Colin 1975 *Underdevelopment in Kenya: The Political Economy of Neo-Colonialism.* Berkeley: University of California Press.

Linz, Juan J., and Alfred Stepan, eds. 1978 *The Breakdown of Democratic Regimes: Latin America*. Baltimore: Johns Hopkins University Press.

Loaeza, Soledad 1988 *Clases medias y política en México.* Mexico: Colegio de México.

Loaeza, Soledad, and Claudio Stern 1987 *Las clases medias en la coyuntura actual.* Mexico, DF: Centro de Estudios Sociologicos, Colegio de México.

Lofchie, Michael F. 1989 *The Policy Factor: Agricultural Performance in Kenya and Tanzania.* Boulder, CO: Lynne Rienner Publishers.

López Monjardín, Adriana 1991 "Organization and Struggle among Agricultural Workers in Mexico." In *Unions, Workers, and the State in Mexico*, ed. Kevin J. Middlebrook. San Diego: Center for US–Mexican Studies, University of California.

Lustig, Nora 1990 "Economic Crisis, Adjustment and Living Standards in Mexico, 1982–85." *World Development* 18, no. 10: 1325–1342.

1992 *Mexico: The Remaking of an Economy.* Washington, DC: The Brookings Institution.

McAdam, Doug, John D. McCarthy, and Mayer N. Zald 1988 "Social Movements." In *Handbook of Sociology*, ed. Neil Smelser and Ron Burt. Beverly Hills, CA: Sage Publications.

McClintock, Cynthia 1989 "The Prospects of Consolidation in a 'Least Likely' Case: Peru." *Comparative Politics* 21, no. 2:127–148.

Malloy, James M. 1989 "Policy Analysts, Public Policy and Regime Structure in Latin America." *Governance: An International Journal of Policy and Administration* 2, no. 3:315–338.

Maxfield, Sylvia 1989 "International Economic Opening and Government–Business Relations." In *Mexico's Alternative Futures*, ed. Wayne A. Cornelius, Judith Gentleman, and Peter H. Smith. San Diego: Center for US–Mexican Studies, University of California.

Mazrui, Ali A. 1983 "Political Engineering in Africa." *International Social Science Journal* 35, no. 2:279–294.

Meier, Gerald M., ed. 1991 *Politics and Policy Making in Developing Countries: Perspectives on the New Political Economy.* San Francisco: ICS Press.

Meller, Patricio 1991 "Adjustment and Social Costs in Chile during the 1980s." *World Development* 19, no. 11:1545–1561.

Meyer, Lorenzo 1989 "Democratization of the PRI: Mission Impossible?" In *Mexico's Alternative Political Futures*, ed. Wayne A. Cornelius, Judith Gentleman, and Peter H. Smith. San Diego: Center for US–Mexican Studies, University of California.

Middlebrook, Kevin J. 1989 "The CTM and the Future of State–Labor Relations." In *Mexico's Alternative Political Futures*, ed. Wayne A. Cornelius, Judith Gentleman, and Peter H. Smith. San Diego: Center for US–Mexican Studies, University of California.

Middlebrook, Kevin J., ed. 1991 *Unions, Workers, and the State in Mexico.* San Diego: Center for US–Mexican Studies, University of California.

Migdal, Joel S. 1988 *Strong Societies and Weak States: State–Society Relations and State Capabilities in the Third World.* Princeton: Princeton University Press.

Milimo, John T., and Yacob Fisseha 1986 "Rural Small Scale Enterprises in Zambia: Results of a 1985 Country-Wide Survey." Working Paper no. 28. Department of Agricultural Economics, Michigan State University.

Mills, Michael 1988 "Kenya: Public Expenditure Review: Government Employment and Personnel Expenditures." Unpublished paper.

Molinar Horcasitas, Juan, and Jeffrey A. Weldon 1994 "Electoral Determinants and Consequences of National Solidarity." In *Transforming State–Society Relations in Mexico: The National Solidarity Strategy*, ed. Wayne A. Cornelius, Ann L. Craig, and Jonathan Fox. San Diego: Center for US–Mexican Studies, University of California.

Montgomery, John D., and Dennis A. Rondinelli 1990 "Managing Economic Reform: An Alternative Perspective on Structural Adjustment Policies." *Policy Sciences* 23:73–93.

Mueller, Susanne D. 1984 "Government and Opposition in Kenya, 1966–9." *Journal of Modern African Studies* 22, no. 3:399–427.

Muigai, Githu 1993 "Amending the Constitution: Lessons from History." *The Advocate*, 2, no. 3 (February): 6–14.

Mutahaba, Gelase 1989 *Reforming Public Administration for Development: Experiences from Eastern Africa.* West Hartford, CT: Kumarian Press.

Mutahaba, Gelase, Rweikiza Baguma, and Mohamed Halfani 1993 *Vitalizing African Public Administration for Recovery and Development.* West Hartford, CT: Kumarian Press.

Mwega, F.M., and J.W. Kabubo 1993 "Kenya." In *The Impact of Structural Adjustment on the Population of Africa*, ed. Aderanti Adepoju. London: United Nations Population Fund.

Myrdal, Gunnar 1968 *Asian Drama: An Inquiry into the Poverty of Nations*. New York: Twentieth Century Fund.

Naim, Moises 1991 "The Launching of Radical Policy Changes: The Venezuelan Experienc∍." Unpublished manuscript.

    1993 *Paper Tigers and Minotaurs: The Politics of Venezuela's Economic Reforms*. Washington, DC: The Carnegie Endowment for International Peace.

Ndulu, Benno J. 1986 "Governance and Economic Management." In *Strategies for African Development*, ed. Robert J. Berg and Jennifer Seymour Whitaker. Berkeley: University of California Press.

Nef, Jorge 1988 "The Trend toward Democratization and Redemocratization in Latin America: Shadow and Substance." *Latin American Research Review* 13, no. 3:131–153.

Nelson, Courtney, Tyler Biggs, Lester Gordon, Charles Mann, and Jennifer Widner 1991 "AID and African Capacity Building." CAER Discussion Paper no. 9. Cambridge, MA: Harvard Institute for International Development.

Nelson, Joan M. 1989 "Overview: The Politics of Long-Haul Economic Reform." In *Fragile Coalitions: The Politics of Economic Adjustment*, ed. Joan M. Nelson and contributors. New Brunswick, NJ: Transaction Books.

Njobvu, Elesani 1992 "Economic Policy Making in Zambia." Personal correspondence, Cambridge, MA.

Nordlinger, Eric 1981 *On the Autonomy of the Democratic State*. Cambridge, MA: Harvard University Press.

North, Douglass C. 1990 *Institutions, Institutional Change and Economic Performance*. Cambridge: Cambridge University Press.

North, Douglass C., and R. Thomas 1973 *The Rise of the Western World*. Cambridge: Cambridge University Press.

O'Donnell, Guillermo 1973 *Modernization and Bureaucratic Authoritarianism*. Berkeley: Institute of International Studies, University of California.

    1979 "Tensions in the Bureaucratic–Authoritarian State and the Question of Democracy." In *The New Authoritarianism in Latin America*, ed. David Collier. Princeton: Princeton University Press.

O'Donnell, Guillermo, Philippe C. Schmitter, and Laurence Whitehead, eds. 1986a *Transitions from Authoritarian Rule: Comparative Perspectives*. Baltimore: Johns Hopkins University Press.

    1986b *Transitions from Authoritarian Rule: Latin America*. Baltimore: Johns Hopkins University Press.

Offe, Claus 1985 "New Social Movements: Challenging the Boundaries of Institutional Politics." *Social Research* 52, no. 4:817–868.

Olowu, Dele 1991 "Administrative Responses to Economic Crisis in Africa: A Summary of the Research Findings." *International Journal of Public Sector Management* 4, no. 3:44–59.

Olson, Jr., Mancur 1965 *The Logic of Collective Action: Public Goods and the Theory of Groups*. New York: Schocken Books.

Oyugi, Walter O. 1990 *Decentralization Development Planning and Management in Kenya: An Assessment*. Washington, DC: Economic Development Institute of the World Bank.

PACTO 1987 *The Mexican Pact of Economic Solidarity*. Mexico.

Paul, Samuel, David Steedman, and Francis X. Sutton 1989 "Building Capacity for

Policy Analysis." Working Paper no. 220 (July). Washington, DC: Country Economics Department, World Bank.

Pegatienan, H. Jacques 1990 "Graduate Training in Economics in Francophone West and Central Africa." African Economic Research Consortium (AERC) Special Paper no. 7 (February). Nairobi: Initiatives Publishers.

Pérez Arce, Francisco 1990 "The Enduring Union Struggle for Legality and Democracy." In *Popular Movements and Political Change in Mexico*, ed. Joe Foweraker and Ann L. Craig. Boulder, CO: Lynne Rienner Publishers.

Popoola, D. 1993 "Nigeria: Consequences for Health." In *The Impact of Structural Adjustment on the Population of Africa*, ed. Aderanti Adepoju. London: United Nations Population Fund.

Programa Nacional de Solidaridad 1990 "El combate a la pobreza: Lineamientos programáticos." Mexico: El Nacional.

1992 *Solidarity in Mexico*. Mexico.

Putnam, Robert D. 1993 *Making Democracy Work: Civic Traditions in Modern Italy*. Princeton, NJ: Princeton University Press.

Ramírez Saiz, Juan Manuel 1990 "Urban Struggles and their Political Consequences." In *Popular Movements and Political Change in Mexico*, ed. Joe Foweraker and Ann L. Craig. Boulder, CO: Lynne Rienner Publishers.

Reich, Robert B., ed. 1988 *The Power of Public Ideas*. Cambridge, MA: Ballinger.

Reimers, Fernando 1990 "The Impact of the Debt Crisis on Education in Latin America." *Prospects* 20, no. 4:539–554.

1991a "The Impact of Economic Stabilization and Adjustment on Education in Latin America." *Comparative Education Review* 35, no. 2:319–353.

1991b "The Role of Organization and Politics in Government Financing of Education: The Effects of Structural Adjustment in Latin America." *Comparative Education* 27, no. 1:35–51.

Republic of Kenya 1986 "Economic Management for Renewed Growth." Sessional Paper no. 1 of 1986. Nairobi.

1990 *Economic Survey*. Nairobi: Ministry of National Planning and Development.

1991a "Kenya's Reforms: Policies, Plans, and Outcomes." Document prepared for Consultative Group Meeting, Paris, November.

1991b *Statistical Abstract*. Nairobi.

1992a *The Kenya Civil Service Reform*. Nairobi.

1992b "Background Papers for the Strategic Plan for Financing Health Care in Kenya." Ministry of Health, Nairobi.

Reynolds, Clark 1970 *The Mexican Economy: Twentieth Century Structure and Growth*. New Haven: Yale University Press.

Robinson, Pearl 1992 "The National Conference Phenomenon in Francophone Africa." Paper presented at the Annual Meeting of the African Studies Association, Seattle, Washington (November).

Rochon, Thomas R., and Michael J. Mitchell 1989 "Social Bases of the Transition to Democracy in Brazil." *Comparative Politics* 21, no. 3:307–322.

Roemer, Michael, and Christine Jones, eds. 1991 *Markets in Developing Countries: Parallel, Fragmented, and Black*. San Francisco, CA: ICS Press.

Rothchild, D., and Naomi Chazan 1988 *The Precarious Balance: State and Society in Africa*. Boulder, CO: Westview Press.

Rothchild, D., and Michael W. Foley 1988 "African States and the Politics of Inclusive

Coalitions." In *The Precarious Balance: State and Society in Africa*, ed. Donald Rothchild and Naomi Chazan. Boulder, CO: Westview Press.

Rubin, Jeffrey W. 1987 "State Policies, Leftist Oppositions, and Municipal Elections: The Case of COCEI in Juchitán." In *Electoral Patterns and Perspectives in Mexico*, ed. Arturo Alvarado. La Jolla: University of California at San Diego, Center for US–Mexican Studies.

Saidi, Paul 1992 "Economic Policy Making in Ghana and Côte d'Ivoire." Personal correspondence, Cambridge, MA.

Salinas de Gortari, Carlos 1990 *Segundo Informe de Gobierno*. Typescript, Mexico.

1992 Speech presented at the 63rd Anniversary of the PRI, March 4.

Sandbrook, Richard 1986 "The State and Economic Stagnation in Tropical Africa." *World Development* 14, no. 3:319–332.

Sandel, Michael 1984 "The Procedural Republic and the Unencumbered Self." *Political Theory* 12, 81–96.

Sheahan, John 1987 *Patterns of Development in Latin America: Poverty, Repression, and Economic Strategy*. Princeton: Princeton University Press.

1991 *Conflict and Change in Mexican Economic Strategy*. San Diego: Center for US–Mexican Studies, University of California.

Sigmund, Paul E. 1990 "Chile." In *Prospects for Democracy in Latin America*, ed. Forrest D. Colburn. Princeton, NJ: Center for International Studies, Princeton University.

Silva-Herzog, Jesus 1988 *Some Problems in Implementing Economic Policy*. San Francisco: International Center for Economic Growth.

Silverman, Jerry M. 1990 "Public Sector Decentralization, Economic Policy Reform and Sector Investment." Study Paper no. 1 (November). Washington, DC: Public Sector Management Division, World Bank.

Skocpol, Theda 1979 *States and Social Revolutions: A Comparative Analysis of France, Russia, and China*. Cambridge: Cambridge University Press.

Smith, Peter 1979 *Labyrinths of Power: Political Recruitment in Twentieth Century Mexico*. Princeton: Princeton University Press.

1986 "Leadership and Change: Intellectuals and Technocrats in Mexico." In *Mexico's Political Stability: The Next Five Years*, ed. Roderick A. Camp. Boulder, CO: Westview Press.

1989 "The 1988 Presidential Succession in Historical Perspective." In *Mexico's Alternative Political Futures*, ed. Wayne A. Cornelius, Judith Gentleman, and Peter H. Smith. La Jolla: University of California at San Diego, Center for US–Mexican Studies.

Smoke, Paul 1993 "Local Government Fiscal Reform in Developing Countries: Lessons from Kenya." *World Development* 21, no. 6:901–923.

Soberón, Guillermo, Julio Frenk, and Jaime Sepúlveda 1986 "The Health Care Reform in Mexico: Before and After the 1985 Earthquake." *American Journal of Public Health* 76, no. 6 (June): 673–680.

Society (Nairobi) 1993 Various.

Solidaridad 1992 *La Solidaridad en el desarrollo nacional*. Mexico.

Srinavasan, T.N. 1985 "Neoclassical Political Economy: The State and Economic Development." *Politics and Society* 17, no. 2:115–162.

Stepan, Alfred 1971 *The Military in Politics: Changing Patterns in Brazil*. Princeton, NJ: Princeton University Press.

Stephens, Evelyne Huber 1989 "Capitalist Development and Democracy in South America." *Politics and Society* 17, no. 3:281–352.

Street, Susan 1993 "Educational Decentralization in Mexico: A State or Societal Project?" *Forum for Advancing Basic Education and Literacy* 2, no. 3 (May): 13.

Summers, Lawrence H. 1991 "The Challenges of Development: Some Lessons of History for Sub-Saharan Africa." Remarks prepared for delivery at the NIIA, Lagos, Nigeria, November 8.

Throup, David 1989 "The Construction and Destruction of the Kenyatta State." In *The Political Economy of Kenya*, ed. M.G. Schatzberg. Baltimore: Johns Hopkins University Press.

Tilly, Charles 1985 "Models and Realities of Popular Collective Action." *Social Research* 52, no. 4:717–747.

Timmer, Peter, ed. 1991 *Agriculture and the State: Growth, Employment, and Poverty in Developing Countries.* Ithaca, NY: Cornell University Press.

Tokman, Victor E. 1989 "Policies for a Heterogeneous Informal Sector in Latin America." *World Development* 17, no. 7:1067–1076.

Touraine, Alain 1985 "An Introduction to the Study of Social Movements." *Social Research* 52, no. 4:749–787.

UNDP (United Nations Development Programme) Various *Human Development Report.* Oxford: Oxford University Press.

UNESCO 1980–1993 *Statistical Yearbook.*

UNICEF 1988 "Impact of Structural Adjustment Policies on the Well-Being of Vulnerable Groups in Kenya." Report of the Proceedings of a Workshop, November 3–5.

Unidad de La Crónica Presidencial 1992 *Diccionario biográfico del gobierno mexicano.* Mexico City: Fondo de Cultura Económica.

van De Walle, Nicolas 1992 "Rent Seeking and Democracy in Africa, With an Illustration from Cameroon." Paper prepared for the Colloquium on the Economics of Political Liberalization in Africa, Harvard University, March 6–7.

Vernon, Raymond 1964 *Public Policy and Private Enterprise in Mexico.* Cambridge, MA: Harvard University Press.

Wade, Robert 1990 *Governing the Market: Economic Theory and the Role of Government in East Asian Industrialization.* Princeton: Princeton University Press.

Walzer, Michael 1980 "Civility and Civic Virtue in Contemporary America." In *Radical Principles*, ed. Michael Walzer. New York: Basic Books.

Waterbury, John 1992 "The Heart of the Matter? Public Enterprise and the Adjustment Process." In *The Politics of Economic Adjustment*, ed. Stephan Haggard and Robert R. Kaufman. Princeton: Princeton University Press.

Weaver, James H., and Kevin M. O'Keefe 1991 "Whither Development Economics?" *SAIS Review* 11, no. 2:113–133.

Weber, Max 1946 "Politics as a Vocation." In *From Max Weber: Essays in Sociology*, ed. H.H. Gerth and C. Wright Mills. New York: Oxford University Press.

Weekly Review (Nairobi) 1985–1993 Various.

Whitehead, Laurence 1989 "Political Change and Economic Stabilization: The 'Economic Solidarity Pact'." In *Mexico's Alternative Political Futures*, ed. Wayne A. Cornelius, Judith Gentleman, and Peter H. Smith. San Diego: Center for US–Mexican Studies, University of California.

Widner, Jennifer 1992a "State Structures and Reform Strategies." Paper prepared for the

Colloquium on the Economics of Political Liberalization in Africa, Harvard University, March 6–7.

1992b *The Rise of a Party-State in Kenya: From Harambee! to Nyayo!* Berkeley: University of California Press.

Williams, Mark 1994 "Converging Interests and Policy Reform: The Politics of Economic Deregulation in the Mexican Freight Transport Sector." Paper prepared for the 18th International Congress of the Latin American Studies Association, Atlanta.

Williamson, John 1990a *Latin American Adjustment: How Much Has Happened?*. Washington, DC: Institute for International Economics.

Williamson, Oliver E. 1985 *The Economic Institutions of Capitalism.* New York: The Free Press.

Winrock International 1991 *African Development: Lessons from Asia.* Arlington, VA: Winrock International Institute for International Development.

Winson, Anthony 1989 *Coffee and Democracy in Modern Costa Rica.* New York: St. Martin's Press.

World Bank 1983a *World Development Report 1983.* Oxford: Oxford University Press.

1983b *Kenya: Country Economic Memorandum.* Washington, DC.

1984a *Towards Sustained Development in Sub-Saharan Africa.* Washington, DC.

1984b *World Development Report 1984.* Oxford: Oxford University Press.

1988 *Social Sector Cost Sharing in Kenya.* Nairobi.

1989 *Sub-Saharan Africa – From Crisis to Sustainable Growth.* Washington, DC.

1990 *World Development Report 1990.* Oxford: Oxford University Press.

1990–1993 *World Tables*

1991a *World Development Report 1991.* Oxford: Oxford University Press.

1991b *Kenya: Re-Investing in Stabilization and Growth Through Public Sector Adjustment.* Washington, DC.

1992 *World Development Report 1992.* Oxford: Oxford University Press.

1993 *World Development Report 1993.* Oxford: Oxford University Press.

Wunsch, James S. 1990 "Centralization and Development in Post-Independence Africa." In *The Failure of the Centralized State: Institutions and Self-Governance in Africa,* ed. James S. Wunsch and Dele Olowu. Boulder, CO: Westview Press.

Wunsch, James S., and Dele Olowu, eds. 1990 *The Failure of the Centralized State: Institutions and Self-Governance in Africa.* Boulder, CO: Westview Press.

Yates, P. Lamartine 1981 *Mexico's Agricultural Dilemma.* Tucson: University of Arizona Press.

Young, Crawford 1982 *Ideology and Development in Africa.* New Haven: Yale University Press.

1988 "The African Colonial State and its Political Legacy." In *The Precarious Balance: State and Society in Africa,* ed. Donald Rothchild and Naomi Chazan. Boulder, CO: Westview Press.

1992 "Democratization in Africa: Contradictions of a Political Imperative." Paper prepared for the Colloquium on the Economics of Political Liberalization in Africa, Harvard University, March 6–7.

Index

administrative capacity, 10, 12, 31,
  37–44, 78, 127–128, 180, 182, 193
  in Kenya, 15–16, 17, 143–153, 184
  in Mexico, 15–16, 17, 128–143, 184
Africa Capacity Building Foundation
  (ACBF), 35
African Development Bank, 36
African Economic Research
  Consortium (AERC), 35–36
agrarian reform
  in Kenya, 62
  in Mexico, 48, 86–91, 159–160
  see also agriculture
agriculture, 24
  in Kenya, 62–3, 73, 76, 103–106, 123
  in Mexico, 50, 54, 87–91
AIDS, 37
Amnesty International, 170
Angola, 23
Argentina, 19, 20, 21, 22, 25, 26, 27,
  28, 29, 32, 34–35, 36, 52
austerity, 2, 7, 10, 23, 28, 37–44,
  127–128
  see also budget deficit; economic
  crisis; stabilization; structural
  adjustment
authoritarianism, 7, 17, 29, 32, 156,
  185, 194
  see also regime

Benin, 30
black market, see informal economy
Bolivia, 19, 20, 21, 22, 25, 26, 27, 28,
  29, 32, 33, 35, 37, 38, 39, 40, 42,
  44, 117, 199n28
Botswana, 36
Brazil, 18, 20, 21, 22, 25, 26, 27, 28, 29,
  32, 37, 38, 39, 40, 42, 44, 117,
  199n28
budget deficit, 24–25, 26, 34
  in Kenya, 26, 72–73, 99–102, 103,
  105, 123, 144–145

in Mexico, 26
  see also austerity; public investment
bureaucracy, 2, 5, 41, 43–44, 46, 128
  in Kenya, 11, 13–14, 16, 76, 80, 108,
  191–192
  in Mexico, 11, 13–14, 49, 80, 93, 108,
  112, 189, 191–192
  see also civil service
camarilla, 114
Cameroon, 19, 21, 22, 25, 26, 27, 28,
  39, 40, 41, 42
Canada, 113
capacity, see state capacity
capital flight
  in Kenya, 78, 80
  in Mexico, 51, 52–53, 54, 80
Cárdenas, Cuauhtémoc, 60, 162–163,
  167
Cárdenas, Lázaro, 87, 157
Central America, 33
Central Organization of Trade Unions
  (COTU), 177
Chad, 25
Chiapas, 90, 91, 160–161
Chile, 19, 21, 22, 25, 26, 27, 28, 29, 32,
  34–35, 36, 37, 38, 39, 40, 42, 44,
  117, 140
China, 140
Citizens in Movement (UNE), 167
civic associations, 6, 23, 30, 45, 183, 193
  in Kenya, 14, 64, 69, 76, 96,
  168–178
  in Mexico, 59–60, 157–161, 163–164
civic society, 6–8, 155–156
  in Kenya, 16–17, 168–178, 179
  in Mexico, 16–17, 58–61, 77,
  156–161, 179
civil service, 10
  in Kenya, 62–63, 65, 69, 72, 73, 78,
  100, 121, 123, 191
clientelism, 6, 7, 30
  in Kenya, 14, 63, 65, 101, 122